THE
CROMWELLIAN SETTLEMENT
OF IRELAND

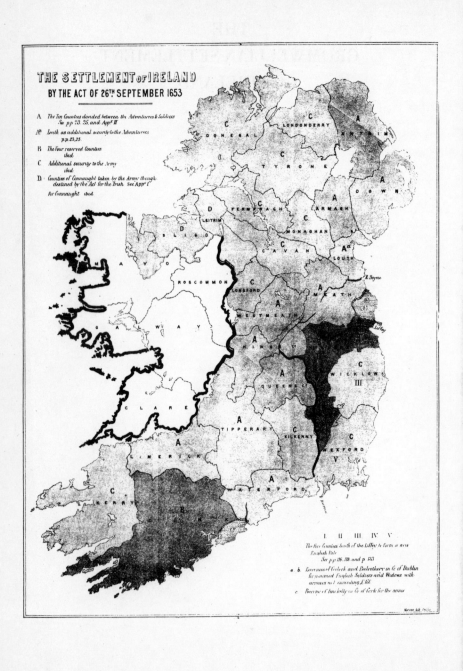

THE SETTLEMENT OF IRELAND
BY THE ACT OF 26TH SEPTEMBER 1653

A. The Ten Counties divided between the Adventurers & Soldiers
  See pp 23. 25. and App.x II

A.o Louth as additional security to the Adventurers
  p.p. 23, 25.

B. The Four reserved Counties
  ibid.

C. Additional security to the Army
  ibid.

D. Counties of Connaught taken by the Army though
  destined by the Act for the Irish. See App.x I

  Re Connaught ibid.

I. II. III. IV. V.
The Five Counties South of the Liffey to form a new
English Pale
  See pp 116. 118. and p 553

a. b. Tenements of Golock and Balrothery in Co. of Dublin
  for maimed English Soldiers and Widows with
  arrears not exceeding £151.

c. Barony of Imokilly in Co. of Cork for the same

THE

CROMWELLIAN SETTLEMENT

OF

IRELAND.

BY

JOHN P. PRENDERGAST, ESQ.

I R E   L A N D.

Arms of the Commonwealth, on the Proclamation of the Lord Deputy and
Council of 14th October, 1653, regulating the Transplantation.

[*From a copy at Kilkenny Castle.*]

CONSTABLE · LONDON

First published in Great Britain 1865
by Longman, Green, Longman, Roberts & Green
This edition published in Great Britain 1996
by Constable and Company Limited
3 The Lanchesters, 162 Fulham Palace Road
London W6 9ER
ISBN 0 09 476620 7
Printed in Great Britain by
St Edmundsbury Press Ltd
Bury St Edmunds, Suffolk

A CIP catalogue record for this book
is available from the British Library

PREFACE.

———◆———

Of all possessions in a country Land is the most desirable. It is the most fixed. It yields its returns in the form of rent with the least amount of labour or forethought to the owner. But, in addition to all these advantages, the possession of it confers such power, that the balance of power in a state rests with the class that has the balance of Land.

The laws of most of the states of Europe since the days of the Northern invasions have been made by the landowners. They have been enabled to prescribe to the mass of the people on what conditions they shall live on the land, or whether indeed they shall live there at all.

The term " Settlement," of such great import in the history of Ireland in the Seventeenth century, means nothing else than the settlement of the balance of land according to the will of the strongest ; for force, not reason, is the source of law. And by the term Cromwellian Settlement is to be understood the history of the dealings of the Commonwealth of England with the lands and habitations of the people of Ireland

after their conquest of the country in the year 1652.
As their object was rather to extinguish a nation than
to suppress a religion, they seized the lands of
the Irish, and transferred them (and with them all
the power of the state) to an overwhelming flood of
new English settlers, filled with the intensest national
and religious hatred of the Irish.

Two other settlements followed, which may be
called the Restoration Settlement and the Revolution
Settlement. The one was a counter revolution, by
which some of the Royalist English of Ireland and a
few of the native Irish were restored to their estates
under the Acts of Settlement and Explanation.* The
other (or Revolution Settlement) followed the victory
of William III. at the Battle of the Boyne. By it the
lands lately restored to the Royalist English and few
native Irish were again seized by the Parliament of

---

* Such was the national hatred of the Royalists of England to the
Irish (who fought, and lost country and everything for the King),
that even in their common exile abroad they rejoiced at Cromwell's
proceedings in stripping the Irish of their lands :—

"We are at a dead calm [writes Sir Edward Hyde, afterwards
Earl of Clarendon, from Paris, in 1654] for all manner of intelligence. Cromwell, no doubt, is very busy. Nathaniel Fiennes is
made Chancellor of Ireland ; and they doubt not to plant that
kingdom without opposition. And truly, if we can get it again,
we shall find difficulties removed which a virtuous Prince and
more quiet times could never have compassed." Sir Edward Hyde
to Mr. Betius, Paris, 29th May, 1654.—Clarendon's "State Tracts,"
vol. iii., p. 244. Folio. Clarendon Press, Oxford.

England, and distributed among the conquering nation. At the Court for the Sale of Estates forfeited on account of the war of 1690, the lands could be purchased only by Englishmen. No Irishman could purchase more than the site for a cabin ; for to the condition of cottagers it was intended that the relics of the nation should be reduced.*

The Penal Laws, which lasted nearly in full force till the breaking out of the first American War, were nothing but the complement of the Forfeited Estates Act. Their main purpose was, on the one hand, to prevent the Irish from ever enlarging their landed interest beyond the low state to which it had been reduced after the sales by the Forfeited Estates Court—for which reason they were forbid to purchase land; and, on the other hand, to contrive by all political ways, and particularly by denying them the power to make settlements of their property by deed or will, and by making their lands divisible equally among their sons at their death, to crumble and break in pieces the remnant that had escaped confiscation, and thereby to deprive them of all power and consideration in the state.† It will thus be seen that these three Settle-

* They could be purchased by Protestants (*i. e.* English) only. 1st Anne, st. 1, c. 26, sect. 8, English Statute. Two acres was the utmost an Irishman could take a lease of.—Ib. sect. 10.

† "As to the intention of the Act,ª it is plain the legislature had a double view; first, to disable Papists from enlarging their

ª 8th Anne, c. 3, A. D. 1710.

ments are only parts of one whole, and that the Cromwellian Settlement is the foundation of the present
settlement of Ireland.

The term Settlement being understood in this sense,
the present sketch is conversant directly with the measures taken by the Parliament of England in dealing
with the land. The history of the Irish Rebellion of
1641, the personal character of Cromwell and the
chief actors, the account of the war from 1649 to
1653, are no further touched upon than has been
thought necessary to the main purpose of the sketch.
But it will be seen from the Introduction, and in treating the details of the Cromwellian Settlement, how
large a share of the history of Ireland is involved in
the Land question.

From the days of the first invasion, the King and
Council of England intended to make English landed
proprietors in Ireland the rulers of Ireland, as William
the Conqueror had made the French of Normandy
landlords and rulers of the English. Though the Government of England were interrupted in this course
by the wars of Edward I. for the subjection of the
Scotch, by the wars of Edward III. and his successors

landed interest, so as they should soon moulder away in their hands:
the second view was to encourage them to become converts by throwing some temporal invitation in their way." *Vicars against Car-
rol*, in the Exchequer, 10th February, 1728. "Several Special Cases
on the Laws against the further Growth of Popery in Ireland. By
Gorges Edmond Howard, Esq." 8vo. Dublin, 1775, p. 37.

for the crown of France, and finally by the civil wars
of England, called the "Wars of the Roses," the design was never abandoned. And when Henry VIII.,
disencumbered of any foreign war or domestic treason,
had time to destroy the house of Kildare, he projected
the clearing of Ireland to the Shannon, and colonizing
it with English. But the new conquest of Ireland
only really began in the reigns of his three children,
Edward VI., Queen Mary, and Queen Elizabeth, when
the conquest of the lands of the Irish for the purpose
of new colonizing or planting them with English was
resumed, after an interval of more than three hundred
years. During this interval the English Pale, or that
part of Ireland subject to the regular jurisdiction of
the King of England and his laws, had been gradually
contracting—partly by the English of Ireland throwing
off the feudal system, and partly by reconquests effected
by the Irish, until in the reign of Henry VI. the Pale
was nearly limited by the line of the Liffey and the
Boyne. Beyond the Pale the English and the Irish
dwelt intermixed. And in all the plans for restoring
the regular administration of the King's laws in Ireland, previous to the reign of Edward VI., it was always proposed that the English of Ireland should be
brought back to their ancient military discipline, and
should conquer from the Irish the lands in their possession, in order that they might be given to English
under grants on feudal conditions by the King.

But the English of Ireland clearly foresaw that the

effect of the complete conquest of the Irish would be
to give the Government of Ireland to the English of
England. Their armed retainers, called Gallowglasses
and Kerne, would be put down, as there would no longer
remain the pretence of defending the land from the
King's Irish enemies. With the regular administration
of English law would come back wardships, marriages, reliefs, escheats, and forfeitures, which they
were only too happy to have thrown off in the days of
Edward II.; and the final result would be to bring
over new colonists from England, who would be rivals
to supplant them in the favour of the Government, and
in all the offices of the State. The English of Ireland,
consequently, were secretly indisposed to effect the
reconquest, and it was not until they were subdued
that the second conquest began.

The first blow to the English of Irish birth was the
limiting the power of the Parliament. In the reign of
Henry VII., Sir Edward Poynings forced from the
Irish Parliament a statute whereby the Privy Council
of England were made virtually part of the Parliament
of Ireland; for thenceforth it could originate no statutes,
and could pass only such as had been first approved by
the Privy Council of England. The Parliament had in
fact long become devoted to the Earls of Kildare, who
had thereby become too powerful for the Kings of England. The next and final blow to the power of the English of Ireland was the fall of the House of Kildare, when
Silken Thomas, Earl of Kildare, and his five uncles,

were executed at Tyburn for treason, at the end of Henry VIII.'s reign. The head of the ancient English of Ireland had now fallen ; their Parliament had been already deprived of its power ; the main obstacles to the designs of England were removed ; and in the following reigns the reconquest of Ireland by plantation began.

At first it was the native Irish that were stripped, as the O'Moores, the O'Connors, and the O'Neils. The Earl of Desmond's great territories, extending over Limerick and Kerry, Cork and Waterford, were next confiscated and planted. Finally, in James I.'s reign, the native Irish, not only of Ulster, but of Leitrim, and wherever else they continued possessed of their original territories, were dispossessed of portions of their lands, varying from one-third to three-fourths, to form plantations of new English. During the reign of Queen Elizabeth, the old English of Ireland, though they agreed in point of religion with the native Irish, always adhered to the English in any rebellion of the Irish, as in a national quarrel. In James I.'s reign, as all the planters were of the new religion, the old English found themselves supplanted by them in all the offices of the State, as the Irish found themselves supplanted by them in their native homes.

It is needless here to recapitulate the long-continued injuries and insults by which the ancient English of Ireland were forced into the same ranks with the Irish in defence of the King's cause in 1641. Chief among them were the attempts to seize their estates under the plea of defective title, in order to plant them with new English. It was thus Lord Strafford got Connaught and parts of Tipperary and Limerick into his power, with the intention of forming a new plantation at the expense of the De Burgos and other old English. One of the old English, in 1644, thus graphically expresses their feelings :—" Was it not the usual taunt of the late Lord Strafford and all his fawning sycophants, in their private conversations with those of the Pale, that they were the most refractory men of the whole kingdom, and that it was more necessary (that is, for their own crooked ends) that they should be planted and supplanted than any others;" and that " where plantations might not reach, Defective Titles should extend." He had known many an officer and gentleman, he adds, who had left a hand at Kinsale in fighting in defence of the Crown of England, when the Spaniards and the Earl of Tyrone were defeated by Lord Mountjoy, to be afterwards deprived of his pension for having refused to take the oath of supremacy and allegiance in the Protestant form, though, as one of them answered, on being questioned before the State for matter of recusancy (as they termed it), " It was not asked of me the day of Kinsale what religion I was of."*

* " Queries propounded by the Protestant Party concerning the Peace now treated of in Ireland, and the Answers thereto made on behalf of the Irish Nation," pp. 11, 12. Small 4to. Paris : 1644.

The Scotch and English, however, having rebelled against the King in 1639 (for the march of the Scottish rebels to the Border in that year was on the invitation of the leaders of the popular party in England, though they themselves did not openly take the field till 1642),* the Irish rose in his favour. They were finally subdued, in 1652, by Cromwell and the arms of the Commonwealth ; and then took place a scene not witnessed in Europe since the conquest of Spain by the Vandals. Indeed, it is injustice to the Vandals to equal them with the English of 1652 ; for the Vandals came as strangers and conquerors in an age of force and barbarism, nor did they banish the people, though they seized and divided their lands by lot ;† but the English, in 1652, were of the same nation as half of the chief families in Ireland, and had at that time had the island under their sway for five hundred years.·

The captains and men of war of the Irish, amounting to 40,000 men and upwards, they banished into Spain, where they took service under that king; others of them, with a crowd of orphan boys and girls,

---

* To obtain a clear account of the leading causes and principal events of this era in England in a short compass, with all the evidence to support his view, I know nothing equal to " The Britannic Constitution," by Roger Acherley, Esq., of the Middle Temple, folio, London, 1727 (chap. ix., " Breaches of the Constitution in the Reign of Charles I.").

† See Robertson's "History of the Emperor Charles V.," Appendix to Introduction.

were transported to serve the English planters in the
West Indies; and the remnant of the nation; not banished or transported, were to be transplanted into
Connaught, while the conquering army divided the
ancient inheritances of the Irish amongst them by
lot.

This scene, never before described, is the subject
of the present sketch. By what accident it became
my study may deserve mention.

I had for about ten years belonged to the Leinster
Circuit, travelling through the counties of Wicklow,
Wexford, Waterford, Kilkenny, and Tipperary, when,
in the year 1846, I received a commission from England to make some pedigree researches in the latter
county. Furnished with an old pedigree, which had
been given to an ancestor of the family by the Ulster
King of Arms, when quitting Ireland, as an exile, after
the battle of the Boyne, I visited the place where the
family had been anciently seated.

Twelve miles south of Clonmel, on the right bank
of the Suir, under a range of hills that there bars
the course of that river from north to south, and sends
it thirty miles eastward to issue below Waterford,
as one of " the Three Sisters," to the sea, I found a
ruined castle, and beside it a still more ruined chapel,
and desecrated graveyard. The castle had evidently
been built to guard the pass over the hills to Lismore.
Among many broken tombstones of the family of the
pedigree, within the roofless walls, lay a large one,

fractured across the centre, recording the name and virtues of a captain in the army, who, as far as could be deciphered, had received the public thanks; but the stone was gapped, and, the next word being "borough," it seemed as if he had been a Member of Parliament. One of the crowd who watched the attempt to decipher the inscription sent a boy for the fragment, which marked a potato ridge in the adjoining conacre field. It filled the gap, and the inscription now showed that he had received the public thanks [*of the great Duke of Marl*] borough for his distinguished services at the siege of Aire, in Flanders, in 1710.

The prospect of the mountain, the river, and the plain, together with the scene of ruin all around, so characteristic of the country, excited my interest; and the pedigrees (for in the neighbourhood I discovered another) were now studied with care. The family, it seems, had come over from Pembrokeshire with Strongbow, and by an alliance with the De Berminghams had obtained large possessions both in Tipperary and in Waterford (counties which the chain of hills here divides); so large, indeed, that the country people, whose imagination supplies a tradition for everything, call the family, whose memory they tenaciously preserve, the Clan a Gothag, or Clan of the Smoke; for they say that the founder of the family, the first invader, halted on the summit of the pass, from whence could be seen the Suir flowing north and south on one side,

and the Blackwater in the same direction on the other;
and, lighting a fire, he said that he would follow and
conquer with the smoke. It was a calm summer day,
and the smoke rose, and spread both ways.

There they remained, possessed of lands in Tipperary and Waterford, from the days of King John.
In the year 1650, Cromwell, leaving his winter quarters in Youghal at an unusually early season of the
year for campaigning in Ireland (the 29th of January),
crossed the Suir at Cahir, nine miles to the north of
this castle; and sending a detachment towards it, it
was surrendered, but was yielded back on condition
of the defences being taken down. A few soldiers
were left to see this done. The rest of the detachment had not proceeded far before they heard confused noises behind; and they hurried back, thinking
that the tenants of the castle were murdering their comrades. But it was only the noise of a pack of buck-
hounds, kept in the bawn, or fortified curtilage. So
they brought off the owner and his hounds to Cromwell, then on his march to the siege of Kilkenny, who
was thus afforded some good sport, whereby the gentleman so ingratiated himself with Cromwell, according to the pedigree, that he afterwards interfered in
his favour. And among the few letters of the Lord
Protector there remains one in favour of a gentleman of the same name " of the County of Tipperary,"
requesting that he might be spared from transplantation.

His estate, however, passed to the Adventurers. Whole families of the name, as I afterwards found, were transplanted into Connaught. Thence some of them petitioned to be allowed to come back, merely to get in their last harvest; but they were refused; they were only suffered to send some servants. Soon afterwards they sold their assignments in Connaught for a trifle to the officers of transplantation, and fled in horror and aversion from the scene, and embarked for Spain. At the Restoration, the heir, who had served under the King's ensigns abroad, returned; and, expecting to be restored to his estate, complained to the Council that he found the Adventurer who was in possession of the family estate cutting down all the timber, endeavouring, evidently, to make the most of his time, in case he should lose the lands by this new revolution. As the timber on all forfeited lands was, by Cromwell's Acts, reserved to the State, the Council had issued a proclamation, on the Restoration, to prevent the cutting down of trees. The affidavit of the heir still remains, informing the Council that, when he showed the Adventurer the proclamation, he and his men answered him, " that they did not value the said proclamation, and that they would not leave standing a tree of all the wood but one, whereon he, this deponent, should hang."

Deprived of their estates, which were never restored, different branches of the family became tenants

XVIPREFACE.

under the Adventurers of the lands they had once owned as lords. Some of them, still adhering to the Crown, forfeited their leases after the battle of the Boyne, and became exiles. Others held on. One of the family—the grandfather of him whose pedigree I was commissioned to investigate—happened to be conducting agent for one of the candidates at the election at Clonmel for the county of Tipperary caused by the accession of George III. He tendered his vote. "You know you married a Papist," said the opposing agent, and thus denied his right. The other challenged him for the insult. They retired at once to the Green of Clonmel, behind the Courthouse, where the man insulted on account of his wife's supposed religion was shot dead, the other with difficulty escaping, on a horse, from the excited crowd across the River Suir, which runs by the Green. I did not understand, until later, that a Protestant who married an Irishwoman, if she did not conform to English religion within one year of the marriage, sank to the helot-like condition of his wife's people; he was deprived of all rights; he became "a constructive Papist;" and "a Protestant of this class was, in the eye of the law, a more odious Papist (to use the words of the Court) than a real and actual Papist by profession and principle."*

* The case of *Rives against Roderic,* in the Exchequer, Hilary Term, 1729. Howard's " Cases on the Laws against the further Growth of Popery in Ireland," p. 60. 8vo. Dublin: 1775.

On my return to Dublin, I had recourse to the
Records, to trace the pedigree. The Rolls of Chancery begin only in the reign of Edward II., almost
all the earlier ones having been burnt by a fire that
destroyed St. Mary's Abbey, where they were then
deposited. Many early links, however, were obtained
from the Tower of London, whither appeals in Writs
of Right by members of the family, and in one case of
Wager of Battle, carried from Ireland to Westminster
in the reign of Edward I., had been preserved. From
Edward II. to the 34th of Henry VIII. comparatively little information was to be obtained, as in that
interval the regular administration of English law
was suspended, except in the Pale; and the English
in the provinces ruled their differences by March Law,
the Irish by Brehon Law, and some of the towns (as,
for instance, Galway) by the Civil Law.

But after the fall of the House of Kildare, the Feudal Law was resumed, and Inquisitions taken upon the
death of every landowner " found," or recorded in
Chancery, his death ; what estates he died seised of ;
who was his heir, and whether under age, and unmar-
ried ; for in that case the King became entitled to the
guardianship and marriage of the heir, and to the rents
of the estate during the minority, without account.
Thus, from 1540 to 1640 nothing was easier than to
trace the chain. But here these documents ended, and
a gap ensued, which it was long difficult to bridge. The
Statutes, after a similar gap, began in 1662 with the Act

of Settlement. After some study it proved unintelligible. It was founded on transactions of which there was no explanation. The histories of Ireland afforded next to nothing.

The search for information had been for some time abandoned as nearly hopeless, when I remembered that in the King's Inns' Library there were pamphlets amounting to thousands, but not catalogued. Each day, after court, a certain number were gone through, until at length the whole was examined. Between 1641 and 1650, there were plenty of pamphlets about Ireland; but they concerned the War; and it was not such I wanted. I had come to perceive the importance of the history of the Landed Settlement of Ireland, and I desired those that concerned the period from 1650 to 1659. I only found the following, viz.:—
"The Great Case of Transplantation in Ireland Discussed," in the year 1655, with an answer by Colonel Lawrence, and a reply by Vincent Gookin (the author of the "Case"); and Colonel Lawrence's "Interest of England in the Well Planting of Ireland with English People Discussed," in 1656.

My interest was now redoubled, for I had formed some conception of the Settlement. I went back to the Rolls' Office, to ask Mr. Hatchell, so long Deputy-Keeper, if he knew anything of the history of the Settlement; and if not, who did? He answered, he knew nothing of it, "but perhaps Groves might." He was an old clergyman, who had been one of the Record

Commission of 1810. Mr. Groves knew nothing, but said Mr. Shaw Mason might—he had been Secretary to the Commission; but Mr. Mason knew no more than Mr. Groves.

I now thought of searching the Record Commissioners' Reports, and found that there were several volumes of the very date required, 1650–1659, in the custody of the Clerk of the Privy Council, preserved in the heavily embattled Tower which forms the most striking feature of the Castle of Dublin. They were only accessible at that day through the order of the Lord Lieutenant or Chief Secretary for Ireland. I obtained at length, in the month of September, 1848, an order. It may be easily imagined with what interest I followed the porter up the dark winding stone staircase of this gloomy tower, once the prison of the Castle, and was ushered into a small central space that seemed dark, even after the dark stairs we had just left. As the eye became accustomed to the spot, it appeared that the doors of five cells made in the prodigious thickness of the Tower walls opened on the central space. From one of them Hugh Roe O'Donel is said to have escaped, by getting down the privy of his cell to the Poddle River that runs round the base of the Tower. The place was covered with the dust of twenty years; but, opening a couple of volumes of the Statutes,—one as a clean spot to place my coat upon, the other to sit on,—I took up my seat in the cell, exactly opposite to the one just mentioned, as it looked to the

south over the Castle garden, and had better light.
In this Tower, I found a series of Order Books of the
Commissioners of the Parliament of the Commonwealth
of England for the Affairs of Ireland, together with
Domestic Correspondence and Books of Establishments
from 1650 to 1659. They were marked on the back by
the letter A over a number, as will be observed in the
various references in the notes to the present sketch.*
Here I found the records of a nation's woes. The first
page I happened to open presented the following:—

" Forasmuch as the within Mrs. Mary Wolverston, by reason of
the bad weather that hath happened, was disabled to travel with her
provision and carriages into Connaught by the tyme limited in the
within passe, these are therefore to desire all whom it may concern
to permit the said Mary, and the within named persons her servants,
with such corne and other necessary provisions as she or they shall
have with them, quietly to pass into Connaught aforesaid to their
habitations, she and they behaving themselves as becometh.

"THOMAS HERBERT, Clerk of the Council.

" *Dated the* 14*th October,* 1654."†

---

* See the Catalogue of these Books, among the papers contained
in the Council Office, in the volume of Reports from the Record
Commissioners from 1816 to 1826, Appendix, p. 227.

† $\frac{A}{5}$. The Wolverstons were at this time owners of the noble
demesne called Stillorgan Park, three miles south of Dublin, derived
through the Cruise family, who were possessed of it in the beginning
of the 13th century. (" History of the County of Dublin, by John
D'Alton, Esq., Barrister at Law," p. 840. 8vo. Dublin: 1838.) It
subsequently got the name of Carysfort Park, from becoming the
property of the Earls of Carysfort.

I felt that I had at last reached the haven I had been so long seeking. There I sat, extracting, for many weeks until I began to know the voices of many of the corporals that came with the guard to relieve the sentry in the Castle yard below, and every drum and bugle call of the regiment quartered in the Ship-street barracks. At length, between the labour of copying, and excitement at the astonishing drama performing as it were before my eyes, my heart by some strange movements warned me it was necessary to retire for a time. But I again and again returned at intervals, sometimes of months, sometimes of years. Other depositories were ransacked. I got free range of the Exchequer, full of interesting historical documents, and containing the Minute and Order Books of Cromwell's Court of Claims. I had access to the Records of the late Auditor and Surveyor-General's offices in the Custom House Buildings, in the custody of W. H. Hardinge, Esq., whose works on the Official Maps and Surveys of the 1641 and 1688 Forfeitures, now publishing in the " Transactions of the Royal Irish Academy," will become, for their extent and accuracy, the basis of much authentic history. Some of the Order Books of the Council are to be found here ; and the correspondence of the Revenue Commissioners of the fifteen precincts into which Ireland was divided by the Commissioners of the Commonwealth abound in curious details. Every circuit I visited, through the kind permission of the late Marquis of Ormond, the muniment room of Kilkenny Castle, containing a series of private and public historical documents, some coæval with the first Conquest—a pleasure enhanced by a friendship with their accomplished keeper, the Rev. James Graves, Honorary Secretary to the Kilkenny Archæological Society.*

This depository is still surprisingly rich, though drayloads of papers concerning the Cromwellian and Restoration eras were carried away by Carte, to enable him to write the "History of the Life of James Duke of Ormond,"—papers which now form the Great Carte Collection in the Bodleian Library at Oxford. These were visited, as also the British Museum and State Paper Office, which, however, did not yield much. I must add the Library of Charles Haliday, Esq., at his Lucullan villa, Monkstown Park, rich in all the rarest literature relating to Ireland, with a collection of pamphlets and fugitive pieces from the earliest time to the present, probably unequalled,† over the door of

---

* Author, jointly with J. G. A. Prim, of the "History of the Cathedral of St. Canice, Kilkenny." 4to. Dublin : Hodges and Smith, 1857. Mr. Graves is now editing, under the sanction of the Master of the Rolls, a Council Roll of 18th Richard II., A. D. 1395, preserved in Kilkenny Castle.

† Plutarch, after describing the elegance of Lucullus's villas, praises him for the libraries he had collected, and the number of volumes he had caused to be copied for him in elegant hands. His libraries were open to all. The Greeks repaired at pleasure to the galleries and porticos, as to the retreat of the Muses, and there spent whole days in conversation on matters of learning, delighted to re-

which might be written, " The Books of Charles Haliday and his friends."* As the materials grew, so grew the difficulty of selecting and framing an account. Other occupations also interfered.

It seemed as if I had now gone through every depository. I had got a tolerably clear view of that great work, the Transplantation of a Nation, which the Commissioners of the Parliament found it such a labour to execute. But to express the despondency I felt at attempting to describe it, I might almost use the language of the Commissioners themselves in effecting it,—" The children were now come to the birth, and much was expected and desired, but there was no strength to bring forth."†

In the beginning of the year, 1864, however, the Earl of Charlemont intrusted me with the care of the noble collection of books, coins, and papers in Charlemont House, Dublin, formed by his grandfather,

---

tire to such a scene from business and from care. Lucullus often joined these learned men in their walks, and gave them his advice about the affairs of their country ; so that his house was in fact an asylum and senate house to all the Greeks that visited Rome. " Life of Lucullus."

* Rabelais inscribed in all his books the following :—" Francisci Rabelæsi, medici, καὶ τῶν αὐτοῦ φίλων." Notwithstanding his devotion to commerce, there are to be found valuable papers from Mr. Haliday on the early history of Dublin and its port, in the " Transactions of the Royal Irish Academy." His researches into the history of the Danes of Ireland would be a most important addition to the history of the kingdom.

† See at p. 31, *post.*

James, first Earl of Charlemont, a man no less distinguished in arts than for patriotism,—the General in
Chief of the Irish Volunteers.   The library was a rich
one (particularly in early English and Italian literature) ; but, as I had had constant access to so many fine
Public libraries, it did not seem likely that I should
meet with anything in print that had not come under my
notice.   What, then, was my surprise to find twelve
small quarto volumes, in old sheepskin covers, comprising the London weekly newspapers between 1641
and 1659, the same substantially in form as those of
the present day !   There is the leading article (those
of the year 1650, for instance, have "Young Tar-
quin" for their subject, sometimes called "the Scotch
King," nicknames for Charles II., to render him odious
to the English), proceedings in Parliament and the
Law Courts, and correspondence from Paris, Sweden,
Rome, &c., and Ireland—the letters from Ireland supplying some of those lively touches that such cotemporary accounts alone can give.

It was plain that all the information that could be
hoped for had now been obtained ; and if not brought
forth, the subject might sleep for another period as
long as the last—some of the information might, perhaps, be buried for ever with the possessor.*   Much

* "When a learned man dies," said the Master of the Temple,
in his speech at the grave of the great jurisconsult, John Selden,
in 1654, in the Temple Church—"when a learned man dies, much
learning dies with him ;" adding, "If learning could have kept

of it had been collected with the view of being able
some time or other to treat the subject of the Settlement of real property in Ireland, historically considered, before the body of the Bar ; but as neither of
the two chairs founded by the Benchers had the law
of real property allotted to it, and still wishing to
interest my own profession in a favourite pursuit, a
select audience of them was addressed.* The interest

---

a man alive, our brother had not died."—Wood's " Athenæ Oxo-
nienses," vol. ii., " John Selden," p. 134.   Folio.   London : 1721.

    * This lecture was delivered on the 9th of June, 1864, at
the Four Courts, Dublin.   The following was the notice issued :—

       "THE CROMWELLIAN SETTLEMENT OF IRELAND.

    " A lecture, to be based on Acts and Ordinances of the Parlia-
ment of the Commonwealth of England, on unpublished Orders and
Declarations of the Lord Deputy and Council for the Affairs of Ireland, and on other original sources.   To be illustrated by transcript
maps of Strafford's Survey, taken in 1637, on occasion of the confiscation of Connaught and part of Tipperary ; also by transcripts of
the Down Survey, for setting down the regiments of the Army of
the Parliament of England, by troops and companies, in 1654 and
1655 ; by original certificates of Adventurers' allotments, and by
conveyances from the soldiers of whole troops and companies of their
debentures to their officers ; likewise by coloured maps, showing, in
different tints, the baronies assigned in Connaught for the new settlements of the ancient nobility, gentry, and farmers of the Irish nation,
corresponding in character to their old habitations in the three other
provinces from whence they were transplanted; and showing the
division of those three provinces between the Adventurers, for their
advances towards putting down the rebellion, and between the
officers and soldiers for arrears of pay.

and appreciation shown by men so well qualified to judge gave assurance that the subject could not be without interest to the public.

JOHN P. PRENDERGAST.

3, *Tower Terrace, Sandymount, Dublin,*
   May 1, 1865.

CONTENTS.

CONCLUSION.

THE THREE BURDENSOME BEASTS.

APPENDIX.

INTRODUCTION.

"THE Irish are one of the most ancient nations," says Spenser, "that I know of at this end of the world;" and come of "as mighty a race as the world ever brought forth."*

They belong to that great Gaelic or Celtic race that ages ago inhabited Erin, Britain, Gaul, and the northern part of Spain.

Men of big hearts, and big bodies,† the Gauls were long the terror of Rome. Bursting over the Alps, they sacked the city (B. C. 388). Camillus paid a ransom for it, and they retired; and Camillus got the name of Second founder of Rome. Others of them, following the course of the Danube, burst into Greece, and attacked the Temple of Delphi for its treasures (B. C. 279). Another body crossed over into Asia Minor. Three of their tribes divided the country among them. Antiochus at length put a stop to their attacks on the Greek cities,‡

---

* "View of the State of Ireland, written by Edmund Spenser, Esq., in the yeare 1596," pp. 26 and 32. Folio. Printed at Dublin: 1633.

† "Ingentes animos ingenti corpore versant."—The men of Tipperary are said to have hearts as big as bulls, and to their foes as fierce; but to woman or friend as tender as thrushes.

‡ See the touching song, in Greek, of three young Ionian ladies of Miletus, who voluntarily quitted life rather than meet these Gauls:—

"Then let us hence, Miletus dear! Sweet native land, farewell!
The insulting wrongs of lawless Gauls we fear whilst here we dwell."

Bohn's "Greek Anthology," translated, 12mo., London, 1852, p. 449.

and confined them to the central mountains of Asia Minor ; for this he got the title of Soteer, or Saviour (B. C. 277). There they long dwelt, the only free people amid nations of slaves. The chiefs of the clans met yearly on a plain, surrounded by ancient oaks. Here St. Jerome found them speaking their own language, six hundred years after their first settlement. Of these were "the Galatians," or Celts, to whom St. Paul addressed his Epistle.

About one hundred years before the birth of Christ, the Cimbric Gauls again threatened Rome. Marius, fresh from his conquest at Carthage, defeated them. It bespeaks the greatness of the peril that the Romans gave him for this victory the name of Third founder of Rome. They were a warlike race. Whoever wanted to buy headlong courage hired the Gauls. They were in the pay of Carthage ; they were the chosen soldiers of Pyrrhus, that king of blasted triumphs, who loved fighting for fighting's sake. It was in going to the rescue of his Gaulish troops, overmatched in the market-place of Argos, that an old woman killed him in one of its narrow streets, by a tile thrown from the roof. Vast in their hopes, noisy, rhetorical, laughers, talkers, sympathetic,—such is the character of the early race. "The Gauls march openly to their end," says Strabo, " and are thus easily circumvented."

Some people seem always disposed to side with the powerful, but the Gauls, according to the same author, more readily took part with the weak and injured.

Cæsar, meditating schemes for the overthrow of the aristocratical power in Rome, exercised his armies in subduing the Gauls. Having desolated a country, the Romans set about

One might have presumed that these Gauls belonged to Gallia Celtica (they did in fact come from Toulouse, in France) ; if they had been Irish, these virgins need not have felt the least alarm,—for

" No son of Erin would have offered them harm."

civilizing it. They established on the ruins of ancient Gaulish freedom a Roman government and a bastard Roman civilization.

They gave the Gauls baths, circuses, and forums; but they took away from them their arms and the management of their own affairs. Their best citizens were withdrawn from them, to seek their fortunes at the capital of the world. Dearly did they pay for their civilization. Large landed estates, which had ruined Italy, now ruined Gaul.* Weighed down with taxes, and the overpowering shadow of the empire, in their wretchedness the Gauls of France actually welcomed the irruption of the barbarians.†

The Britons, in the course of 400 years of Roman government, were reduced to similar weakness. The descendants of those warriors that startled Julius Cæsar with their enthusiastic bravery and contempt of death, were unable to strike in their own defence, when the Roman armies withdrew to the Continent to support the crumbling empire. When the Irish of Caledonia invaded them, the Britons could do nothing but "groan," and finally called in the Saxons to defend them. It was the same with Spain—this country, that so long maintained itself against the Romans, was overrun by the Vandals, and partitioned in two years. It was the same wherever the Roman power prevailed. Italy, and Rome itself, Gaul, Spain, Britain, were overrun by hordes of barbarians.

Huns, Alans, Vandals, Burgundians, Goths, Ostrogoths, Visigoths, Lombards, Saxons, Franks, poured over Western Europe, like wave succeeding wave. Whole countries were depopulated ; their names were changed, their laws and

---

* "Latifundia perdidere Italiam ; jam vero et provincias." C. Plin. Secundi, Nat. Hist. lib. xviii. 7.

† For an account of the Gauls, see Michelet, "Histoire de France," b. i., cc. 1–3 ; Amadée Thierry, "Histoire des Gaules." 2 vols. 8vo. Paris : 1857.

languages lost; the survivors became the farm slaves of the
conquerors, to be taxed, worked, and flogged at the will of
their masters. These conquerors began to fight amongst themselves; the strong ones knew no law but their own will,
limited only by their power. They built themselves castles
on the heights, clad themselves in iron, and compelled
each man to be either of their band or to be their victim. The
earlier invaders resigned to some later tyrant in the neighbourhood the allotments they had carved out for themselves with
their own swords and held independent of any superior. They
took them back from him as his Tenants on the condition
of serving him with his followers either in robbing, or in
defending him from being robbed, he on his part yielding
them protection.* This was the feudal system, the foundation
of the law of real property in Europe, modified in the course of
centuries, by the growth of towns, by the spread of intelligence,
by the Crusades; happily extinguished utterly in France by the
Revolution of 1789, and wherever the French army carried
the Code Napoleon with its abolition of settlements or *quasi*-
entails, by deed or will, and its freer diffusion of property in
land, accompanied by general self-respect, and increase of
national well-being.

Britain from her remoteness, and by being an island, was
not subject to so many invasions as the Continent of Europe.
She fell, however (A.D. 450) to one of the fiercest of the barbarian nations, the Saxons. They were possessed in the highest
degree of the Land hunger that made the invasions of these
northern hordes so terrible beyond all former conquests.
They seized the houses and farms of the Romanized Britons,
exterminated them and their language, and the very names of

* Robertson, "History of the Emperor Charles V.;" preliminary
chapter and appendix, ib.

their towns and districts, and drove the survivors behind the
River Severn ; and there they shut them up among the mountains of Cambria, surrounded by the Severn and the sea, and
further secured on the land side by the dyke called Offa's
Dyke, just as their descendants, one thousand years later,
penned up the Irish in Connaught behind the Shannon.

Six hundred years after the settlement of the Saxons in
Britain, another race of pirates, who had issued in their boats
from the fiords and bays of Norway and the Baltic, sailed
up the Seine. They made themselves masters of Neustria,
took wives of the native race, and became the French of Normandy. Thence William the Conqueror led his French and
Flemish followers into England. These French of Normandy reduced this great English nation to such slavery,
that they seized the entire lands and government of England, made the inhabitants their serfs, taxable and floggable
at their will, until it became a disgrace to be called an Englishman.*

The English peasantry, deprived of the protection of their
native gentry and national Government, took the only means
they had to make themselves respected : they cut the throats
of the worst of their foreign landlords whenever they caught
them unawares in byways and thickets.† As no one would turn
informer (for national hatred is the firmest bond of association
and secrecy), the vill or townland was then fined where a
Frenchman was found murdered. To escape this fine, the
English peasantry used to cut off the poor gentleman's nose,
slit his cheeks, and so disfigure the corpse, that no one could

---

* "Ut Anglum vocari foret opprobrio." Matthew of Paris, b. i.,
c. 12.

† "Black Book of the Exchequer," by Richard Fitz Nigel (or Lenoir),
afterwards Bishop of Ely, written in 24th of Henry II., A. D. 1172, in the

know whether it was French or English. This practice is alluded to in the ballad of " Robin Hood and Sir Guy of Gisborne," where, after Robin has slain Sir Guy, the ballad proceeds,—

> " Then Robin pulled out an Irish knife,
>   And nicked Sir Guy in the face,
> That he was never of woman born
>   Could know whose head it was."

It was then enacted that the corpse should be deemed French, unless a jury found it was only an Englishman. This was called the presentment of " Englischerie." The French who ruled England charged the English peasantry with treachery and murder as characteristic of their race. They said that abroad over the wide extent of Germany, inhabited by so many races, whenever any very atrocious deed was committed, it was common to hear people say, " Perfidious Saxon!"* But the English peasantry had no natural taste for murder. They

introduction to Madox's " History and Antiquities of the Exchequer," 2 vols. 4to, London, 1769, vol. i., p. 390. It has been truly said—

> " Qui de ses sujets est haï,
>   N'est pas seigneur de son pays."

> " The lord whose tenants cannot well endure him,
>   Finds no place in his country to secure him."

See Randle Cotgrave's French and English Dictionary, A. D. 1610, at the word " Seigneur." Howell's edit. Folio. London : 1673.

    * " Who dare compare the English, the most degraded of all races under heaven [says Giraldus Cambrensis], with the Welsh ? In their own country they are the serfs, the veriest slaves of the Normans. In ours who else have we for our herdsmen, shepherds, cobblers, skinners, cleaners of our dog kennels, ay, even of our privies, but Englishmen ? Not to mention their original treachery to the Britons, that hired by them to defend them they turned upon them in spite of their oaths and engagements,

sheltered and protected the man that avenged his own
wrongs with spirit, as in some degree the champion of their
cause and race ; feeling, perhaps, that if it was not for shooting
a gentleman now and then, there would be no living in the
country for a poor man. This law (and probably these insults
and murders) lasted till the reign of Edward III. Then, when
the services of the English bowmen were wanted to bring
back the revolted French provinces under the hated rule of
England,* they ceased from these national insults, and no doubt
found the English peasantry possessed of bravery, truth, and
all the virtues under the sun.

These French conquerors were settled one hundred years
in England before they invaded Ireland. A body of them,
principally Flemings, had settled in the southern part of

---

they are to this day given to treachery and murder, so that whenever,
&c." The concluding words in the Latin of Giraldus are—" Unde et in
Teutonico regno quotiens enormiter quis delinquere videtur, de natione
quacunque, quasi proverbialiter in suo vulgari dici solet *Untrewe Sax*, hoc
est, infidelis Saxo."   Giraldi Cambrensis Opera, edited by J. S. Brewer,
M. A., vol. iii., p. 27. 8vo. London, Longman & Co.: 1863.

* " The English," says Carte (alluding to the brutal insolence displayed
in the debates in the Parliament of England upon the Live Irish Cattle
Importation Prohibition Bill, in 1666, which he says was urged out of wan-
tonness, and a resolution taken to domineer over that distressed kingdom),
" never understood governing their provinces, and have put them under a
necessity of casting off their government whenever an opportunity offered."
" Life of James Duke of Ormond," vol. ii., p. 317. And he had seen the
treaties which the provinces of Guienne, Poictou, Anjou, &c., had made
with the Kings of France, when by the intolerable pride of the English they
had been forced to throw off their yoke. In these they expressly stipulated,
"that in any distress of the affairs of France they should never be delivered
back into the power of the English." Ib., ib. And the people thus injured
and insulted by them in Ireland, in 1666, were their own blood and nation,
the Adventurers and Soldiers not ten years settled in the country.

Wales along the Bristol Channel, round by St. David's Head, from whence Ireland was in view.

A party of these men, by way of private adventure, sailed over to the aid of the King of Leinster, then at war with the neighbouring Irish kings. The contingent they brought was small in number compared to the Irish army which they joined; but better arms, and discipline acquired in foreign war and in maintaining the rule of conquerors over the English they had enslaved, gave the victory to the side they espoused. Their leader married the King's daughter, and received as her dowry the kingdom of Leinster; his followers obtained estates in the same district; and, an opening being thus made, the French prince then ruling in England followed, with an army of French and Flemings, and established his rule in Ireland.

The country to which the invaders had now arrived struck them as another world.* The rest of western Europe had been for more than a thousand years enslaved, first to the Romans, then to the northern hordes; so that the Feudal system, which is founded on the conquest and colonization of the country by an army of foreigners, had come to be considered as the natural state.

Ireland, however, lying on the verge of the western world in the Atlantic, separated from Britain by the unquiet Irish Sea, scarcely calm for three days in summer,† had escaped Roman and feudal thraldom.

Tacitus had often heard Agricola, his father-in-law, commander of the Roman forces in Britain, say that the country

* "Thus separated from the rest of the known world, and in some sort to be distinguished as another world."—Giraldus, "Topographia Hiberniæ," b. i., chap. 2.

† Ibid., b. ii., chap. 1.

could be conquered and held by one legion, and that the conquest of it much concerned the interests of the Romans in Britain ; for the neighbourhood of a free country rendered the Britons more difficult to govern. It would be well, therefore, that freedom should be as it were taken out of sight, and the Roman armies be seen everywhere.

To this end he kept a Mac Murrogh* in his camp, and moved a legion to the coast of Wales, watching for some opportunity ; but the exigencies of the empire called the Roman forces home without having invaded Ireland.† So that when the companions of Strongbow landed, in the reign of King Henry II., they found a country such as Cæsar found in Gaul 1200 years before ; the inhabitants divided into tribes on the system of clansmen and chiefs, without a common government, suddenly confederating, suddenly dissolving, with Brehons, Shannahs, Minstrels, Bards, and Harpers, in all unchanged, except that for their ancient Druids they had got Christian priests. Had the Irish only remained honest Pagans, Ireland perhaps had been unconquered still. Round the coast strangers had built seaport towns, either traders from the Carthaginian settlements in Spain, or outcasts from their own country, like the Greeks that built Marseilles.‡ At the time of the arrival of the French and Flemish adventurers from Wales, they were occupied by a mixed Danish and French population, who supplied the Irish with groceries, including the wines of Poitou,

---

* " Agricola, expulsum seditione domesticâ, unum ex regulis gentis exceperat, ac specie amicitiæ in occasionem retinebat."—Tacitus, " Life of Agricola."

† " Life of Agricola."

‡ Giraldus Cambrensis says the towns were built by the Ostmen, " Topography of Ireland," Distinction iii., chap. 43. But, as Tacitus says the ports of Ireland were better known to merchants than those of England, the account here given is the more probable one.

—the latter in such abundance, that they had no need of vineyards.*

Unlike England, then covered with castles on the heights, where the French gentlemen secured themselves and their families against the hatred of the churls and villeins, as the English peasantry were called, the dwellings of the Irish chiefs were of wattle or clay. It is for robbers and foreigners to take to rocks and precipices for security ; for native rulers there is no such fortress as justice and humanity.

The Irish, like the wealthiest and highest of the present day, loved detached houses, surrounded by fields and woods. Towns and their walls they looked upon as tombs or sepulchres, where man's native vigour decays, as the fiercest animals lose their courage by being caged.† They wore woollen garments much in the present fashion, and disdained to case themselves in iron, thinking it honourable to fight naked, as it was called, with the mailed French of Normandy and their Flemish and English followers, just as the Gauls fought naked with the well-armed soldiers of Rome.‡

They were fond of music, poetry, and genealogy, and the professors of these arts in each tribe or clan had land hereditarily allotted to them. In the spirited character of the Irish

---

* Giraldus Cambrensis, Distinction i., chap. 5.

† This was the feeling of the ancient Germans.—Gibbon, chap. xix.

‡ Sentleger, Lord Deputy, giving Henry VIII. a description of such troops as he might command out of Ireland to France, after describing the galloglasses, says :—" The other sort, called kerne, are naked men but only their shirts and small coats, and many times when they came to the bicker [fight] but bare naked saving their shirts to hide their privities," p. 444. State Papers (Ireland), H. VIII., vol. ii., Paper 385. In the battle with Lucius Æmilius, the young chiefs of the Gesatæ stripped themselves naked, except only their collars and armlets of gold.—Polybius, b. ii., chap. 2.

the new settlers found themselves in the presence of a people of original sentiments and institutions, the native vigour of whose mind had not been weakened by another mind. Nothing surprised the invaders more than the natural boldness and readiness of the Irish in speaking and answering even in the presence of their chieftains and princes, accustomed as the invaders were to the servile habits of the English, produced, as Giraldus says, either by long slavery, or (more probably he adds) by the innate dulness of men of Saxon and German stock.*

They were equally astonished at the freedom and familiarity of the Irish gentry with their poorer followers, so different from the haughty reserve of an aristocracy of foreign descent towards the lower classes of a subject nation reduced by conquest to the state of villeins and serfs. Free by nature, the Irish were followers of nature and freedom in all things.

Unlike most other nations of the world, the Irish did not bind up their infants in swaddling clothes.† It required the

---

* Giraldus Cambrensis, "Description of Wales," b. i., c. 15; but the same remark was applicable to the Irish even in a greater degree.

† Such was the custom of the Jews:—"And when I was born, I drew in the common air, and fell upon the earth . . . and the first voice which I uttered was crying . . . I was nursed in swaddling clothes." . . . Wisdom of Solomon, chap. 7. And of the Romans:—"Hominem tantum nudum, et in nudâ humo natali die [natura] abjicit ad vagitus statim et ploratum. Ab hoc lucis rudimento, . . . vincula excipiunt et omnium membrorum nexus: itaque feliciter natus, jacet, manibus pedibusque devinctis, flens animal cæteris imperaturum, et a suppliciis vitam auspicatur, unam tantum ob culpam quia natum est."—C. Plinius, lib. vii., chap. 1. "Nature flings down man alone naked on the bare ground on the day of his birth, to begin life with cries and tears. On his entrance into light every limb is chained and bound; and there lies this little weeping animal that is to command all others, born under these happy auspices, and begins its life in chains and punishment, guilty only of being born."

lapse of ages, and the burning eloquence of Rousseau, to induce the world to follow the practice of the Irish, who never
went wrong in this respect; so true is the saying that he
who follows nature never goes out of the way. We learn
from Giraldus, that the Irish midwives did not raise the new-
born babe's nose, nor shape its face, nor stretch and swathe
its little legs. Nature, he says, was in that country allowed to
adjust the limbs she had given birth to; and, as if to prove that
what she was able to form she does not cease to watch over,
it was found that she gave growth and proportion to the Irish
until they arrived at perfect vigour, tall and handsome.* And,
being never swathed in infancy, their limbs had a freer turn,
and their countenances a more liberal air.

The harp that had long been silent in Gaul, and was heard
in Britain only in the mountains of Wales, was universally
played in Ireland; and the gaiety of the airs, and the skill of
the artists, astonished and delighted those accustomed to the
slower airs of the Welsh.†

They amused themselves with hurling, the men of one district playing against those of another, the prize probably, as in
later times, being often some fair girl, arranged to be the bride
of the favourite youth of the winning side.‡

---

* "Topography of Ireland," Distinction iii., chap. 10.

† Ibid., chap. 11.

‡ " There is a very ancient custom here [county of Tipperary] for a
number of country neighbours among the poor people to fix upon some
young woman that ought, as they think, to be married. They also agree upon
a young fellow as a proper husband for her. This determined, they send to
the fair one's cabin, to inform her that on the Sunday following she is to
be horsed, that is, carried in triumph on men's backs. She must then provide whiskey and cider for a treat, as all will pay her a visit after mass for
a hurling match. As soon as she is horsed, the hurling begins, on which
the young fellow appointed for her husband has the eyes of all the company

The great body of the people were of pastoral habits. The different families used the tribal lands in common, following their herds from the winter feeding grounds to the summer pastures in the mountains, shifting their quarters as the need of fresh pasturage for their cows required, and building for themselves light booths of boughs of trees, covered with long strips of green turf.

The tillage ground of each tribe, near which they seem to have had dwellings a little more durable than their moveable summer huts in the mountains, was annually divided among the families by the Caunfinny, according to their stock and requirements.

But, though the great body of the people had no separate properties, the chief families had portions appropriated to them in perpetuity. There were also lands appointed as well for the elected chief, as others for the Tanist who was to succeed him ; other portions were also enjoyed hereditarily by the Brehons, and bards, and physicians of the tribe. The chief also was entitled to tributes of victuals, and certain of his dependents were bound to entertain him and his company for stated times in the year.

But the Irish knew no such thing as tenure, nor forfeiture, nor fixed rent ; at this they repined, though willing to offer

---

fixed on him : if he comes off conqueror, he is certainly married to the girl ; but if another is victor, he as certainly loses her, for she is the prize of the victor."—Vol. ii., p. 250, " A Tour in Ireland in the years 1776, 1777, 1778," by Arthur Young. 8vo. Dublin : 1780. See also his account of Irish dancing, ibid. ; but, with the advance of English power and English religion,

> " These healthful sports that graced the happy scene,
> Lived in each look, and brightened all the green,
> These, far departing, seek a kinder shore,
> And rural mirth and manners are no more."

such tribute of victuals as was required, and to let their chieftains eat them almost out of house and home : hence the
saying, " Spend me, but Defend me."*

The treaty between Henry II. and Roderic, King of Connaught, entered into at Windsor, three years after the king's
return from his " Veni, vidi, vici," visit to Ireland, as Sir
John Davies styles it, justifies his ridicule of the nature of the
conquest attributed to him.

By that instrument, signed on O'Connor's behalf, as King
of Connaught, and Chief King of Ireland, by two of the Pope's
new archbishops of Ireland, O'Connor is made to become the
King's liegeman, and to be King of Connaught, and Chief
King of Ireland, under Henry II. He undertakes that the
Irish shall yield the King of England annually one merchant-
able hide for every ten cows in Ireland, which O'Connor is to
collect for him through every part of Ireland, except that
which is in the possession of King Henry II. and his barons,
being Dublin, Meath, and Leinster, with Waterford as far as
Dungarvan. The rest of the kings and people of Ireland are
to enjoy all their lands and liberties as long as they shall continue faithful to the King of England, and pay this tribute
through the hands of the King of Connaught.†

Two systems were thus established side by side in Ireland,
the Feudal and the Brehon systems ; for the Irish, as Sir John
Davies remarks, merely became tributaries to the King of Eng-

---

* Spenser says, "Coigny is in common use amongst landlords of the Irish
to have a common spending upon their tenants . . . . neither in this was
the tenant wronged, for it was an ordinary and known custom . . . . for
they were never wont (and yet are loth) to yield any certain rent but only
such spendings ; for their common saying is, 'Spend me, but Defend me.' "
" A View of the State of Ireland," by Edmund Spenser, Esq., in the year
1596.

† Rymer's "Fœdera," vol. i., p. 31. Folio. London : 1816.

land, preserving their ancient Brehon law, and electing their chiefs and tanists, making war and peace with one another, and ruling all things between themselves by this law, until the reign of Queen Elizabeth ;* and this, as Spenser remarks, not merely in districts entirely inhabited by Irish, but in the English parts. He speaks as an eye-witness, having seen their meetings on their ancient accustomed hills, where they debated and settled matters between family and family, township and township, assembling in large numbers, and going, according to their custom, all armed.†

There, surrounded by the Irish lords and gentlemen and commonalty, seated on the accustomed stone, or under some ancient tree, the Brehon gave his judgment according to the Brehon code, formed partly of Irish customs, and partly of maxims culled from the Roman Digest.‡

Campion, an English Jesuit, from Cambridge, who travelled in Ireland in Queen Elizabeth's day, saw their schools of Brehon law ; the rising Brehons, stretched at full length, conning their tasks, and learning by rote fragments of Roman and Irish law, at which they continued for many years.§ Spenser admits

---

* " A Discoverie of the State of Ireland, and the true Cause why that Kingdom was never entirely subdued until the Beginning of His Majesties [James I.] most happie Reign." London : 1613, p. 603.

† " View of Ireland," pp. 421, 500.

‡ Sir James Ware, " Antiquities of Ireland," chap. viii.

§ " They speak Latin like a vulgar language, learned in their common schools of leachcraft and law, whereat they begin children and hold on sixteen or twenty years, conning by rote the aphorisms of Hippocrates and the Civil Institutes, and a few other parings of these two faculties. I have seen them where they kept school, ten in some one chamber, grovelling upon couches of straw, their books at their noses, themselves lying prostrate, and so to chaunt out their lessons by piecemeal, being the most part lusty fellows of twenty-five years and upwards."—p. 18, Edmund Campion's " Account of Ireland," written in May, 1571.

that their decisions had great show of equity. Stanihurst, a cotemporary of Spenser's, had witnessed the breaking up of their meetings, and seen the crowd in long lines coming down the hills in the wake of each chieftain, he the proudest that could bring the largest company home to his evening supper.*

It was from a priest who had once been a Brehon that Sir John Davies, in 1610, received the treatise on "Corbes and Herenachs ;"† and few who have read his account of the first assizes held for the county of Fermanagh, in the ruins of the abbey, in the island of Lough Erne, will forget the aged Brehon of the Maguires drawing from his bosom with trembling hand the ancient roll, and refusing to part with it until the Lord Deputy, Sir Arthur Chichester, had given him his hand and faith that it should be restored to him.‡ It was only at this period of the reign of King James I. that the practice of the Brehon law was forbidden in Ireland ;§ for the Statutes of Kilkenny, passed in the 40th of Edward III., only prohibited the use of it in ruling differences between the English. The Irish had no other, as they were denied the use of the English law. But after the subduing of Tyrone's rebellion, the English judges, who had hitherto gone their circuits round the Pale, were sent all round Ireland to administer English law ; and the practice of the Irish code was superseded, and declared to be no law, but a lewd custom.

---

* Ricardus Stanihurst, "De Rebus in Hiberniâ Gestis," p. 37. 4to. Antwerp: 1584.

† "Letter to Robert Earl of Salisbury, touching the State of Monaghan, Fermanagh, and Cavan ; wherein is a Discourse concerning the Corbes and Herenachs of Ireland," 1607, 8vo, Dublin, 1787, p. 246.

‡ Ib., ib., p. 253.

§ In Hilary Term, 3rd James I. (A. D. 1605). See Sir J. Davies, Reports, p. 40.

At the date of the Treaty of Windsor the invaders had planted themselves only on the east coast of Ireland; and King Henry II. by that treaty purported to guarantee their lands to the rest of the Irish. Yet he did not hesitate, unknown probably to the Irish, to cantonize or divide Ireland among ten of his followers, who received by these grants petty kingdoms, to be divided among their comrades and followers, in the expectation that they should bring over fresh Adventurers from England, and that as they grew more numerous, they should gradually supplant the Irish, and strip them of their lands.*

These barons and their followers all held their lands on feudal conditions, liable to homage and fealty, to aids and talliages, to wardships and marriages, to fines for alienation, to primer seisins, rents, reliefs, escheats, and forfeitures—contrivances of the stronger for exacting money from the weaker. They stood instead of legacy and succession duties and stamp duties of modern times. No man could come into his estate without paying a year's rent as a relief, or sell it or settle it without a fine for alienation.

But beyond all other feudal burthens were wardships and marriages. If a gentleman left his heir under age at his death, he could appoint no guardian: the king or superior lord (for each lord exacted from his tenants what the king exacted from him) took possession of the heir and the estate, leaving the widow to maintain the rest of the family out of her dower, while the guardian spent the rents of the estate without liability to account, often letting the castle go out of repair. As incident to the wardship, he had the right to sell it, and with it the right for the purchaser to dispose of the heir or heiress in marriage to the highest bidder. Thus the Earl of Lincoln gave King John 3000 marcs for the marriage of Richard de

---

* Sir John Davies' "Discoverie," &c. p. 652.

Clare in order to marry him to his eldest daughter, Matilda.*
Geoffry de Mandeville gave him 20,000 marcs, that he might
marry Isabella Countess of Gloucester, and possess her lands.†
Sibella de Singera offers the king 200 marcs to marry as she
likes.‡ Heiresses remained in wardship to the king or their
landlord until they married, no matter what their age, and when
they became widows became wards again, and to marry a second time must have their landlords' consent.§ Thus Alice
Countess of Warwick gave the king £1000 for liberty to remain a widow as long as she liked, and not to be forced by the
king to marry, and for the wardship of her sons.‖ One of the
great inducements to settle in towns was the privilege con-
ceded by almost every founder of a borough by his charter,
that the burghers or citizens might marry, themselves, their
sons, and daughters, and widows, without license from their
lords ;¶ a license of late required on the estates of some landlords managed in the English or feudal mode in Ireland.

No man could hunt or hawk on his own estate ; the game
was all reserved for the king ;** he could not even take the
young hawks in his own oaks—this was one of the liberties
won and consecrated by Magna Charta. So strict a game pre-
server was King John, that the beasts and fowl of the forest
seemed to be aware that they were under his protection. In
England the country abounded with them ; they would not

* Preface, p. xxx. " Oblate and Fine Rolls in the Tower of London, in
the Time of King John," Record Publication. 8vo. By T. D. Hardy :
1835.

† Ib., ib.   ‡ Ib., xxxii.   § Ib., ib.   ‖ Ib., ib.

¶ See the charter of the City of Dublin and other charters, in " Cartæ
Privilegia et Immunitates," Irish Record Commission. Folio.

** Walter de Riddlesford offers King John (A. D. 1200) twenty marcs
to have the King's confirmation of his lands, and for license to hunt the hare
and the wolf. " Oblate and Fine Rolls," preface, p. ix, n.

fly from the traveller, but would only move to a short distance
and continue to feed.* This slavery the Anglo-Saxons always
endured; but the Irish never knew the Forest Law or Game
Law, nor could the English ever impose it on them. "If they
had," says Sir John Davies, "it might have been a means
of conquest; for they might have turned the Irish out of the
wild places where they dwelt in freedom, and might have given
them up to the beasts of chase, less hurtful, and less wild than
they."†

The feudal system proceeded on the principle that the lands
were all derived from the king, as the captain of a conquering
army, and had been distributed by him amongst the members
of it on certain conditions (the main object of which was the
maintaining of the conquest), liable to be forfeited if they were
not observed.

The Irish, having never undergone a feudal conquest and
plantation like the rest of Europe, considered the territory as
the common property and patrimony of the clans or nations—
not held from any one, not liable to forfeiture, which indeed
was impossible, as it was owned and occupied by them jointly
or in common.

The chief families had contrived, contrary to the general
principle, to appropriate some portions to themselves, divisible
however at the death of the father among all the sons, legi-
timate and illegitimate alike. The inferior members of the tribe
yielded to the chiefs milk and honey, and even money for the
grazing of their cows, and were bound to maintain their lords,
with their wives, sons, and daughters, their horses, servants,

---

* See a curious account by one of the Flemish soldiers of King John's
expeditionary army to Ireland, in the year 1210, " Histoire des Ducs de
Normandie," vol. i., p. 109. 2 vols. 8vo. Paris : 1840.

Sir John Davies' " Discoverie," &c., p. 664.

their dogs and dog boys, for a specified number of meals or days in their houses when they went among their dependents " coshering," as it was called. But they knew no such thing as rent or services in the feudal sense, as an acknowledgment of holding their land from a landlord, liable to forfeiture if not rendered.

The chief, like the baron, had his law court, but it assembled under his Brehon on the hill.* He had his retainers, and each of them had their kerne, or foot soldiers, ready to appear on summons, quartered on the poorer families of the tribe. The Irish custom of fosterage was in the nature of wardship ; but the object being to make the young chief the beloved of his followers, he was brought up in the bosom of the family of his foster parents, who paid largely for the honour of thus bringing him up from his earliest years in the midst of them.† Nursed up in a sense of his own importance, he became the proud and spirited head of the clan, their pride and joy, and bound to his foster family and they to him by ties of affection stronger than those of blood.

Though their lands were thus left with the Irish, it was the design of the English Government that they should gradually come into the possession of the English, until all should be

---

* " Other lawyers they have liable to certain families, which after the custom of the country determine and judge causes. . . the Breighoon (as they call this kind of lawyer) sitteth him down on a bank, the lords and gentlemen at variance around about him, and then they proceed," p. 19, Edward Campion (1571).

† " They love tenderly their foster children, and bequeath to them a child's portion, whereby they nourish sure friendship, so beneficial in every way, that commonly 500 kine and better are given to winne a nobleman's child to foster." Ib., pp. 13–14. Gifts of the Irishry to foster with the Earl of Kildare, pp. 70 71, " Earls of Kildare," vol. ii., by the Marquis of Kildare. Dublin : 1860.

held in feudal tenure, and the feudal system be spread throughout the kingdom. With this intent, therefore, the Irish were
denied the right of bringing actions in any of the English
Courts in Ireland for trespasses to their lands, or for assaults
and batteries to their persons. Accordingly, it was answer
enough to the action in such a case to say that the plaintiff
was an Irishman,* unless he could produce a special charter
giving him the rights of an Englishman. If he sought damages
against an Englishman for turning him out of his land, for the
seduction of his daughter Nora, or for the beating of his wife
Devorgil, or for the driving off of his cattle, it was a good defence to say he was a mere Irishman. And if an Englishman
was indicted for manslaughter, if the man slain was an Irishman, he pleaded that the deceased was of the Irish nation, and
that it was no felony to kill an Irishman. For this, however,
there was a fine of five marcs, payable to the king; but mostly
they killed as for nothing. If it happened that the man killed
was a servant of an Englishman, he added to the plea of the
deceased being an Irishman, that if the master should ever demand damages, he would be ready to satisfy him.† Not unlike

---

* Thus in 29th Edward I., before the justices in Eyre, at Drogheda,
Thomas le Boteler brought an action against Robert de Almain for certain
goods. The defendant pleaded that he was not bound to answer him, because he was an Irishman, and not of free blood. A jury was summoned,
and found that the plaintiff was an Englishman, and thereupon he had judgment to recover his goods. Sir J. Davies' " Discoverie," p. 639.

† " Lastly, the mere Irish were not only accounted aliens, but enemies,
and altogether out of the protection of the law, so as it was no capital offence
to kill them." And then Sir J. Davies gives a record of a gaol delivery at
Waterford, where " Robert Walsh, indicted of the manslaughter of John,
son of Ivor Mac Gilmore, admits the slaying; but says it was no felony, because Mac Gilmore was a mere Irishman, and not of free blood : But when
the master of the said John shall ask damages for the slaying, he will be
ready to answer him as the law may require." " Discoverie," p. 641.

the story of those hot bloods of Charles II.'s day who ran the waiter through at a tavern with their rapiers, and threw the body out at the window, and then rang the bell for the land-lord, and bade him put him in the bill.

The Irish, too, were forbid to purchase land. Though the English might take from the Irish, the Irish could not even by way of gift or purchase take any from the English. In every charter of English liberty, as it was called, granted to an Irishman, besides the right to bring actions in the king's courts, there was given an express power to him to purchase lands to him and his heirs;* without this he could not hold any so ac-quired. The Exchequer officers constantly held inquisitions for the purpose of obtaining a return that certain lands had been aliened to an Irishman, in order thereupon to seize them into the hands of the Crown as forfeited. Thus, by inquisition taken at Dunboyne, in the first year of King Henry VI., the lands of Moymet and Clonfine in the county of Meath, were found forfeited; and were seized by the king's escheator, as having been aliened by Esmond Butler, son and heir of James Lord and Baron of Dunboyne, deceased, to Connor O'Mulrooney and John Machan, chaplains, and their heirs, they being Irish and of Irish nation.† Not that this was any beneficial con-veyance to these two Irishmen, but simply a feoffment to them as trustees for the purposes of a will or settlement. In 16th of Edward IV., lands near Swords, in the county of Dublin, were seized on a like inquisition, finding them to have been conveyed by Catherine Dowdal to John Belane, chaplain, an Irishman of Irish nation, that is to say, of the O'Belanes, Irishmen, and enemies to our lord the king; although O'Belane was evi-

* Sir J. Davies' " Discoverie," p. 641.

† Fifth Edward IV., c. 24. Transcript of Statute Rolls, made by the Record Commissioners (1810), in the Record Tower, Dublin Castle.

dently only a trustee to answer the uses of Mrs. Dowdal's will.*
The Parliament Rolls are full of cases where the inquisitions
are set aside, for the finding having been malicious and untrue,
the parties complained of not being Irish, but English. They
prove, however, that no Irishman could take lands by conveyance from an Englishman; and this continued to be the law
until the year 1612, when Sir John Davies framed an act abo-
lishing the distinction of nations.† But the prohibition practically prevailed after the passing of the act; for, by Plantation
rule, the English were forbidden, under pain of forfeiture, to
convey any of the lands taken from the Irish in the extensive
plantations of English made in Munster, Ulster, and Leinster,
to any Irishman, and the Irish there could only aliene to English; so that the Irish must be always losing, and the English
gaining, by any change. The prohibition was again extended
to the whole nation by the Commonwealth Government;
and when the lands forfeited for the war of 1690 came to be sold
at Chichester House in 1703, the Irish were declared by the
English Parliament incapable of purchasing at the auction
or of taking a lease of more than two acres. Shortly afterwards, another act disqualified them for ever from purchasing
or acquiring any lands in Ireland, and declared the purchase

---

* Sixteenth Edward IV., c. 80. Ib., ib.

† "Statutes of Ireland," 11th, 12th, and 13th James I., c. v.

‡ But it was when the estate was made the property of the first Protestant discoverer, that animation was put into this law (Robinson, Justice,
in *Lessee M‘Carty* against *Stanley*, King's Bench, Hilary Term, 1771),
Howard's "Popery Cases," Dublin, 1775, p. 209. Discoverers then became like hounds upon the scent after lands secretly purchased by the Irish.
Gentlemen fearing to lose their lands found it now necessary to conform.
"Between 1703 and 1709 there were only 36 conformers in Ireland. In
the next ten years (i. e. after the Discovery Act), the conformists were 150."
Ib., ib., pp. 211-12.

void.* But, notwithstanding these prohibitions, the Irish grew
and increased upon the English, instead of the English upon
the Irish ; and the Irish customs overspread the feudal, until at
length the administration of the feudal law was confined to
little more than the counties lying within the line of the Liffey
and the Boyne.

It may be asked how the Irish contrived to preserve
their lands ? In the first place, then, it is to be remembered that
they kept their arms, and the whole tribe rose in war against the
English of that district whence their lands had been invaded,
or by whom an Irishman had been killed. They ravaged it,
and made prisoner of the highest Englishman they could take,
and held him to ransom, and by this obtained a " health saute,"
or satisfaction to the family of the deceased.*

Had the first English adventurers in Ireland been of the
same mind as the king and nobility in England the Irish might
possibly been subdued, their lands taken from them, and the
nation reduced to serfdom, or exterminated. But the early
settlers learned to love the Irish, and to prefer the freedom of
Irish life and manners to the burdensome feudal system. The
case of the leader of the first English adventurers in Ireland
may serve to explain the relations of the English in Ireland
with the Irish in early times.

Richard Strongbow, Earl of Pembroke, was married to an
Irishwoman ; he had a large body of Irish kinsmen ; he had an
army composed largely of Irishmen, and he and they had been
comrades in war; his territory was nearly sixty miles square,
inhabited almost entirely by Irish. His English captains
and men-at-arms, amongst whom he divided his territory
in fiefs, were much in the same condition. They, many

---

* The payment of " Health Saute" by the English to the Irish, made
high treason, 11 & 12 Edward IV., c. 5 (Unpublished Statutes).

of them, took Irish wives and mistresses—had Irish kinsmen
and comrades. As Strongbow left the Kavanaghs and M'Murroughs, relations of his wife's, in possession of their lands,
liable to serve him with their followers in war, so did his captains other Irish; no difference of religion divided them;
they early learned the language of Ireland; they gave out
their sons to be fostered with their Irish relations; the young
English heir became the pride of his foster father and his
clan; hurled with his Irish cousins;* listened with delight
to the harpers, bards, and minstrels,† and became enamoured
of Irish life, and probably of some fine Irish girl also.‡
The young Englishman, however, remained of his father's
nation, an Englishman; and held his estate on English tenure,
liable to the demands of the Exchequer for aids, reliefs, and
fines. How burdensome this tenure was, may be judged from
the complaints of the English of Ireland. In 1347 they complained to the king, that bad as were the Irish enemies, the ex-
tortions and oppressions done by the king's officers were
worse.§ But, bad as these burdens were, the law of forfeiture

* "It is ordained and established that the English do not henceforth
use the plays which men call hurlings with great sticks and a ball upon the
ground, and other plays called coitings; but that they do apply themselves to draw the bow and throw lances, and other gentlemanlike games
appertaining to arms, whereby the Irish enemies may be better checked," &c.
"Statutes of Kilkenny," 40th Edward III. (A. D. 1367), s. 6.

† Ib., sect. 15.

‡ "It is ordained that no alliance by marriage, gossipred, fostering
of children, concubinage, or by amour, be henceforth made between the
English and Irish . . . and if any shall do to the contrary, he shall have
judgment of life and member as a traitor to our Lord the King." Ib., s. 2.

§ "Petitions delivered to our Lord the King of France and England,
by Friar John L'Archer, Prior of St. John of Jerusalem, in Ireland, and
Master Thomas Wogan, sent in message by the Prelates, Earls, Barons, and
Commons of the land in Ireland." "Red Book of the Exchequer of Ireland."

must have been a more constant source of disquiet. Under convictions of high treason the king could enrich himself and his courtiers with confiscated estates. The De Lacys, beggared by this law, and driven from their principalities of Meath and Ulster, induced Edward Bruce to invade Ireland. John Fitzthomas with an army of Irishmen recovered the kingdom for Edward II., but not until the greater part of it had been in possession of the invading force, supported by some of the English of Ireland, for more than a year, during which time the sitting of the courts and the administration of the feudal laws was suspended. The English of Ireland beyond the immediate neighbourhood of the metropolis took care, under various pretences, to oppose its being resumed; and thenceforth the regular administration of the English law was confined to the limits of the Pale. They represented the whole Irish nation as hostile to the English, and thereby had an excuse for keeping up their forces. These forces of kerne and gallowglasses were maintained by coyne and livery, nearly equivalent to free quarters on their tenants; and their English tenants, being unwilling to endure this infliction, retired to England, and the lands thus deserted were granted by these great lords to Irish.*

"The Irish enemy" now became an excuse for feudal duties neglected, and feudal payments withheld. The government of Ireland became impossible to strangers from England. The English lords of Ireland had always a means of moving the Irish to rebellion by oppressing them, or to attacks on their neighbours, or the king's officers, by secretly egging them on.

The judges, who from the days of the first Settlement had regularly ridden their circuits in Munster to administer the

---

* Preamble to 10 Henry VII., c. 4. Sir J. "Davies' Discoverie," p. 675.

feudal law, now ceased to hold assizes. The danger from the Irish enemy was alleged to be the cause, though there was no reason why the Irish should object to the administration of the law, as it was only administered between the King's English subjects. The journey to the South lay through Kildare and Carlow, under the Dublin and Wicklow mountains, to the bridge of Leighlin, for many ages the only passage over the Barrow. These hills were inhabited by the three nations of the Tooles, the Byrnes, and the Kavanaghs, and the opposite side of the river towards Leighlin Bridge by the O'Moores, so that there was a kind of gantelope to be run between these tribes. It is alleged that the Tooles, the Byrnes, and Kavanaghs, exiled the administration of the king's law from Munster, by preventing the judges riding their circuits past Leighlin Bridge.* But as the English of Munster had much greater reason to fear the return of the king's officers than the Irish, there is good reason to suspect that they were egged on by them. In Henry VIII.'s days, the Earl of Kildare was charged with having always protected these three nations, the Tooles, the Byrnes, and the Kavanaghs, whom he kept at his bidding, it was said, ready to rise and "make war behind" when any of the king's forces marched out of Dublin on any expedition which he secretly wished to counteract.† Now "the Irish enemy" was no nation in the modern sense of the word, but a race divided into many nations or tribes, separately defending their lands from the English barons in their immediate neighbourhood. There had been no ancient national government displaced, no national dynasty overthrown; the Irish had no national flag, nor any capital city as the metropolis

* State Papers, Henry VIII. (Ireland), vol. i., p. 411. Memorial, or "A Note for the Wynning of Leynster," A. D. 1536.
† Ib., ib., p. 410.

of their common country, nor any common administration of law; nor did they ever give a national opposition to the English. All the notions of nationality and independent empire are of a surprisingly modern date. The English, coming in the name of the Pope, with the aid of the clergy, and with a superior national organization, which the Irish easily recognised, were accepted by the Irish. Neither King Henry II. nor King John ever fought a battle in Ireland.

In the early days of English rule in Ireland, the Irish generally lived as tributaries to the king. During the reign of Henry III. and in the beginning of that of Edward I. the kings and captains of nations received regular writs of summons, in precisely the same terms and by the same cursitor or courier as the De Burgos, the Butlers, the Le Poërs, to attend the war in Wales or Scotland, or yield the king an aid in money.* The chief or royal tribe in each of the five provinces became allies of the English at the first invasion, as is plain from their receiving the rights of Englishmen to bring and defend actions. They were legally known as the Five bloods, being the O'Neills of Ulster, the O'Connors of Connaught, the O'Melaghlins of Meath, the O'Briens of Munster, and the M'Murroughs of Leinster.† Different encroachments of English adventurers caused partial insurrections. In Bruce's invasion the Northern Irish formed a more general confederacy, and, owing to their situation, established their independence; but the Irish tenants and kerne of the Fitzgeralds, the Butlers, the De Burgos, the Roches, the Barrys, adhered to their English chiefs in Leinster, Munster, and Connaught.

No soldiers came from England, and it was Irish troops

---

* See some of these writs, " Liber Munerum Publicorum," vol. i., part IV., pp. 6, 12.   2 vols.   Folio.   London : 1826.

† Sir John Davies' " Discoverie," p. 639.

that recovered the dominion of Ireland for the English.* But from thenceforth all the Irish were called in law the king's Irish enemy. So that the very men who filled the troops levied by the English Deputy for service against the Irish were known as such. Thus O'Hanlon and O'Mulloy, who claimed to be hereditary standard bearers of Ulster, and bore the Banner of Queen Elizabeth's army as soon as it crossed the Boyne on alternate days, on its march against Hugh O'Neill, were Irish enemy.† It meant that they were excluded from claiming any rights or privileges under English law ; and was in fact a far less injurious disqualification than that of Irish Papist in the last century. The English of Ireland intermarried with them, fostered with them, and made alliances with them, though the Statutes of Kilkenny made it high treason so to do. But as the English law was now confined within the limits of the English Pale, and no judges went circuit beyond the Barrow, the prohibition was nugatory. If it is only remembered that from the reign of King John no army ever came out of England except the expeditionary army of Richard II., and that the few forces subsequently sent over, until the 29th of Queen Elizabeth, were to subdue rebellions of the English,‡ it will be evident that the term Irish enemy simply meant that the Irish had no legal rights, and that sooner or later they should lose their lands to the English.

The English in all the provinces beyond the Pale saw with joy the regular administration of the English law confined within the line of the Liffey and the Boyne. Many of them had acquired lands not held from the Crown, which they feared would be seized.§ Others had large arrears of fines due by

* Sir J. Davies' " Discoverie," p. 674.
† Sir Richard Cox, " Hibernia Anglicana," vol. i., p. 407.
‡ Sir J. Davies' "Discoverie," p. 617.
§ Ib., p. 676.

them, for which their estates were liable to forfeiture. These men boldly banished the king's sheriffs, escheators, and pursuivants, by making it dangerous for them to approach. The Burkes, or De Burgos, were in this class. They had lands which the king claimed by title derived by the intermarriage of Lionel, son of Edward III., with the heir female of William De Burgo, Earl of Ulster. Lionel came over with a considerable force to seize these lands from the Burkes, but did not march into Connaught. Thenceforth they employed every effort to prevent the king's writ running in Connaught. In this sense, and through fear of losing their lands, they became the king's English rebels.* They allied themselves for this purpose with the king's Irish enemies, but they had no intention of rebelling to eject the English out of Ireland; they were too proud of their English blood. To the eye they looked like Irish, for they dressed and spoke as Irishmen, yet they are described as "tall men who boast themselves to be of the king's blood, and berith hate to the Irishrie."† But besides English rebels, the king had his English lieges beyond the Pale. The English lieges beyond the Pale acknowledged themselves to be the king's subjects, on his peace and war, and held their Irish tenants and forces ready to appear in the field on the king's side. But they had for the most part ceased to pay feudal dues, as there were no sheriffs or escheators to enforce them; though the Butlers of Kilkenny, and the Earls of Kildare and Desmond, as they were about the king's court, and aspired to be lord deputies and treasurers, seem to have sued out livery, and paid some of the feudal charges.

The English of Ireland, however, of all classes except in

* Deputy and Council to the King, A. D. 1610. State Papers, Henry VIII. (Ireland), vol. ii., p. 307.

† Ib., ib., vol. i., p. 327.

the neighbourhood of Dublin, had adopted the Irish language, dress, and manners, and never appeared in English apparel, except when attending Parliament or the Lord Deputy's court;* and no sooner home thence (or from the Court of England), than off with their English apparel, and on with their brogues and saffron shirt, and kerne's coat, and other Irish attire.†

In their justice halls, they administered March law, a mixture of the English law and the Irish law of Kincogish, the latter being a system of fines or satisfaction exacted from the clan or nation of the party committing the injury, payable, part to the party injured, and part to the lord who enforced it.‡

The king and statesmen of England, indignant that the feudal system had been nearly abandoned in Ireland, and that the English settlers had adopted the freer mode of life of the Irish, by an ordinance made in England in the year 1342 (15 Edw. III.), resumed—in other words, confiscated—the estates of all the great English nobility and gentry of Ireland,§

---

* State Papers, Henry VIII. (Ireland), vol. i., p. 477.

† "That the Earl of Clanricarde's sons (not without manifest consent of their father) had stolen across the Shannon, and there cast away their English habit and apparel, and put on their wonted Irish weede." Sir Henry Sidney to the Council in England (A. D. 1576), pp. 119, 120, Collins' "Memorials of the Sidney Family." 2 vols. Folio.

Patrick, the Baron of Lixnaw's eldest son, "Notwithstanding he was trained up in the court of England, sworn servant to her Majesty, in good favour there, and apparelled according to his degree, yet he was no sooner come home, but away with his English attires, and on with his brogs, his shirt, and other Irish rags, being become as verie a traitor as the veriest knave of them all."—A. D. 1586. Holinshed, "Chronicle of Ireland," p. 477.

‡ "The Deputie's Boke," State Papers of Henry VIII., vol. i., Paper 181, p. 447.

§ Sir J. Davies' "Discoverie," p. 660.

intending plainly to send over colonists from England to plant
such parts of their lands as the king should judge convenient, just as was done about 200 years later (in the year
1585), when the estates of the descendant of the Earl of
Desmond, one of the noblemen now aimed at, were confiscated,
and set out to planters from Somersetshire and Devonshire,
from Cheshire and Lancashire. For this purpose the Deputy
summoned the nobility and commons of Ireland to a Parliament at Dublin, largely filled with prelates and lords, and
landed proprietors of English birth, who were eager, no doubt,
for a reformation and improvement of Ireland, founded on
a redistribution of Irish lands to English capitalists. But the
Earls of Desmond and Kildare, and the rest of the English
nobility possessed of Irish estates, refused to attend, and,
with the citizens and burgesses of the principal towns, held
a separate Parliament or Convention at Kilkenny, and remon-
strated against the design. The Earl of Kildare was thereupon arrested, and the Earl of Desmond and many others
indicted, their lands seized, and their titles called in, and cancelled.* But about ten years afterwards (26th Edw. III.),
their lands and liberties were restored; much, however, to
the chagrin of the Parliament of England, who made the king
engage not to restore them if he again got them into his
hand.†

The expedition of Lionel Duke of Clarence, the king's son,
to Ireland, a few years afterwards, was a partial renewal of
the same design. He claimed the greater part of Connaught
from the Burkes, and other lands in other parts of Ireland,
which he intended to take from the present possessors, and to
plant, of course, when recovered, with settlers out of England.

* Sir John Davies' "Discoverie," pp. 660, 680.
† Ib., p. 655.

Preparatory to his invasion of Connaught, he assembled a
Parliament at Kilkenny, where the most rigorous laws were
passed against those English that had adopted Irish customs,
or should adopt them for the future. Those who should take
Irishwomen for wives or mistresses, or should give out their
children to be fostered or reared up in Irish families—who
should maintain Irish harpers, bards, rhymers, or minstrels in
their halls—were to undergo various punishments. For marrying an Irish wife, or for having an Irishwoman for a mistress, the penalty was to be half hanged, disembowelled alive,
and to forfeit his estate.*

" It was manifest from these laws," says Sir John Davies,
" that those who had the government of Ireland under the
Crown of England intended to make a perpetual separation and

---

* " The Statutes of Kilkenny, of the 40th Year of King Edward III.,
enacted in a Parliament held at Kilkenny, A. D. 1367, before Liónel Duke
of Clarence. Now first printed. Edited by James Hardiman, M. R. I. A."
4to. Dublin. For the Irish Archæological Society : 1843. The English
of Ireland became as fond of the harp as the Irish. In the inventories of
the household goods of the gentry confiscated at the Revolution of 1688,
the ancient English families of the Pale are found possessed of " one
Irish harpe." (W. Lynch, author of " Feudal Dignities in Ireland," Sub-
Commissioner of Irish Records, " Dublin Penny Journal," vol. i., p. 335.)
And the Irish " Hudibras," printed in London, 1698, to ridicule and vilify
the Irish, thus describes the gentlemen of the same class :—

> " There was old Threicy [Tracy], and old Darcy,
> Playing all weathers on the clarsey,
> The Irish harp,—whose rusty metal
> Sounds like the patching of a kettle."

Ten years afterwards it survived in Connaught, where the old Irish
gentry are described as careful to have their children taught to speak Latin,
write well, and play on the harp. " Discourse concerning Ireland, and the
different Interests thereof; in Answer to the Exon and Barnstaple Petition."
Small 4to., London, 1697-8, p. 19.

enmity between the English settled in Ireland and the native Irish, in the expectation that the English should in the end root out the Irish." But the numerous English of Irish birth possessed of lands to which the Crown laid claim, or which were liable to forfeiture, had now nearly equal reason with the native Irish to fear the designs of the Government of England. The degenerate English, like the Burkes of the counties of Mayo and Galway, the Poers of Waterford, and others, became only more determined " English rebels." The other English beyond the Pale, though they professed allegiance to the king, were in secret equally disinclined to see the king's escheators, sheriffs, and judges resume their duties among them. They knew the value of being free from the feudal burdens of wardships, marriages, fines for alienation, and all the other taxes which it was the secondary aim of these reforms to restore ; and they did not feel that hatred and contempt for their Irish tenants, neighbours, and kinsmen, required by the Statute of Kilkenny. Nor did the English who came over from England render themselves very agreeable to their countrymen settled in Ireland, or make them very anxious for any reformation that should bring a fresh accession of them from the mother country ; for they were, of course, preferred to all the chief offices of the State, and they despised the English of the birth of Ireland. It appears from this very Statute of Kilkenny (which forbids the use of the contemptuous term), that the newly arrived English had no better name for them than " Irish Dogg,"—insolence which the English of Ireland hurled back by calling them " English hobbe" or churls.* The Irish marked the coarser manners, the cold reserve of the English by birth, by calling them "Buddagh Sassenach," Saxon

---

* " Also . . that no difference of allegiance shall henceforth be made between the English born in Ireland and the English born in England by

clowns;* for they conceive it to be the mark of a gentleman to be free and affable with inferiors and equals : clowns are cold, they thought, but gentlemen courteous.† Thus, both the English of the birth of Ireland and the native Irish had reason to dislike the reforms aimed at by the Statute of Kilkenny ; but it was the English of Ireland that became the main impediment to the reconquest of Ireland, and more malicious to the English‡—more mortal enemies than the Irish themselves,§ as better knowing their power and purposes.‖

During the long wars in France, and afterwards during the civil wars of the Roses, when the English, driven back from their attempted conquests in France, turned in their lust for land and power to rob each other, this reformation of Ireland was suspended. But no sooner were these wars over, and the Government firmly established in England, which was not until Henry VIII.'s reign, than all these projects were renewed.

At the commencement of Henry VIII.'s reign, the regular administration of the law was limited to the four counties adjacent to the capital, called the English Pale. In these only

calling them English hobbe or Irish dog; but that all be called by one name, the English lieges of our Lord the King." 40th Edward III. (Irish), c. 4.

* Stanihurst, in Holinshed's " Chronicle," vol. ii., chap. 8, p. 44. Folio. London : 1586.

† " Les vilains s'entretiennent ; les nobles s'embrassent." Old French proverb.

‡ Spenser's " View of Ireland."

§ Sir J. Davies' "Discoverie."

‖ In Henry VIII.'s reign the Deputy and Council dissuade the king from seeking to confiscate Connaught, as it was " the fearing to be expelled from these their possessions," that kept M'William [the ancestor of the present Marquis of Clanricarde] and his ancestors so long English rebels." State Papers of Henry VIII. (Ireland), vol. ii., p. 309.

were there justices or sheriffs under the king. In the rest of
Ireland no judges had held assizes for more than 200 years. No
escheators or sheriffs had levied the reliefs payable to the king
for each succession ; no fines had been paid for alienations.
The estates of all the old English settlers beyond the Pale
were for this reason alone liable to forfeiture.

The native Irish were in a still worse case. From the days
of the first conquest, they were denied the protection and enjoyment of the English law, with the intent that the English
should in the end root them out of their lands. Many of the
largest English proprietors were absentees, who possessed
land in both countries, and scorned to dwell in this remote and
backward island. In their absence, the Irish reoccupied their
ancient territories. During the civil war of the Roses whole
families had left Ireland for the battle fields in England, and
been swept away. The Irish repossessed themselves of the
deserted lands. But it was against the policy of England that
any Irish should ever possess any lands that had once belonged to an Englishman. About this period much of the
county of Kildare was thus deserted of English, and reoccupied by Irish. The Parliament offered it to any English who
would come, and inhabit it ; and as an inducement, they were
to be tax-free for six years.* In like manner, in the counties
of Kilkenny and Tipperary, many of the native proprietors
had got back into their ancient lands, abandoned by the English. This, if not remedied, would be the destruction of these
counties, which (piously adds the Parliament) God forbid.
For the English seem to have thought God made a mistake in
giving so fine a country as Ireland to the Irish ; and for
near seven hundred years they have been trying to remedy
it. Sir James of Ormond was therefore commissioned to

---

* 28th Henry VI. (Irish), c. 35 (Unpublished Statutes).

recover the lands for himself.* The Earls of Kildare subsequently had grants of all lands they could win from the Irish.† The Irish were therefore never deceived as to the purpose of the English. And though the English Pale had not been extended for 240 years, their firm persuasion in the reign of Henry VIII. was, that the original design was not abandoned. "Irishmen be of opinion among themselves," says Justice Cusack, to the King, "that Englishmen will one day banish them, and put them from their lands for ever."‡ How correctly they judged of their purposes is now evident from the State Papers of that day. Upon the subduing of Thomas Fitzgerald's rebellion there is to be found project after project for clearing Ireland of Irish to the Shannon.§ Almost all concur in proposing that the country south of Dublin, within the line of the Barrow, be inhabited exclusively by English. It was to be a base of operations against the rest of Ireland. Some even contemplated the entire extirpation of the Irish ; but, luckily for the Irish, there was no precedent for it found in the chronicle of the conquest.‖ Add to this the difficulty of finding people to reinhabit it, if suddenly unpeopled. Accordingly, the chiefs and gentlemen of the Irish only were to be driven from their properties, and worn out in exile, while their lands should be given to English. The towns were to

---

* 8th Henry VII. (Irish), c. 25.

† State Papers of Henry VIII. (Ireland), vol. i., p. 177.

‡ Ibid., vol. ii., p. 326.

§ See Cowley's "Treatise," ibid., vol. i., pp. 323-328. Another paper thus concludes—"Consequently, the premises brought to pass, there shall no Irishrie be on this side the water of Shennyn unprosecuted, unsubdued, and unexiled. . . . . . Then shall the English Pale be well 200 Iryshe miles in length, and more." Ibid., ib., p. 452.

‖ "The lande is very large, by estimation as large as Englande, so that to enhabit the whole with new inhabiters, the number would be so great

be all cleared, their walls repaired, and rendered defensible against the attacks of the exiled Irish.* And the projectors of these improvements were, of course, to be rewarded by lands thus recovered. The king, however, seems to have been satisfied with confiscating the estates of the Earl of Kildare and his family. Fierce and bloody though he was, there was something lion-like in his nature. Notwithstanding all these promptings, he left to the Irish and old English their possessions, and seemed anxious even to secure them, but failed to do so for want of time. Swarms, however, of English adventurers were hungering and thirsting after Irish lands, and there was no difficulty in driving a high-spirited people, full of well-grounded suspicions, into rebellion. The O'Moores and O'Connors rebelled in Edward VI.'s reign. Their territories were formed by Philip and Mary into the King's and Queen's Counties, and their lands passed to English. The Earl of Desmond's great territories in Munster were forfeited in Queen Elizabeth's reign, and were set out to companies of planters out of Devonshire, Dorsetshire, and Somersetshire—out of Lancashire, and Cheshire—organized for defence, and to be supported by standing forces. Each new plantation produced fresh rebellions, from the pride and insolence of the new planters, the cupidity of

that there is no prince christened that commodiously might spare so many subjects to depart out of his regions. . . . . . But to enterprise the whole extirpation and totall destruction of all the Irishmen of the lande, it would be a marvaillous and sumptious charge and great difficulty, considering both the lack of enhabitors, and the great hardness and misery these Irishmen can endure, both of hunger, colde, and thirst and evill lodging, more than the inhabitauntes of any other lande. And by president of the conquest of this lande we have not heard or redde in any cronycle that at such conquestes the hole inhabitauntes of the landes have been utterly extirped and banished. Wherefore," &c. Lord Deputy and Council to the King, ibid., vol. ii., p. 176.

* Cowley's " Treatise," ibid., vol. i., p. 326.

standers-by, and the fears and resistance of the neighbouring Irish ; till at length, in Hugh Earl of Tyrone's rebellion, in 1598, the most of the native Irish were engaged, and great numbers of degenerate or rebellious English.

This rebellion was subdued in the closing hours of Queen Elizabeth's life ; and James I. ascended the throne with the country at his disposal.

And here, before entering on his settlement of Ireland, it may be worth inquiring what were the crimes of the Irish to cause the English for so many ages to treat them as alien enemies, to refuse them the right to bring actions in the courts set up by the English in Ireland, and to adhere to their cherished scheme of depriving the nation of their lands. The Irish gave no national resistance to the English ; they had no dynasty to set up ; no common government to restore ; no national capital to recover. They never contemplated independence or separation. The doctrine that allegiance and protection were reciprocal was not yet established—the rights of man not yet suspected. There was no inveterate repugnance between the races ; on the contrary, they were too ready to intermarry, and the heaviest penalties could not prevent these alliances. The designs of extirpation were on the side of the English—the fears of it on the side of the Irish. The Irish only too quickly forgave the robbery of their lands. The Fitzgeralds and the Butlers soon became to them as much their natural leaders and captains as the O'Briens, the M'Carthys, and O'Neills.* No one ever questioned their titles. Sir J. Davies has said that the Irish, after a thousand conquests, pretended title still. This was to transfer the feelings en-

---

* Thus, in 1520, the Earl of Surrey urges that James Lord Butler be sent over to Ireland, as the Earl of Ormond has gout, and cannot take the field ; " and his men will never go forth unless they may have the said Erl, or ellys his sonne and heire with them, to be their capitaine." State Papers of Henry VIII., vol. i. (Ireland), p. 49.

gendered by the Plantations of the reigns of Queen Elizabeth and James I. to a period when no such feelings were
known. If they had entertained them, they might easily have
expelled or massacred the English when the jurisdiction of the
English Government was limited for 200 years to the line of
the Liffey and the Boyne. No forces came from England;
there was no standing army of English; yet the English lived
unharmed among the Irish, as secure of their castles and lands
as native Irish. Campion, Spenser, and Davies have noted
with no friendly hand the faults of the Irish; but the murdering of English landlords is not in the catalogue; on the contrary, their devotion to them was unbounded. Thousands
sacrificed themselves to maintain the Kildares and the Des-
monds in their right. And the love of lord and tenant was reciprocal. When the Earl of Kildare and his five uncles had
been cut off by a kind of Turkish butchery,* the Irish of
Leinster pined for the return of the heir; they longed to see
young Gerald's banner displayed, and coveted more to see a
Geraldine reign and triumph than to see God come among
them;† and the last Earl of Desmond declared he had rather
forsake God than forsake his men.‡

Their crime was to be possessed of lands the English

---

* Hanged and disembowelled alive at Tyburn on 3rd of February, 1538.

"Butchered to make a London holiday."

Some or all of the uncles were guiltless of their nephew's rebellion. But
the king was told there should never be peace and good order in Ireland
"till the bludde of the Garroldes were wholly extinct." Lord Audley to
Thomas Cromwell, 13 Sept., 1535. "Lives of the Earls of Kildare," by
the Marquis of Kildare, vol. i., p. 152. For details of the punishment
for treason, see *post*, p. 106, n.

† State Papers of Henry VIII. (Ireland), vol. ii., p. 147.

‡ Carleton (Bishop of Chichester), "Thankful Remembrance of God's
Mercy to the Church of England," p. 48. 4to. London: 1624.

coveted. Moreover, the English could not endure that the Irish should enjoy their lands in a freer manner than themselves ; and the Irish could not submit to give them up, or to change their free and independent title into feudal tenure. The English planted in Ireland soon learned to prefer Irish freedom to feudal thraldom. This became a fresh crime in the Irish—they corrupted the English, and both became odious, and the lands of each were to be confiscated.

James I. ascended the throne at the very hour of Hugh O'Neill Earl of Tyrone's submission. The country was a ruin, from the devastations of " the fifteen years' war." He recognised the insecurity of the properties of the Irish as the capital error of all the former governments, from the days of the Conquest. He saw also how largely the fears of the degenerate English for their estates, held under defective title, had contributed to the disturbance of Ireland. His first act was to proclaim a general oblivion and indemnity. He restored the Earl of Tyrone to his estates; he promised the Irish that they should thenceforth hold their lands as English freeholds, instead of under the law of tanistry, and assured the degenerate English that their estates should be confirmed to them for the future against the claims of discoverers, on easy terms of composition. By these measures the perpetual war which had continued between the nations " for four hundred and odd years," and was caused, says Sir John Davies, by the purpose entertained by the English " to roote out" the Irish, was to be brought to an end. But before many years were passed these first good resolutions were abandoned. The right of the Irish to their lands was derided, and we find Sir John himself sharing in the spoil.* In the mean time the king's design with re-

* In the Plantation of Ulster he got, in the county of Fermanagh, 1300 acres; in the county of Tyrone, 2000 acres ; in the county of Armagh, 500 acres. Pynnar's " Survey of Ulster by Commission under the

gard to the Irish was to restore to the chiefs and principal
gentlemen such demesnes as they kept in their own occupation, to hold as tenants by knight's service under the king ;
and to fix the inferior members of the clan, hitherto living
the wandering life of the creaghts, in settled villages, paying
certain money rents to their lords, instead of their former uncertain spendings,—the object being to break up the clan
system, and to destroy the power of the chiefs.

This plan seems to have been matured by the summer of
1607. On the 17th of July in that year, Sir Arthur Chichester, Lord Deputy, accompanied by Sir John Davies and
other commissioners, proceeded to Ulster, with powers to in-
quire what lands each man held. There appeared before
them in each county which they visited the chief lords and
Irish gentlemen, the heads of creaghts, and the common people,
the Brehons and Shannahs, a kind of Irish heralds or chro-
niclers, who knew all the septs and families, and took upon
themselves to tell what quantity of land every man ought to
have ; they thus ascertained and booked their several lands,
and the Lord Deputy promised them estates in them.* "He
thus," says Sir John Davies, " made it a year of jubilee to the
poor inhabitants, because every man was to return to his own
house, and be restored to his ancient possessions, and they all
went home rejoicing."†

Notwithstanding these promises, the king, in the following
year issued his scheme for the Plantation of Ulster, urged to
it, it would seem, by Sir Arthur Chichester, who so largely
profited by it, though the highest councillor in the kingdom

Great Seal of Ireland, A. D. 1618–1619." Harris's " Hibernica," 8vo,
Dublin, 1717, p. 131.

    * Letter of Sir John Davies to the Earl of Salisbury, A. D. 1607.
" Historical Tracts," by Sir John Davies, 8vo, Dublin, 1787, p. 258.

    † Ibid., ib., p. 238.

told him to his face in the king's presence that it was against
the honour of the king and the justice of the kingdom.* It
could not be said that the flight of O'Neill and O'Donnell, Earls
of Tyrone and Tyrconnell, gave occasion to this change; for
the king immediately issued a proclamation† (which he renewed on taking formal possession of the Earls' territories),‡
assuring the inhabitants that they should be protected and
preserved in their estates, notwithstanding the flight of the
Earls: nor the outbreak of Sir Cahir O'Doherty in the month
of May, 1608, as it was confined to the neighbourhood of Londonderry, which he attacked, killing the governor, who had
dared to strike him. The truth would seem to be, that the
English, with their feudal prejudices, regard the land in a
higher light than man, and consider the improvement of the
country to consist in better tilled fields and straightened fences,
and not in the happiness of the countrymen; the more especially as they assume that the Irish cannot effect these works,
and that the lands must accordingly be assigned to themselves,
careful not to remember that the energies of the Irish are destroyed by their sense of impending exile. Manors of 1000,
1500, and 3000 acres were offered by this project to such
English and Scottish as should undertake to plant their lots
with British Protestants, and engage to allow no Irish to dwell
upon them. For the security of the Plantation, all Irish who
had been in arms were to be transplanted with their families,
cattle, and followers, to waste places in Munster and Connaught, and there set down at a distance from one another;

---

* " Analecta Sacra, Nova et Mira de Rebus Catholicorum in Hiberniâ
pro Fide et Religione Gestis. Collectore et Relatore T. N. Philadelpho-
Coloniæ," 1617, 12mo, p. 239.

† Dated Rathfarnham, 7th Sept., fifth James I. " Printed Calendar
of Patent Rolls of James I.," p. 419.

‡ Dated 9th November of same year. Ib., p. 420.

while those who should be suffered to remain were to remove from the lands allotted to the planters, to places where they could be under the eye of the Government officers.

The Irish gentlemen who did not forfeit their estates received proportions (intended to be three-fourths of their former lands, but often only one-half or one-third, as the English "were their own carvers"), as immediate tenants of the king. Their lands were liable to forfeiture if the chief took from any of his former clansmen any of his ancient customary exactions of victuals; if he went coshering on them as of old; if he used gavelkind, or took the name of the great O, whether O'Neill or O'Donnell, O'Carroll or O'Connor. On his death, his youthful heir was made ward to a Protestant, to be brought up in Trinity College, Dublin, from his twelfth to his eighteenth year in English habits and religion,—often after this enforced conformity, all the more embittered, like Sir Phelim O'Neill, against English religion. The wandering creaghts were now to become his tenants at fixed money rents. He covenanted that they should build and dwell in villages, and live on allotted portions of land, "to them as grievous as to be made bond slaves." Unable to keep their cattle on the small portions of land assigned to them, instead of ranging at large, they sold away both corn and cattle.* Unused to money rents, though of victuals they formerly made small account because of their plenty, they were unable to pay their rents; and their lords finding it impossible to exact them, and being thus deprived of their living, numbers of them fled to Spain. Similar Plantations followed in Leitrim, Longford, King's County, and Wexford, except that in some (as in Leitrim) one-half of the lands of the Irish were seized.

* Letter of Sir Arthur Chichester to the King, 30th October, 1610. Sir Henry Ellis's " Original Letters." Third series.

If the fair promises of James I. were of no value to the native Irish, his commission to secure the defective titles of the English availed them but little more. Notwithstanding large sums paid during his reign, as compositions to obtain perfect titles, Discoverers with eagle eyes (to use the language of a Committee of the House of Commons of Ireland to Lord Strafford, in 1634), piercing into the grants made to them under this commission, took advantage of the errors of the persons employed in passing of patents and estates from the Crown, and disheartened them from making their possessions beautiful or profitable.* And King Charles I., occupied in devising means to raise moneys without the aid of Parliament, connived at the Earl's proceedings in the confiscation of the estates of the old English of Connaught, though they had bought off the claim of the Crown, three hundred years old, de-rived through the De Burgos, whose daughter and heir Lionel, son of Edward III., had married. Lord Strafford found flaws in the execution of the previous commissions, and got the king's title found. More unscrupulous than James I., who took one-fourth from the native Irish, Strafford resolved to take one-half of the lands of the old English of Connaught, with the intention of founding there " a noble English Planta-tion."† And when Lord Holland, in the Privy Council in England, declared that taking so much might induce them to call the Irish regiments out of Flanders, Lord Strafford an-swered that if taking one-half should move that country to

* " Strafford's Letters," vol. i., p. 310. For a good account of the various technical errors for which the Patents were declared to be void, see " Fiction Unmasked," by Walter Harris, Esq., 12mo, Dublin, 1752, pp. 60-83.

† Sir Richard Cox, Secretary to King William III., and afterwards Chancellor of Ireland, in his " Hibernia Anglicana," vol. ii., p. 56. Folio. London : 1690.

rebellion, the taking one-third or one-fourth would hardly insure the Crown their allegiance ; and if they were so rotten and unsound at heart, wisdom would counsel to weaken them, and line them thoroughly with Protestants as guards upon them.*

His despotic proceeding in the confiscation of Connaught was made one of the grounds of his impeachment ; but the managers for the Parliament abandoned it.† It had served its purpose by swelling the train of the Earl's accusers ; and, in their Declaration concerning the Rise and Progress of the Irish Rebellion, the Commons of England made it a ground of complaint against the king that he had allowed the Connaught proprietors to compound with him for their estates.‡

* "Strafford's Letters," vol. ii., p. 33.
† Rushworth's "Historical Collections," vol. viii., p. 717.
‡ Ibid., vol. v., pp. 346-7.

Observe.

The signs, $\frac{A}{5}$, $\frac{A}{85}$, $\frac{A}{90}$, &c., &c., so frequently used in the foot notes to the following work, refer to the series of books of the Lord Deputy and Council, otherwise called "The Commissioners of the Parliament of the Commonwealth of England for the Affairs of Ireland," preserved in the Record Tower, Dublin Castle, as described at page xx of the Preface.

THE CROMWELLIAN SETTLEMENT

OF

IRELAND.

————◆————

PART I.

CIRCUMSTANCES IMMEDIATELY LEADING TO THE CROMWELLIAN SETTLEMENT OF IRELAND.

————

THE GREAT IRISH REBELLION OF 23RD OCTOBER, 1641.

THE forty years between the defeat of the Irish at Kinsale, on the 2nd January, 1601–2, and the great War or Rebellion which broke out on the 23rd October, 1641, have been represented as the period of the greatest peace, improvement, and prosperity known in Ireland since the days of the first invasion. And so it was in one sense; but in another the period of the greatest misery. The land was improved. Castles and bawns sprang up among new formed fields. The planters, happy and energetic, thought all the world was happy too. Under the labours of about twenty years, their lands began to smile. Little they thought or cared how the ancient owner, dispossessed of his lands, must grieve as he turned from the sight of the prosperous stranger to his pining family; daughters without prospect of preferment in marriage; sons, without fit companions, walking up and down the country with their horses and greyhounds, coshering on the Irish, drinking and gaming, and ready for any rebellion;* most of his high-born friends wandering in poverty in France or Spain, or enlisted in their armies. There was prosperity, but it was among the supplanting strangers—misery among the displanted and transplanted Irish. There was peace, but it was the peace of despair, because there remained no hope except in arms, and their arms were taken from them.

The case was little better among the old English gentry of Leinster, Munster, and Connaught, once possessed of the finest lands, and all the power and privileges of the kingdom. They were now supplanted in all the offices of state by the later invaders of Queen Elizabeth's, and James the First's, and Charles the First's reigns, all Protestants. The towns, always hitherto the sure defence of the English power, were equally unhappy in this prosperous time. The seaport towns were built by the Danes, the inland ones raised and walled under charters from the kings of England or of feudal lords. They were so strictly English, that no Irish could originally by law dwell in them. They were considered by Sir Henry Sydney the Queen's unpaid garrisons, which had ever stood staunch in all wars as well of English rebels as of Irish enemies. The ancient burgher families were now supplanted by English Protestants in the office of mayors, sheriffs, and recorders ; and where these

---

* Act of 10th and 11th Charles I., chap. 16 [Irish], A. D. 1636, "For the Suppression of Cosherers and idle Wanderers." It speaks of "the many young gentlemen of this kingdom that have little or nothing to live on of their own. . . . but live coshering on the country and sessing themselves and their followers, their horses and their greyhounds, sometimes exacting money to spare them and their tenants, and to go elsewhere for their *eeaught* and *adraugh*, viz., supper and breakefaste . . . . being commonly active young men, and such as seek to have many followers . . . . . . apt upon the least occasion of insurrection or disturbance . . . . to be heads and leaders of outlaws and rebels, and in the meantime do support their excessivedrinking and gaming by several stealths."

could not be had, and Roman Catholics took the offices, the members of the corporation were summoned before the Lord Deputy, and fined £100 each, and imprisoned, for not taking the oath of supremacy when tendered to them.* Churchwardens enumerated in lists the Irish of every parish that did not attend the English service, and these were tendered to grand juries at sessions of the peace and assizes to be presented for fines. If the old English or Irish grand jurors outnumbered the new English, there were no presentments made; for they made it a matter of conscience not to be accessory to fining their fellow-worshippers for an act of duty. They were then all "censured" by the Court of Castle Chamber by heavy fines, and put in prison, till at times the jails were choked with them.†

Suddenly, on the night of the 23rd of October, 1641, the Irish of Ulster, under the leading of Sir Phelim O'Neil, rose in insurrection, seized the forts of Charlemont and Mountjoy, and all the places of strength in the North except Derry and Carrickfergus, made prisoners of some of the planters, and caused the rest to fly towards Derry or Dublin. The planters were like criminals seized with the goods in their possession : the owners had come to claim their properties. So terrified were they, that for the first three days and nights no cock was heard [by them] to crow, no dog to bark, nay, not even when the rebels came in great multitudes.‡ The English power was

---

* P. 325, "Analecta de Rebus Catholicis in Hibernia" (Collections relating to Catholic affairs in Ireland), 12mo. Dublin : 1617.

† "Last Michaelmas term the jurors who were imprisoned for refusing to find verdict against their fellow Catholics were packed in jail like herrings in a barrel; their fines reached to £16,000, which, instead of going to the poor of the parishes, went to private favourites." Ibid., p. 49. Those of the county of Cavan alone were fined £8000. Ibid., p. 59.

‡ Deposition of the Rev. Dr. Maxwell, Rector of Tynan, in the county of Armagh. Borlase's "History of the Execrable Irish Rebellion," p. 418.

overthrown in three-fourths of Ireland in a night; and before Christmas, 1641, they only held Londonderry, Carrickfergus, and Drogheda, in the North; and Cork, Youghal, Kinsale, and Bandon, in the South. Though the Irish were at first a popular rout of unarmed clowns, the English durst scarce peep out of the gates of their great garrisons of Dublin and Drogheda.*

It was not until the month of February, 1642, that Lord Ormond marched out of Dublin with a large force, to relieve the gentlemen in the neighbourhood of the capital confined to their castles. It has been represented that there was a general massacre, surpassing the horrors of the Sicilian Vespers, the Parisian Nuptials, and Matins of the Valtelline, but nothing is more false. The English, whose conscience made them expect such retribution, had often foretold this outburst of injured and outraged humanity. They themselves massacred the Danes; but the Irish, to use the words of an old divine, have ever lacked gall to supply a wholesome animosity to the eternal enemies and revilers of their name and nation.† They were content to recover their ancient lands. While these designs, therefore, were freely attributed to them, their very accusers

---

* P. 11, "Queries propounded by the Protestant Party concerning the Peace now treated of in Ireland, and the Answers thereto made on behalf of the Irish Nation." 4to. Paris: 1644.

† "Six hundred years ago we found the native Irish murdering and pillaging, burning towns, carrying off heiresses and wives, too; and it cannot be said that the leaven is quite out of them yet. A hundred years, more or less, are a trifle in the cure of so deep a disease. . . . . So long as there are ——s [naming the latest sacrifice on the scaffold to the maintenance of the unendurable feudal land monopoly], *there will be stout Saxons, who, by fair means or by foul, will carry the day, or send them to work and be honest across the ocean.* We wish, of course, the animal could be tamed [i. e., reduced to the serfish condition of the rural population of England], and kept at home; *but it is no use wishing when a whole race has an innate taste for conspiracy and manslaughter.*"—"Times," 10th May, 1859.

furnish proof of the falseness of the charge; for they show that, when they had the opportunity to effect their alleged purpose, they let their enemies go. Contemporaneous accounts, especially those that give results against the bias of the writers, are mostly the true ones. All these prove there was no massacre. Thus, a minister of God's Word, writing in December, 1641, with the express object of rousing the indignation of the English by an account of the atrocities done by the Irish, in order to draw forth charitable aid to their victims, says, " It was the intention of the Irish to massacre all the English. On Saturday they were to disarm them; on Sunday, to seize all their cattle and goods; on Monday, at the watchword ' Skeane,' they were to cut all the English throats. The former they executed; the third only [that is, the massacre] they failed in."*

Against such intentions, provided only they were true, there could of course be no cruelty too great. Accordingly, the English of Dublin petitioned the Parliament of England, in December, 1641, that the towns should be cleared of Irish and forfeited, and given to English ; that all the cows, cattle, and provisions of the country should be brought into them, or driven under their guns, out of reach of the Irish, to starve

" The Lion of St. Jarlath's . . . surveys with an envious eye . . . the Irish exodus, . . . and *sighs over the departing demons of assassination and murder*. . . So complete is the rush of departing marauders, whose lives were profitably occupied in shooting Protestants from behind a hedge, that silence reigns over the vast solitude of Ireland. . . . Just as . . . civilization gradually supersedes the wilder and fiercer creatures by men and cities, so decivilization, such as is going on in Ireland, wipes out mankind to make room for oxen."—" Saturday Review," Nov. 28th, 1863.

* " A Brief Declaration of the Barbarous and Inhuman Dealings of the Northern Irish Rebels . . . ; written to excite the English Nation to relieve our poor Wives and Children that have escaped the Rebels' savage Crueltie. . . By G. S., Minister of God's Word, in Ireland." Small 4to. London: 1641.

them ; and pardon and reward offered to any rebel that should bring in the head of his fellow-rebel, and promotion to respect and honour for the head of a chief ringleader, provided the traitor would turn Protestant.*

That the massacre rested hitherto in intention only is further evident from the proclamation of the Lords Justices of the 8th of February, 1642 ; for, while offering large sums for the heads of the chief Northern gentlemen in arms (Sir Phelim O'Neil's name heading the list, with a thousand pounds), the Lords Justices state that the massacre had failed. Many thousands had been robbed and spoiled, dispossessed of house and lands, many murdered on the spot ; but the chief part of their plots (so the proclamation states), and amongst them a universal massacre, had been disappointed.†

But after Lord Ormond and Sir Simon Harcourt, with the English forces, in the month of April, 1642, had burned the houses of the gentry in the Pale,‡ and committed slaughters of unarmed men,§ and that the Scotch forces, in the same month, after beating off Sir Phelim O'Neil's army at Newry,

* " Remonstrance from Ireland to the High Court of Parliament in England for the speedy oppression of the Rebels without cost, and the probable way of moving the Rebels to submit themselves, and to cut one another's own Throats, and to bring in the Heads of the chief Actors, thereby to get their pardon. Presented by a Member of the House of Commons in Ireland." Small 4to. First printed at Dublin. Reprinted at London : 1641.

† The proclamation is given at length in Borlase's " History of the Execrable Irish Rebellion."

‡ Page 117, " The humble Protestation of the Catholics of the English Pale of Ireland against a Proclamation dated 8th February, 1641–2."— " Desiderata Curiosa Hibernica, or Select State Papers," &c. Dublin : 1772.

§ " A full Relation of the good Success of Lord Ormond and his Army, from their going out of Dublin on 2nd April, 1642, till the 17th of the same, when they returned thither again." Small 4to. London : 1642.

drowned and shot men, women, and priests, in that town, who had surrendered on condition of mercy,* then it was that some of Sir Phelim O'Neil's wild followers, in revenge, and in fear of the advancing army, massacred their prisoners in some of the towns in Tyrone. The subsequent cruelties were not on one side only, and were magnified to render the Irish detestable, so as to make it impossible for the king to seek their aid without ruining his cause utterly in England. The story of the massacre, invented to serve the politics of the hour, has been since kept up for the purposes of interest. No inventions could be too monstrous that served to strengthen the possession of Irish confiscated lands.

The truth seems to be, that the English were to the full as bloody as the Irish; but, as regarded the acts of the English, law,† which is nothing but the will of the strongest, made killing no murder. Incited by those who hungered after Irish estates, and therefore determined to render them desperate,

* " Monday, May 5th, [1642] :—The common soldiers, without direction from the general-major, took some eighteen of the Irish women of the town [Newry], and stript them naked, and threw them into the river, and drowned them, shooting some in the water. More had suffered so, but that some of the common soldiers were made examples of". . .—" A True Relation of the Proceedings of the Scots and English Forces in the North, of Ireland." 4to. London : 1642.

" Mr. Griffin, Mr. Bartly, Mr. Starkey, all of Ardmagh, and murdered by these bloudsuckers on the sixt of May. For, about the fourth of May, as I take it, we put neare fourty of them to death upon the bridge of the Newry, amongst which were two of the Pope's pedlers, two seminary priests, in return of which they slaughtered many prisoners in their custody."—" The Levite's Lamentation," pp. 13, 14.

† " Amongst acts some produce great evils. The Strongest wished to arrest the course of acts prejudicial [to themselves], and for that reason turned those acts into crimes. The will of the strongest, clothed with outward forms, received the name of law."—" Bentham's Principles of Morals and Legislation," edited by Dumont, vol. i., p. 153.

and drive all into rebellion, they proclaimed all of them rebels,—old English of the Pale as well as the ancient natives; confiscated in advance 2,500,000 acres of their lands ; invented crimes for them, thereby maddening the people of England, until extermination was preached for gospel, and the sparing of any of them was declared a crime. So that when the Bishop of Meath, in a sermon in Christ Church, Dublin, in 1642, pleaded for mercy for women and children, an English officer, publicly by print in London, justified his quitting the army of Ireland, inasmuch as the plea was made by the bishop in the presence of the Lords Justices, and not reproved, and they must, therefore, be traitors to the English interest.*

The Puritans heard of the Irish rebellion with feelings of great anger; for it gave the king an opportunity to demand fresh forces to be employed into Ireland, which he might turn against the Parliament, when he had subdued or made a treaty with the Irish. The king was already suspected of such a design. One of the charges against the Earl of Strafford, who had been impeached the previous year, was that he purposed to bring an army from Ireland to England ; and it was believed that his brother only spoke the Earl's sentiments when he said that the English nation would never be well till they were conquered over again.† They had also knowledge of the king's design to supersede Borlase and Parsons, the Lords Justices, who were in the interest of the Parliament, by Lord Ormond ; and then Lord Ormond having command of the army, and a

---

* " An Apology made by an English Officer of Quality for leaving the Irish Wars, declaring the design now on foot to reconcile the Irish and English, and expelling the Scotch, to bring their Popish Forces against the Parliament."

† Trial of the Earl of Strafford, " Rushworth's Collections," vol. viii., pp. 725, 728 ; and " Declaration of the Commons of 25th July, 1643, concerning the Rise and Progress of the Rebellion in Ireland." Ibid., vol. v., p. 353.

majority in the Parliament of Ireland, formed by a junction of the Protestant Royalist gentry with the old English gentry of Ireland, all Catholic and Royalist, the king could raise taxes there, dissolve the Parliament of England, and use all his prerogative uncontrolled against the English Puritans.

It was this secret coming to the knowledge of Sir Phelim O'Neil that induced him to rise with the native Irish, that they might anticipate the other parties, and have the credit of greater zeal for the king.* But the Parliament defeated the king's design : unwilling to trust him with an army for Ireland, or with the funds to pay it, they offered 2,500,000 acres of Irish lands to be forfeited, as security to those who should advance moneys towards raising and paying a private army for subduing the rebels in Ireland. The moneys, instead of being paid into the king's exchequer, were to be paid to a committee, composed half of members of the House of Commons, and half of subscribers to this joint fund, who were to nominate the general and the officers, the king having nothing to say to the force but to sign the officers' commissions. All the Irish

---

* P. 22, " Case of Ireland Stated," by Hugh Reilly. The Marchioness of Antrim [Lady Catherine Manners, heiress of Rutland, and widow of G. Villiers, first Duke of Buckingham] said that Lord Ormond hated her husband, believing he had blabbed the plot to Sir Phelim O'Neil. Ibid., p. 23.

† " Petition of divers well affected to the House of Commons, offering to raise and maintain forces on their own charge against the rebels of Ireland, and afterwards to receive their recompense out of the rebells estates," Feb. 11, 1642, p. 553, 4th Rushworth's Collections ; Act for the speedy reducing of the rebels in Ireland, 16 Charles I. [English], c. 33.

" The adventurers, with their moneys raised under the Act, were to have carried over a brigade of 5000 foot and 500 horse into Munster against the rebels, which business they were to have carried on by officers chosen by themselves, whereby they had the oversight of that business, and laying out their own money for the best advantage of the service."—Reasons of the Committee of Adventurers for refusing to lend moneys on the Ordinance of 15th August, 1645.

saw that this army of adventurers were coming, like the first invaders under Strongbow, to conquer estates for themselves and their employers, and therefore could not but oppose them for the sake of their wives and children, who must be deprived of their homes. They must therefore fight against England, thus represented, and the king be deprived of their aid. The king objected to the Act: it took away from him the power of pardoning the Irish, and he suggested that it must only render them desperate, which in truth was the very purpose of the Parliament, but he dared not refuse his assent.* The measure was received in England as a triumph over the king and the Irish. The subscribers, or adventurers as they were called, were to have estates and manors of 1000 acres given to them in Ireland at the following low rates :—In Ulster for £200, in Connaught for £300, in Munster for £450, and in Leinster for £600, and lands proportionably for less sums. The rates by the acre were four shillings in Ulster, six shillings in Connaught, eight shillings in Munster, and twelve shillings in Leinster.

If this plan were carried out, it was to put an end for ever, according to Sir John Bulstrode Whitelock, the Speaker of the House of Commons, to that long and bloody conflict foretold (with so much truth) by Giraldus Cambrensis.† According to another, it would bring in such sums of money (which are the sinews of war) as would bring the war to a speedy end; the more certainly as many of the officers of the force would themselves become adventurers, and thus, in the language of Tacitus describing the soldiers of Catiline, they would carry fortune, honour, glory, and riches at their swords' points. The work of Queen Elizabeth and James the First, it was said,

* P. 557, ibid.

† " Speech at a Conference between the Lords and Commons on 13th February, 1641-2, concerning the Proposition of divers Gentlemen, &c., for the speedy Reducing," &c. Small 4to. London : 1642.

would now be perfected. The Irish would be rooted out by a new and overwhelming plantation of English : another England would speedily be found in Ireland, and that prophecy be proved false that Ireland will not be reformed till the day of judgment.*

The adventurers had their private army of 5000 foot and 500 horse at Bristol, under the orders of Lord Wharton, ready for the invasion of Munster, in the summer of 1642. But the conflict between the king and Parliament growing embittered, he delayed the giving the commissions for the officers ;† and the civil war having broken out, the Parliament directed Lord Wharton and his force to march against the king ; and on the 23rd October, 1642 (the first anniversary of the Irish rebellion), they were defeated at the battle of Edge Hill, with the rest of the English rebels. The adventurers, finding that the funds they had raised to conquer lands in Ireland were thus misused by the Parliament, it was difficult to obtain further subscriptions, though the measure of land was enlarged to the Irish standard, and afterwards doubled for any adventurer that would pay in a sum equal to a fourth of his original subscription. But the conflict in England prevented any forces from coming thence for seven years. It was not until they had put a conclusion to their strife by cutting off the king's head and dethroning the dynasty, that Cromwell, as Lord Lieutenant of Ireland, and general-in-chief of the Commonwealth armies, landed at Ringsend, near Dublin, on the 14th August, 1649, in order to carry on the war in Ireland. He remained

---

* " Fidelity, Valour, and Obedience, of the English declared by way of Pacification of His Majesty, and a desire of reunion between His Majesty and the Parliament, as also, that the present forces now ready to bicker here in England, may be turned against the barbarous Irish rebels. By Walter Meredith, Gent." Small 4to. London : 1642.

† 4th " Rushworth's Collections," p. 776.

here for nearly nine months, being called back to England on the 29th May, 1650, just after the capture of Clonmel.

The war lasted more than two years longer; for it was not until the 27th September, 1653, that the Parliament were enabled to declare the rebellion subdued, and the war appeased and ended.[*]

THE DIFFICULTIES OF THE IRISH WAR, AND THE TERMS OFFERED TO THE IRISH.

The immediate cause of the settlement of the soldiery in Ireland was the waste caused by the war, and the difficulty the government were in about satisfying them their large arrears, or finding them current pay.

Spenser has described the English method of war in Ireland. He was an eye-witness of the measures pursued by his master and patron, Lord Grey de Wilton, to subdue Munster, in 1580. By this method a most populous and plentiful country, he says, was suddenly left void of man and beast, so that (to use the language of the Irish annalists) the lowing of a cow nor the voice of a herdsman was not heard from Dunquin, in Kerry, to Cashel, in Munster.[†] It consisted in so placing garrisons as to confine the Irish to some narrow fastnesses. The English then destroyed the cattle and growing crops in the neighbourhood, and removed away or spoiled all those that bordered on those parts, that the enemy might find no succour; and the Irish being closely penned up, and their cattle prevented from running abroad, they were soon consumed and the people starved.[‡] "In one year and a half," says

---

[*] " Ordinance for the Satisfaction of the Adventurers for Lands in Ireland, and the Arrears due to the Soldiery there, 27th September, 1653."— Scobell, " Acts and Ordinances."

[†] " Annals of the Four Masters," at the year 1582.

[‡] " View of the State of Ireland, written dialoguewise between Eudoxus and Irenæus, by Edmund Spenser, Esq., in the Year 1596," p. 526, vol. i.

Spenser, "they were brought to such wretchedness, as any stony heart would have rued the sight. Out of every corner of the woods and glynns they came forth on their hands, for their legs could not bear them,—they looked like anatomies of death, and spoke like ghosts crying out of the grave ; they flocked to a plot of water-cresses as to a feast, though it afforded them small nourishment, and ate dead carrion, happy when they could find it, and soon after scraped the very carcases out of the graves."* Yet this gentle poet only describes this war-fare, and all its horrors, in order to recommend it for adoption by the Earl of Essex in the war then on foot against Hugh O'Neil, Earl of Tyrone. And though Essex did not carry out this ruthless plan, Lord Mountjoy, who superseded him, did, burning the houses and destroying the corn and cattle, till the dead lay unburied in the fields in thousands.†

Carrion and corpses became the food of the survivors ; and, more horrible still, children were killed and eaten, and the poor wretches who killed them were tried and hanged for it by those that drove them to such horrors."‡ Archbishop Ussher, who was ordained on the very day that Tyrone's war was ended by the defeat of the Irish and Spaniards at Kinsale, and therefore speaks of what was within his own knowledge, re-lates how women were known to lie in wait, and to rush out, like famished wolves, upon a rider, to drag him from his saddle and to seize and devour the horse.§ The war in Ire-

---

of " Collection of Tracts and Treatises illustrative of Ireland." 2 vols. 8vo. Alexander Thom. Dublin : 1860.

* Ibid., id.

† Fynes Morison's " Itinerary ;" and " The History of Hugh O'Neil, Earl of Tyrone's, Rebellion, and its Suppression," p. 237. Folio. London : 1617.

‡ Idem, p. 271.

§ " Life of Primate Ussher, by Dean Barnard," p. 67. 12mo. London : 1656.

land in 1650 was of the same nature ; but the resistance was more general; for the ancient English, and all the towns, who were upon the Queen's side in Tyrone's, and all former wars, were now united with the Irish. The process consequently was longer, because the English forces were comparatively fewer : the methods were the same. It may seem strange to hear counted as military weapons issued from the store at Waterford, among swords, pikes, powder, shot, bandaliers and match, " eighteen dozen of scythes with handles and rings, forty reape hooks, and whetstones and rubstones proportional ;"* but with these the soldiers cut down the growing crop, in order to starve the Irish into submission.†

Not less strange is it to hear of the Bible being served out of store, with their other ammunition, to the army ; yet they had no bloodier implement in all their arsenal of war.‡

On the 1st January, 1651–2, the Parliament (so the Commissioners report) had in Ireland an army of 30,000 men, but they had 350 garrisons and military posts to maintain, and 100 more to plant ; while the Irish had an equal number of men, all of

* $\frac{A}{82}$, p. 281.

† " Dublin, 1st July, 1650.—Last Monday, Colonel Hewson, with a considerable body from hence, marched into Wicklow. Colonel Hewson doth now intend to make use of scythes and sickles that were sent over in 1649, with which they intend to cut down the corn growing in those parts which the enemy is to live upon in the winter time, and thereby, for want of bread and cattle, the Tories may be left destitute of provisions, and so forced to submit and quit those places.—Dublin, 1st July, 1651."—Letter of the Commissioners for Ireland to the Parliament, $\frac{A}{2}$, p. 7.

‡ " Dublin, 3rd August, 1652.—Ordered, that the Governor of Dublin do give warrant to the commissary of the stores in Dublin *to issue the Bibles now in the stores to the several companies of foote and troopes of horse within the said precinct of Dublin according to muster, that is to say, one Bible to every file ;* and that the several commissaries of the musters within the said precinct have order every muster to see the said Bibles accounted for by the officer so commanding the said troope or company ; and when they find the said Bibles to be wanting upon musters as aforesaid, to certify the

them, except those in their towns and garrisons in Connaught, in woods, bogs, and other fastnesses of the greatest advantage to them, and from which there was no dislodging them. They describe the country as almost everywhere interlaced with great bogs, with firm woody grounds like islands in the middle, approached by a narrow pass where only one horse could go abreast, easily broken up, so as no horse could attack them ; but in and out the Irish could pass over the wet and quaking bog by ways known only to themselves, whereby they could attack or escape at pleasure. To place garrisons near their fastnesses, to lay waste the adjacent country, allowing none to inhabit there on pain of death, was the course taken to subdue the Irish.* The consequence was, that the country was reduced to a howling wilderness. Three-fourths of the stock of cattle were destroyed. In 1653, cattle had to be imported from Wales into Dublin ;† it required a license to kill lamb ;‡ tillage had ceased : the English themselves were near starving. Soldiers and officers were encouraged, there-

same to the governor and commissioners of the revenue in the respective precincts, that defalcation may be made of the said troopes or companys pay for such Bibles as are wanting." $\frac{A}{2}$, p. 294.

"Drogheda, 17th August, 1652.—You are desired forthwith to deliver out of the stores under your charge *one hundred Bibles* unto Mr. Robert Clarke, or whom he shall appoint to receive the same, *to be by him disposed of for the use of the forces* and others as may bee *for the propagation of the Gospell within the precinct of Galway* as hee shall see cause.

"To the storekeeper at Limerick or Galway." $\frac{A}{2}$, p. 304.

* "Some particulars humbly offered to consideration, in order to the breaking of the enemy's strength, and lessening the charge of England in managing the affairs of Ireland. Commissioners for Ireland to the Council of State in England, dated 1 January, 1652." $\frac{A}{2}$, p. 288.

† Petty's "Political Anatomy of Ireland," 1672, vol. ii., p. 26, " Tracts and Treatises on Ireland." Alexander Thom, Dublin : 1860.

‡ " Upon the petition of Mrs. Alice Bulkeley, widow, and consideration had of her ould age and weakness of body : It is thought fitt and ordered

fore to till the lands round their posts ;* and such of the Irish not in arms as would come down from their fastnesses and raise crops within the line of a garrison, until the Parliament of England should declare their intentions towards the Irish nation, were promised the benefit of their crop.† The revenue from all sources, even in 1654, did not amount to £200,000 (exact, £198,000). The cost of the army exceeded £500,000.‡ It became important, therefore, to come to some terms with the Irish. The Commissioners for Ireland reported that the natives were of opinion that the Parliament intended them no mercy. At length, on 12th May, 1652, the Leinster army of the Irish surrendered on terms signed at Kilkenny,§ which were adopted successively by the other principal armies between that time and the September following, when the Ulster forces surrendered. By these Kilkenny articles, all except those who were

that she be and she is hereby permitted and lycensed to kill and dresse so much lambe as shall be necessary for her own use and eating, not exceeding three lambes for this whole year, notwithstanding any declaration of the said Commissioners of Parliament to the contrary. Dated at Dublin, 17 March, 1652." $\frac{A}{82}$, p. 721.

* Waste and untenanted lands to be let to officers and soldiers of the garrison for five years, from 25th March, 1653, at reasonable rents, free of contribution, on condition that they till and manure, and sow one-third of arable land with corn, and occupy. $\frac{A}{82}$, p. 601.

† "The stock of cattle in this country are almost spent, so that above four parts in five of the best and most fertile lands in Ireland lye waste and uninhabited, which threatens great scarcity here ; for prevention whereof, declarations have been issued forth for encouragement of the Irish to till their lands, promising them the enjoyment of their crop, as also for enforcing those that are removed to the mountains to return. Dublin, 1 July, 1651. Commissioners for Ireland to the Council of State in England." $\frac{A}{2}$, p. 12.

‡ "Memoir on the Mapped Surveys of Ireland from 1640 to 1688, remaining in the late Auditor-General for Ireland's Office," by W. H. Hardinge, "Transactions of the Royal Irish Academy" for 1862, p. 7.

§ $\frac{A}{90}$, p. 103.

guilty of the first blood were received into protection, on laying down their arms ; those who should not be satisfied with the conclusions the Parliament might come to concerning the Irish nation, and should desire to transport themselves with their men to serve any foreign state in amity with the Parliament, should have liberty to treat with their agents for that purpose. But the Commissioners undertook faithfully and really to mediate with the Parliament to their utmost endeavours, that they might enjoy such a remnant of their lands as might make their lives comfortable who lived amongst them, or for the maintenance of the families of such of them as should go beyond seas.

SCHEMES FOR THE NEW PLANTING OF IRELAND.

Under this destructive system of war, the country was becoming a waste, without cattle, and without inhabitants. The taxation to support the army was continually increasing on the parts of the country under protection, and amounted to double the rent in the former times of peace. Soldiers who had taken farms were throwing them up.* The Irish under protection were quitting the English quarters with their cattle, unable to endure the grinding taxation, and flying to the moun-

---

* 11 January, 1653. On reading the petition of the inhabitants of the barony of Shilelogher, in the county of Kilkenny, complaining of the assessment, the Commissioners of Revenue were directed, if they found that the persons who took waste lands in the said barony have deserted them, they are to compel such persons to stand to their agreements, and the rents and contributions payable by such persons to be allowed to the petitioners for the better enabling them to pay their monthly contribution [i. e. a like amount to be deducted from the monthly assessment of the barony, as the parties deserting their holdings ought to have paid]. $\frac{A}{82}$, p. 542.

7 January, 1653. On reading the petition of the inhabitants of the barony of Cranagh, in the county of Kilkenny, ordered, if it be true as is suggested that many have thrown up their farms which they had taken,

tains again; and the charge to be supplied from England was continually increasing. There was only one remedy for these evils—to plant and inhabit the country, and reduce the army.

The officers of the army were eager to take Irish lands in lieu of their arrears,* though it does not appear that the common soldiers were, who had small debentures and no capital, and no chance of founding families and leaving estates to their posterity. But the adventurers must be first settled with, as they had a claim to about one million of acres, to satisfy the sums advanced for putting down the rebellion on the faith of the Act of 17 Charles I. (A. D. 1642), and subsequent Acts and Ordinances, commonly called "The Acts of Subscription." By these, lands for the adventurers must be first ascertained, before the rest of the country could be free for disposal by the Parliament to the army.

Pressed with these considerations, the Commissioners for Ireland, on the 1st of January, 1652, proposed to the Council of State in England, that the adventurers should cast lots for their lands presently, notwithstanding the war was not over; and they suggested that four allotments, one in each province, amply sufficient to pay the adventurers, should be made, and that they should then cast lots to ascertain in which of them their proportions should be fixed; the first lot to consist of the counties of Limerick, Kerry, and Clare in Munster; and Galway in Connaught; the second, of the counties of Kilkenny, Wexford, Wicklow, and Carlow, in Leinster; the third, of the counties of Westmeath and Longford in Leinster, and Cavan and Monaghan in Ulster; the fourth of the counties of Fermanagh

casting them as a burthen upon the said barony, that such persons stand to their bargains, and discharge the rents and duties falling on their holdings. $\frac{A}{82}$, p. 523.

* "Some proposals humbly offered by a General Council of officers to the General and Commissioners of Parliament. 22 October, 1652." Ib., p. 47.

and Donegal in Ulster, and Leitrim and Sligo in Connaught.*
By which it appears, that they had not as yet determined on
the transplantation of the Irish to Connaught, but still adhered
to the plan of the Adventurers Act, that the lands should be
taken equally out of the four provinces. They also proposed
that the soldiers should have land in their quarters, as well for
their arrears as in lieu (for part at least) of their present pay.
They would thus be encouraged to follow husbandry, and to
maintain their own interest as well as that of the Commonwealth.† The adventurers, therefore, were directed on 30th
January, 1652, to attend the Committee of Parliament sitting
in the Speaker's Chamber at Westminster, and propose a form
of speedy plantation.

The adventurers had been very urgent during the whole
course of the war for lands to be set out to them. In 1645, they
demanded to be put in possession of the houses belonging to
the Irish in Cork, Kinsale, and Youghal, with lands adjacent, and to be given other lands in Munster as they should
be conquered from the rebels.‡ Now they declared, if the Parliament insisted on a speedy plantation, they were undone. The
war was not over—people feared the Tories. No plan was
proposed for their security. The Irish were to be removed.
Men were hard to be got in England for tenants and labourers,
as they saw that the government would have to give people land
in Ireland for nothing, as there must be many millions of acres
still left after satisfying the adventurers and soldiers, which
must be waste and untenanted, unless given away to prevent
them from being reoccupied by the Irish. That labourers were
scarce, by reason of the many forests and chaces lately disaf-

* $\frac{A}{2}$, p. 290.　　　† $\frac{A}{2}$, p. 289.

‡ P. 11, "Reasons offered by a Committee of Adventurers for refusing
to lend Moneys on the Ordinance of 15th August, 1645, for raising Moneys
for Ireland for six months from November, 1645." Small 4to: London.

forested in England, and then under improvement. They
accordingly demanded to be paid in lands, in such parts of Munster, Kilkenny, and (if need be) in other parts of Leinster most
contiguous, as they should choose; that they should have the
city of Waterford, and such towns as they should point out,
preserved for them; that they should be well guarded.

But they refused to be put under conditions to plant in any
limited time, and demanded that they should be free of taxes
while planting. Unless they should be greatly favoured, they
must be forced to plant on such terms that the labourers would
grow rich, and the adventurers poor, as many did in New
England. And if the first adventurers should prove unsuc-
cessful, it might cast such a damp upon the spirits of others,
like a dismal discomfit in the beginning of a battle, as they
would hardly be brought on again on any conditions.*

The government, however, still pressed for a speedy plantation. They wished to limit them to three years, and the
lands not then planted and inhabited to be forfeited. To which
the adventurers gave for final answer, that it would take 40,000
labourers and their families to execute such a work, for whom
no housing was provided, no guards against Tories, and that to
attempt it would be to destroy the plantation.†

The officers of the army were at the same time urging that
the army should have lands set out to them forthwith for their
arrears. There was no way of preventing a further increase
of the charge that weighed upon England, but by planting the
country, and reducing the forces by degrees, and with as much
speed as might be consistent with safety. And they proposed

* Proposals of the Adventurers, dated April 5, 1652. Carte, MSS.,
Bodleian Library, "Ireland," vol. x., pp. 230-236.

† "Adventurers' remarks upon the Proposals of the Committee of Parliament for the Planting of Ireland, sitting in the Speaker's Chamber, 23rd
December, 1652." Ib., p. 257.

that one or more counties should be allotted to the adventurers, adequate to their demands, and others to the army, that so the planting by the adventurers and by the gradually disbanding army might go on together. As the utmost speed was necessary for the relief of England, they proposed that the army should have lands for their arrears at the same rates as they were given by the Act of 1642 to the adventurers, called the Act rates, namely, lands in Leinster at 12s. per acre; in Munster, at 8s.; in Connaught, at 6s.; and in Ulster, at 4s. To value the several estates and farms in a convenient time, would require more fit valuers than could be found, would cost more than the revenue could bear, and the army and its pay (drawn from England) must continue. Moreover, it would be a very uncertain valuation, the lands being in many places waste, the inhabitants destroyed or gone, so as there were none to give evidence of the value when they were inhabited. And, lastly, the Ordinance of the year 1643, allowing officers of the army to become adventurers to the extent of their pay on the same terms as the adventurers, was a precedent for paying the whole army their arrears now at the Act rates.* All very good reasoning to give them the lands at extraordinary cheap rates.

DEPARTURE OF THE SWORDMEN FOR SPAIN.

Foreign nations were apprised by the Kilkenny Articles that the Irish were to be allowed to engage in the service of any state in amity with the Commonwealth. The valour of the Irish soldier was well known abroad. From the time of the Munster plantation by Queen Elizabeth, numerous exiles had taken service in the Spanish army. There were Irish regiments serving in the Low Countries. The Prince of Orange

* $\frac{A}{82}$, p. 391.

declared they were born soldiers ;* and Henry IV. of France publicly called Hugh O'Neil the third soldier of the age,† and he said there was no nation made better troops than the Irish when drilled. Sir John Norris, who had served in many countries, said he knew no nation where there were so few fools or cowards. Agents from the King of Spain, the King of Poland, and the Prince de Conde, were now contending for the services of Irish troops. Don Ricardo White, in May, 1652, shipped 7000 in batches from Waterford, Kinsale, Galway, Limerick, and Bantry, for the King of Spain.‡ Colonel Christopher Mayo got liberty in September, 1652, to beat his drums to raise 3000 for the same King.§ Lord Muskerry took 5000 to the King of Poland.‖ In July, 1654, 3500, commanded by

* "There lives not a people more hardy, active, and painful. . . . . . neither is there any will endure the miseries of warre, as famine, watching, heat, cold, wet, travel, and the like, so naturally, and with such facility and courage that they do. The Prince of Orange's Excellency uses often publiquely to deliver that the Irish are souldiers the first day of their birth. The famous Henry IV., late king of France, said there would prove no nation so resolute martial men as they, would they be ruly, and not too headstrong. And Sir John Norris was wont to ascribe this particular to that nation above others, that he never beheld so few of any country as of Irish that were idiots and cowards, which is very notable." P. 219, "Advertisement for Ireland," MS., folio (A. D. 1615), Library of Trin. Coll. Dublin, F. 3, 16.

† "Se ipsum primum esse significans," &c., "meaning himself to be the first, and the illustrious Count de Fuentes the second; as testified to this day by the most noble the Count D'Ossunia, late Viceroy of Naples and Sicily, in whose presence he said so." Lynch's "Alithinilogia," vol. ii. p. 50.

‡ $\frac{A}{82}$, p. 205.   § Ib., p. 331.

‖ "On reading the within petition of John Gould, in behalf of the Lord Muskerry, who has license to transport 5000 men out of Ireland to the service of any prince in amity with the Commonwealth, praying that while his lord is now in treaty with the Polish ambassador for those men . . . . they may not be transplanted : It is ordered, &c. . . . . . Dublin, 12 February, 1655." $\frac{A}{4}$ p. 426.

Colonel Edmund Dwyer, went to serve the Prince de Condé.[*]
Sir Walter Dungan and others got liberty to beat their drums
in different garrisons to a rallying of their men that laid down
arms with them in order to a rendezvous, and to depart for
Spain.[†] They got permission to march their men together to
the different ports, their pipers perhaps playing "Ha til, Ha til,
Ha til, mi tulidh"—We return, we return no more ;[‡] or more
probably, after their first burst of passionate grief at leaving
home and friends for ever was over, marching gaily to the
lively strains of Garryowen. Between 1651 and 1654, thirty
four thousand (of whom few ever saw their loved native land
again) were transported into foreign parts.[§]

IRELAND ASSIGNED TO THE ADVENTURERS AND SOLDIERS.

These discussions occupied the whole of the year 1652 ;
but caused in point of fact no loss of time, for the war was
still raging, and there could be no planting.

Towards the close of the year 1653, the island seemed
sufficiently desolated to allow the English to occupy it. On
the 26th of September in that year, the Parliament passed an
Act for the new planting of Ireland with English.

The government reserved for themselves all the towns, all
the church lands and tithes; for they abolished all archbishops,
bishops, deans, and other officers, belonging to that hierarchy,

---

[*] $\frac{A}{32}$, p. 112.   [†] $\frac{A}{84}$, p. 342.

[‡] The tune with which the departing Highlanders usually bid farewell to
their native shores. Preface to Sir Walter Scott's "Legend of Montrose."

[§] Sir W. Petty's "Political Anatomy" (published A. D. 1672), p. 27.
"The chiefest and eminentest of the nobility and many of the gentry have
taken conditions from the King of Spain, and have transported 40,000 of
the most active spirited men, most acquainted with the dangers and discipline of war." P. 20. "The Great Case of Transplantation in Ireland discussed," [by Vincent Gookin] Small 4to. London: 1655.

and in those days the Church of Christ sat in Chichester House on College-green.* They reserved also for themselves the four counties of Dublin, Kildare, Carlow, and Cork. Out of the lands and tithes thus reserved, the government were to satisfy public debts, private favourites, eminent friends of the republican cause in Parliament, regicides, and the most active of the English rebels, not being of the army.

They next made ample provision for the adventurers. The amount due to the adventurers was £360,000. This they divided into three lots, of which £110,000 was to be satisfied in Munster, £205,000 in Leinster, and £45,000 in Ulster, and the moiety of ten counties was charged with their payment;—Waterford, Limerick, and Tipperary, in Munster; Meath, Westmeath, King's and Queen's Counties, in Leinster; and Antrim, Down, and Armagh, in Ulster. But, as all was required by the Adventurers Act to be done by lot, a lottery was appointed to be held in Grocers' Hall, London, for the 20th July, 1653, to begin at 8 o'clock in the morning, when lots should be first drawn in which province each adventurer was to be satisfied, not exceeding the specified amounts in any province; lots were to be drawn, secondly, to ascertain in which of the ten counties each adventurer was to receive his land—the lots not to exceed in Westmeath £70,000, in Tipperary £60,000, in Meath £55,000, in King's and Queen's Counties £40,000 each, in Limerick £30,000, in Waterford £20,000, in Antrim, Down, and Armagh, £15,000 each. And, as it was thought it would be a great encouragement to the adventurers (who were for the most part

---

* " Whereas Mr. Thomas Hicks is by the Church of Christ meeting at Chichester House approved as one fully qualified to preach and dispense the gospel . . . . he is appointed to preach the gospel at Stillorgan, and other places in the barony of Rathdown, in the county of Dublin, as often as the Lord shall enable him, and in such places as the Lord shall make his ministry most effectual. Dated 12th September, 1659. THOMAS HERBERT, Clerk of the Council." " Book of Establishments," p. 181.

merchants and tradesmen), about to plant in so wild and dangerous a country, not yet subdued, to have soldier planters near them, these ten counties, when surveyed (which was directed to be done immediately, and returned to the committee for the lottery at Grocers' Hall), were to be divided, each county, by baronies, into two moieties, as equally as might be, without dividing any barony. A lot was then to be drawn by the adventurers, and by some officer appointed by the Lord General Cromwell on behalf of the soldiery, to ascertain which baronies in the ten counties should be for the adventurers, and which for the soldiers.

The rest of Ireland, except Connaught, was to be set out amongst the officers and soldiers, for their arrears, amounting to £1,550,000, and to satisfy debts of money or provisions due for supplies advanced to the army of the Commonwealth amounting to £1,750,000. Connaught was by the Parliament reserved and appointed for the habitation of the Irish nation; and all English and Protestants having lands there, who should desire to remove out of Connaught into the provinces inhabited by the English, were to receive estates in the English parts, of equal value, in exchange.*

---

* " For the satisfaction of the Adventurers for Lands in Ireland, out of the arrears due to the Souldiery here, and of other Publique Debts." Scobell's " Acts and Ordinances," chap. xii.

PART II.

THE TRANSPLANTATION.

THE FIRST TRUMPET.

WHEN the Irish forces laid down arms in 1650, they could scarce have anticipated the measures adopted towards them, two years later, by the Parliament of England. Many of the Irish gentry embarked, in the years 1650 and 1651, for Spain. Those who stayed behind had families, that prevented them from following their example; they returned to their former neighbourhoods, took up their abode in the offices attached to their mansions, or shared the dwellings of some of their late tenants,—their mansions being occupied by some English officer or soldier,—and employed themselves in tilling the lands they had lately owned as lords. Let us conceive the dismay of a poor nobleman, with his wife and daughters, thus employed on the evening of the first market day, after the 11th October, 1652, when some neighbour came to announce the news proclaimed by beat of drum and sound of trumpet in the adjoining town.* It was, in fact, the proscription of the nation. If

---

* "The Parliament of the Commonwealth of England having by one Act lately passed (entitled an Act for the Settling of Ireland) declared that *it is not their intention to extirpate this whole nation*, but that mercy and pardon for life and estate be extended to all husbandmen, plowmen, labourers, artificers, and others of the inferior sort, in such manner as in and by the said Act is set forth; for the better execution of the said Act, and that timely notice may be given to all persons therein concerned, it is ordered that the Governor and Commissioners of Revenue or any two or more of them,

he had been a colonel or a superior officer in the army, as almost all the highest were, it was a sentence of confiscation and banishment; and a separation from his now beggared wife and daughters, the partners of his miseries, unless he had the means of bringing them abroad with him.

The Earl of Ormond, Primate Bramhall, and all the Catholic nobility, and many of the gentry, were declared incapable of pardon of life or estate, and were banished. The rest of the nation were to lose their lands, and take up their residence wherever the Parliament of England should order.* On 26th September, 1653, all the ancient estates and farms of the people of Ireland were declared to belong to the adventurers and the army of England; and it was announced that the Parliament had assigned Connaught (America was not then accessible), for the habitation of the Irish nation, whither they must transplant with their wives, and daughters, and children, before the 1st of May following (1654), under penalty of death, if found on this side of the Shannon after that day.

It might, perhaps, be imagined that this fearful sentence was a penalty upon the supposed bloodthirstiness of the Irish. But for blood, death, not banishment was the punishment; and the class most likely to be guilty of blood,—the ploughmen, labourers, and others of the lower order of poor people,—were ex-

within every precinct in this nation, do cause the said Act of Parliament with this present declaration to be published and proclaimed in their respective precincts *by beat of drumme and sound of trumpett*, on some markett day, within tenn days after the same shall come unto them within their respective precincts.

"Dated at the Castle of Kilkenny, this 11th October 1652.

"Edmund Ludlow,   Miles Corbet,

"John Jones,   R. Weaver."

$\frac{A}{82}$, p. 367.

* Act for the Settling of Ireland, passed 12th August, 1652. Scobell's "Acts and Ordinances."

cepted from transplantation. The nobility and gentry of ancient descent, proprietors of landed estates, were incapable of murder or massacre ; but it was they that were particularly required to transplant. Their properties were wanted for the new English planters. There is an anecdote told by an Englishman of the order of the Friars Minors, who must have dwelt, disguised probably (a not uncommon incident) as a soldier or servant, in the household of Colonel Ingoldsby, Governor of Limerick, that explains the reason why the common people were to be allowed to stay, and the gentry required to transplant. He heard the question asked of a great Protestant statesman ("magnus hereticus consiliarius"), who gave three reasons for it :—First, he said, they are useful to the English as earth-tillers and herdsmen ; secondly, deprived of their priests and gentry, and living among the English, it is hoped they will become Protestants ; and, thirdly, the gentry without their aid must work for themselves and their families, or, if they don't, must die, and if they do, will in time turn into common peasants.*

The truth is, that, having engaged to take 2,500,000 acres from the gentry of Ireland, the Parliament feared they might seek to recover their own again, unless they went through with the business, and swept the nation beyond the Shannon.

---

* " Threnodia Hiberno-Catholica, sive Planctus universalis totius Cleri et Populi Regni Hiberniæ," &c. [" The Wail of the Irish Catholics ; or, Groans of the whole Clergy and People of the Kingdom of Ireland, in which is truly set forth an Epitome of the unheard of and transcendental Cruelty by which the Catholics of the Kingdom of Ireland are oppressed under the Arch Tyrant Cromwell, the Usurper and Destroyer of the three Realms of England, Ireland, and Scotland," p. 25.   By F. Maurice Morison, of the Minors of Strict Observance, Lecturer in Theology, an Eye-witness of those Cruelties.   Innsbruck.   A. D. 1659, 12mo.   The book is dedicated to his worthy patron, Don Guidobald, Archbishop of Salzburg, and to the dean and canons there.

The Parliament made one exception. Those Irish who could show by active proof that they had borne a constant good affection to the Parliament of England during the ten years' contest, were to be exempt from transplantation. To render it more difficult, however, the claim was barred if it was shown the claimant had dwelt on an estate in the Irish quarters, or that the rents were remitted to him though dwelling in the English quarters. The exception, too, of husbandmen, ploughmen, and others of the lower ranks, did not save them for the use of the English, as was intended; for all swordmen were to transplant, and in this term were included all who had attended muster, though compelled by their landlords, and any who kept watch and ward, which comprised almost every one. For their share in the war, or not proving a constant good affection to the Parliament of England, the proprietors of lands were to suffer a loss of the greater part of their estates, and to receive an equivalent for the residue in Connaught for the support of themselves and their families.

THE SECOND AND LAST TRUMPET, WITH THE DOOM OF THE IRISH NATION.

Connaught was selected for the habitation of all the Irish nation by reason of its being surrounded by the sea and the Shannon, all but ten miles, and the whole easily made into one line by a few forts.* To further secure the imprisonment of the nation, and cut them off from relief by sea, a belt four miles wide, commencing one mile to the west of Sligo, and so winging along the coast and Shannon, was reserved by the Act of 27th September, 1653, from being set out to the Irish, and was to be given to the soldiery to plant. Thither all the Irish were to remove at latest by the first day of May, 1654, ex-

* 9th March, 1654-5. Order. Passes over the Shannon between Jamestown and Sligo to be closed, so as to make one entire line between Connaught and the adjacent parts of Leinster and Ulster. $\frac{A.}{85}$

cept Irishwomen married to English Protestants before the 2nd December, 1650, provided they became Protestants; except also boys under fourteen, and girls under twelve, in Protestant service and to be brought up Protestants; and, lastly, those who had shown during the ten years' war in Ireland their constant good affection to the Parliament of England in preference to the King. There they were to dwell without entering a walled town or coming within five miles of some, on pain of death. All were to remove thither by the 1st of May, 1654, at latest, under pain of being put to death by sentence of a court of military officers, if found after that date on the English side of the Shannon.*

Connaught was at this time the most wasted province in the kingdom. Sir Charles Coote the younger, disregarding the truce or cessation made by order of the King with the Irish in 1644, had continued to ravage it, like another Attila, with fire and sword.† The order was for the flight of the Irish nation thither in winter time, their nobles, their gentry, and their commons, with their wives and little children, their young maidens and old men, their cattle, and their household goods.

The officers of the army were themselves struck with the difficulties of executing the orders of the Parliament of England. The gentry and farmers were then engaged in getting

---

* "The further Instructions confirmed by this Act." Act for the Satisfaction of the Adventurers for Lands in Ireland and Arrears due to the Souldiery there. 26 September, 1653. Scobell's "Acts and Ordinances," Anno 1653, chap. xii.

† P. 58, vol. 1st, "Alithinologia; sive Veridica Responsio, &c. [in English] A true Answer to the Attack of R. F. [Richard Farrel], Capuchin, full of Lies, Fallacies, and Calumnies against a large body of the Clergy, Nobility, and Irish of every rank, presented to the Propaganda in the year 1659. By Eudoxius Alithinologus [John Lynch, Priest, Archdeacon of Tuam.]" Printed at St. Malos, 1664. 2 vols. 4to.

in the harvest they had been encouraged to plant on account
of the scarcity. The whole nation, panic-struck at having to
travel during the winter to Connaught, and to abandon the
lands they were still in occupation of, were deprived of all
motive to go on with their tillage. The country must next
year be a waste, for the soldiers could not be put in possession in time to sow. Then there was the possibility that the
Irish generally might decline to remove, and incur all penalties, and prefer death itself to transplanting under such difficulties.

The officers communicated their thoughts to the commissioners for the Government of Ireland, who communicated
them to the Council of State in England.

The Commissioners for Ireland, to use their own expres-
sions, were overwhelmed with a sense of their difficulties, and
of their own unworthiness and weakness for so great a service.
They felt they had neither wisdom nor strength for such
matters; and that they might truly say, " The children are now
come to the birth, and much is desired and expected, but there
is no strength to bring forth."

They therefore fasted, and enjoined the same thing on all
Christian friends in Ireland, and invited the commanders and
officers of the army to join them in lifting up prayers
with strong crying and tears to Him to whom nothing is too
hard, that His servants, whom He had called forth in this
day to act in these great transactions, might be made faithful,
and carried on by His own outstretched arm against all opposition and difficulty, to do what was pleasing in His sight.*

Meantime they proceeded, as in duty bound, to carry out
the law. They issued their orders, dated the 15th October,

* Letter, dated 9th November, 1653, from the Commissioners for Ireland " to the commanders of the respective precincts, to be communicated to
the rest of our Christian friends there." $\frac{A}{90}$, p. 555.

1653, for the better carrying on the great work. Fathers and heads of families were to proceed before 30th January, 1654, to Loughrea, to commissioners appointed to set them out lands competent to the stock possessed by them and by the tenants and friends who were to transplant with them. They were there to build huts against the arrival of their wives and families, who were to follow before the first of May. The commissioners were to be guided by a statement, or Particular, which each proprietor, before leaving home, was to present to the revenue officer of the precinct for his certificate. It set forth the abode, names, ages, stature, colour of the hair, and other marks of distinction, of the transplanter and his family, and of all his tenants and friends who were to accompany him into Connaught, together with the number of their cattle, quantity and quality of tillage, and other substance.* From the grey-haired sire to the blue-eyed daughter of four years old, the family portraiture is given in these transplanters' certificates. Sometimes there is a long list of tenants and friends, and sheep and cattle, accompanying the chief proprietor of the district into exile, like the pictures of the descent of the Israelites into Egypt. In others, a landlord, who perhaps had rendered himself distasteful to his tenants, has none to accompany him ; for tenants were not required to adhere to their landlord ; they might sit down in Connaught as tenants under the state. Occasionally in these certificates is described a gentleman, like Sir Nicholas Comyn, of Limerick precinct, "numb at one side of his body of a dead palsy, accompanied only by his Lady, Catherine Comyn, aged thirty-five years, flaxen-haired, middle stature ; and one maid servant, Honor ny McNamara, aged twenty years, brown hair, middle stature ; having no substance, but expecting the benefit of his qualifica-

* From a printed copy (original), preserved in the muniment room, Kilkenny Castle.

tion." Or orphans; as, "Ignatius Stacpoole, of Limerick, orphant, aged eleven years, flaxen haire, full face, low stature; Katherine Stacpoole, orphant, sister to the said Ignatius, aged eight years, flaxen haire, full face; having no substance to relieve themselves, but desireth the benefit of his claim before the Commissioners of the Revenue."*

James, Lord Dunboyne, in the county of Tipperary, describes himself as likely to be accompanied by twenty-one followers, and as having four cows, ten garrans, and two swine.† Dame Katherine Morris, of Lathragh, in the same county: thirty-five followers, one and a half acre of summer corne, ten cows, sixteen garrans, nineteen goats, two swine. Lady Mary Hamerton, of Roscrea: forty-five persons, three and a half acres of summer corn, forty cows, thirty garrans, forty-six sheepe, two goats.‡ Pierce, Lord Viscount Ikerrin: seventeen persons, sixteen acres of winter corne, four cows, five garrans, twenty-four sheep, two swine. For each acre of winter corn, three acres of land were to be assigned, summer corn and fallow being included; for each cow or bullock (of two years old and upwards), three acres; for each yearling one acre; for each garran, nag, or mare (of three years old and upwards), four acres; for every three sheep, one acre; and for goats and swine proportionably.§ These assignments were only conditional; for at a future day other commissioners were to arrive and sit at Athlone, to determine the claims, i. e. the extent of lands the transplanter had left behind him, and to distinguish the qualifications, i. e. the extent of disaffection to the Parliament, by which the proportion to be confiscated was to be regulated, and an equivalent, called a

* Pp. 12, 13, Book of Transplanters' Certificates, in the Record Tower, Dublin Castle.

† Ib. Among the records of the late Auditor-General's Office in the custody of W. H. Hardinge, Esq., Custom House Buildings.

‡ Ib. ib.   § $\frac{A}{90}$, p. 629.

Final Settlement was to be given in Connaught. These first assignments were technically called Assignments de Bene Esse.

REMONSTRANCES OF THE IRISH.

And now there went forth petitions from every quarter of the kingdom, praying that the petitioners' flight might not be in the winter time; or alleging that their wives or children were sick, their cattle unfit to drive,—that they had crops to get in. Some were still collecting men for transport to Spain. Others had claims to exemption under articles of war. All sought a dispensation.

The petitioners were the noble and the wealthy, men of ancient English blood, descendants of the invaders—the Fitzgeralds, the Butlers, the Plunkets, the Barnwalls, Dillons, Cheevers, Cusacks, names found appended to various schemes for extirpating or transplanting the Irish after the subduing of Lord Thomas Fitzgerald's rebellion in 1535,—who were now to transplant as Irish. The native Irish were too poor to pay scriveners and messengers to the Council, and their sorrows were unheard, though under their rough coats beat hearts that felt pangs as great at being driven from their native homes as the highest in the land. The first dispensations were limited within the 1st of May, the Commissioners for the Affairs of Ireland not being empowered to dispense from compliance with the Act of Parliament. But they represented to the Council of State in London that all tillage would cease unless people were encouraged to put in a crop with the prospect of reaping it. Powers were accordingly given to them to grant dispensations for the wives and children and necessary servants of those who should crop their land, who were to be permitted, in case the father or head of the family should have complied with the orders of the state, and have removed into Connaught, to stay behind with not more than one or two servants to watch the corn in the ground, and to attend to the threshing and "inning" of it.* But from the 1st of May, 1654, their estates would be either taken possession of by the soldiers, or let by the state to other tenants, to whom they must pay for the standing of their crop from that date till removed, an eighth or a fifth sheaf, according to the custom of the country.

The estate now called Woodlands, the seat of Lord Annaly, adjoining the Phœnix Park, Dublin, formerly known as Luttrelstown, was the seat of the Luttrels, from the days of King John until sold, about seventy years ago, by Luttrel, Lord Carhampton, to the ancestor of Lord Annaly.

Thomas Luttrel, the owner, though strongly attached to the English interest, as appeared by his getting a decree at Athlone, in 1658, of good, though not constant good, affection,† was obliged, as an Irish Papist, to make way, when Lord Ormond handed over Dublin and the sword of state, in 1647,

---

* " *Commissioners for Ireland to Colonel Foulk, Governor of Tredagh, and the Commissioners of Revenue there.*

" Gentlemen,—The Commissioners of the Commonwealth of England for the Affairs of Ireland have read your letter of the 25th instant, declaring that several persons removing from your parts into Connaught desire some time to stay for their wives, children, and stock, for the better enabling them to travel, and that it is your judgment that by their short stay the contribution will be the better secured. They have commanded me to signify that you may suspend the transplantation of such wives and children (whose husbands and parents are to go into Connaught) for such time as you shall judge fit, not exceeding the 1st July next, and may permit the stay of their cattle until they be in a condition to drive, allowing but one servant to look after the respective herds or flocks, and such servants to be neither proprietors nor such as have been in arms against the Commonwealth.

" Thos. Herbert, Clerk of the Council.

" *Cork House, 27th April, 1654.*" $\frac{A}{90}$, p. 668.

† $\frac{A}{22}$, p. 149.

to the Parliament, for Lord Broghill, who was afterwards suc-
ceeded as tenant to the state by Colonel Hewson, Governor
of Dublin. In 1652, Luttrel got permission to occupy the
stables and till the land.*

On the 30th of September, 1654, he was dispensed from
being transplanted until the 1st of December following, in
" regard his whole livelihood and his family's depended on
improving the crop of corn that was then in taking off the
ground."† On the 15th of March, 1655, upon his inability,
through his weakness by sickness, to travel into Connaught,
he was further dispensed till the 1st June.‡ Before this time,
however, he had departed, leaving his wife behind; for on the
18th of May she was dispensed until the 1st of June following, on her representation that her husband was already
transplanted, and that she had a great charge of children and
stock which were not yet in a condition to drive.§

But often the owners were transplanted, and got liberty to return to reap their crop, or to send back their servants. Thus,
John Talbot, ancestor of Lord Talbot de Malahide, had to yield
his castle to Chief Baron Corbet, and transplant, and in April,
1655, got a pass for safe travelling from Connaught to the
county of Dublin to dispose of his corn and other goods,
giving security to return within the time limited.‖

Considerable difficulties arose about these allowances between the families of the transplanted, left behind to watch the
crop and the soldiers. On the 1st of May, 1654, the first
considerable disbanding took place; and from the moment any
district was assigned to the soldiers, they became uncontrolled
masters of it. Thus, the officers and soldiers whose lots had
fallen in the district called the Rower, in the county of Kilkenny, were declared entitled to have an allowance for the

---

* $\frac{A}{82}$ p. 515; ib., p. 534.　　† $\frac{A}{4}$ p. 17.　　‡ $\frac{A}{6}$, p. 134.
§ Ib., p. 217.　　‖ Ib., p. 173.

standing of the corn on the lands fallen to them for their arrears, from the 1st of May last (1654) till December following, according to the custom of the country, not exceeding a fifth sheaf;* and the transplanted inhabitants of the county of Waterford, finding that their wives and children were interrupted in the securing of their crops, petitioned the government from Connaught for protection.† The government thereupon ordered that the Commissioners of Revenue of the precinct where the respective crops of corn were should permit the wives, and such servants of theirs as were permitted to stay, to receive the benefit of their crop, having discharged the contribution due thereout, and allowing the new proprietors an eighth sheaf, or such proportion as is usually made in those parts, according to the custom of the country. But the cruelest act of these rough soldiers was that they and the state tenants entered, and proceeded without mercy to turn out the wives and children of these transplanted proprietors and their servants engaged in watching their last crop, without giving them even a cabin to shelter in, or allowing them grass for their cows on lands so lately their own.‡ The

* $\frac{A}{4}$, p. 6.   † Ib., p. 50.

‡ " *To the Commissioners of the Revenue of the respective Precincts.*
" *Dublin,* 26 *May,* 1654.

" GENTLEMEN,—Whereas we have been informed that several persons that have taken leases of lands from the Commonwealth belonging to Irish inhabitants that are to be transplanted into Connaught from the 1st of May, instant, and upon orders of possession for the same, have entered by virtue of their said leases, and turned out the former Irish possessors and their servants, without allowing them any cabbins or other habitacōns for such necessary servants as they leave behind them for looking after their corn in the ground, and inning and thrashing of the same, contrary to the provisions made in the order for transplantation, we therefore hereby order that you take care that in cases where the said Irish are denied such liberty as abovesaid, you cause convenience of room to be allowed for servants dwelling and thrashing the said corn now in the ground, with grazing on the

ancient owners became, in fact, strict tenants at will to the
state from the time that the Parliament declared the forfeited
lands to belong to the soldiers and adventurers, though, as
would appear from Sir John Burke's complaint, they had
been promised, or understood they were entitled to, a six
months' notice to quit.*

In the case of Thomas Luttrel, of Luttrelstown, in the
county of Dublin, we have a proprietor reduced, with his
family, to occupy the stables while taking the last crop, and
thence transplanted to Connaught.

APPLICATIONS FOR DISPENSATIONS FROM TRANSPLANTATION.

The applications for dispensations were innumerable, and
the Commissioners were overwhelmed with them.

Margaret Barnwall had long been troubled with a shaking
palsy.† Mary Archer had an aged father, who would be suddenly brought to his grave wanting his accustomed accommo-

---

said lands fit for such sort of cattle as will be needful for carrying in the
corn in harvest.

　　　　"We remain your loving friends,

$\frac{A}{90}$, p. 702.　　　　"CHAS. FLEETWOOD, MILES CORBET, JOHN JONES."

* "Upon consideration had of the agreement made by the Commissioners of Revenue with the petitioner, Sir John Bourke, and others in
like condition with him, that he should, upon six months' notice, remove
out of the possession of the lands in the petition mentioned, and the petitioner having been required to remove into Connaught upon the general
declaration for transplanting, the Councill do not think fit to do anything
in his case, but do expect that the petitioner should conform himself to
former orders for removing into Connaught.

"16th Oct., 1654.　　　"THOS. HERBERT, Clerk of the Council."
$\frac{A}{4}$, p. 67.

† $\frac{A}{6}$, p. 266.

dation.* Lady Margaret Atkinson was of great age, and no
one to support her but her son, Sir George Atkinson, a Protestant.† Lady Culme prayed not to be deprived of her
servant.‡ Elinor Butler, widow, had a charge of helpless children.§ Dowager Lady Lowth was of great age and impotency.‖
John, Lord Baron Power, of Curraghmore, had for twenty
years past been distracted, and destitute of all judgment.¶
Piers Creagh, of Limerick, was hated by his countrymen for

* $\frac{A}{12}$, p. 65.

† " Upon consideration of the petition of Sir G. Atkinson on the behalf
of his mother, the Lady Margaret Atkinson, desiring that his said mother
might be dispensed with from transplantation, and remain in the province
of Ulster ; and consideration being had of the report of Colonel Mark-
ham, Captain Shaw, and Thomas Richardson, Esq., unto whom it was
referred, who have certified that in regard of the said Ladys great age, as
also that she hath no friend to support her save only her said son, a Protestant, and for that it appears by Sir Charles Coote's certificate that she
hath always lived inoffensively in said quarters, they are of opinion she
should not be removed into Connaught or Clare without special direction ;
and that she may in the meantime continue to reside with her said son.
It is therefore ordered that she be dispensed with from transplantation until
1st May, and that she be permitted to enjoy that proportion of her estate
according to her qualification.

" T. HERBERT, Clerk of the Council.
" *Dublin, 30th October*, 1654." $\frac{A}{4}$, p.116.

‡ $\frac{A}{12}$, p. 214.

§ " Upon the consideration of the petition of Ellinor Butler, widow, and
the order of the Commissioners of the Revenue of Waterford, and the report of Colonel Lawrence, &c. &c., and it being his opinion that the pe-
tioner's own person and her helpless children should be dispensed with
as to her present transplantation ; *and that she be permitted to bring back
her cattle from Connaught* towards the maintenance of herself and children :
We, the said Deputy and Council, agree, &c., that she be permitted to bring
back her said cattle without molestation, &c. *Dublin*, 16th *October*, 1654.'
$\frac{A}{4}$, p. 64.

‖ $\frac{A}{4}$, p. 211.   ¶ Ib., p. 363.

his former known inclination to the English Government.* Robert Plunket had given information against several prisoners
now in the Marshalsea, who are of great alliance to the Irish,
and his safety would be risked in Connaught† (a common statement). Lord Viscount Ikerrin had great weakness and infirmity
of body.‡ Dominic Bodkin, Nicholas oge French, and Richard
Kerroan (Kirwan), inhabitants of Galway, pleaded their singular
good services, whereby they had prejudiced their private interests, and contracted malice from those of their own nation,
amongst whom they were now to live, which might prove dangerous to them ;§ Major Charles Cavanagh and his brother
James,—their inoffensive demeanor to the English.‖ Anne
White, widow, of the town of Wexford, sought to spend the remnant of her days there on the certificate of Colonel Lawrence,
Governor of Waterford, who had observed her charity for
four or five years past, her good affection to English officers
and others quartered in her house—a very useful person to that
town ; and if any of her religion might live in any garrison, none more deserving than she.¶ Cicely Plunket,—that her
husband was a schoolboy at the breaking out of the rebellion,
and had since lived inoffensively ; that her husband was upon
his transplanting, but that his whole substance depends upon
her corn in her haggard, and prayed time for making benefit of
her corn and provision for herself and her children.** Margaret
Cusack, that she was seventy-eight years of age, and dropsical.††
Mary Butler, widow of Mr. Richard Butler, of Ballinakill, in
the county of Tipperary, her affection to the English forces,
and having discovered an ambushment of the Irish to cut off
the English.‡‡ John Rose, of Warrenstown in the barony of

---

* $\frac{A}{4}$, p. 112.   † $\frac{A}{85}$, p. 531.   ‡ Ib., p. 384.

§ $\frac{A}{30}$, p. 160.   ‖ $\frac{A}{6}$, p. 9.   ¶ Ib., p. 170.

** Ib., p. 248.   †† Ib., p. 188.   ‡‡ Ib., p. 219.

Dunboyne, his having suffered much in the beginning of the rebellion for his affection to the English interest, and served as a trooper under Captain Bland against the rebels, and was wounded and also that he was of English parents.* Henry Burnell, for his tedious and languishing sickness, sought time till 1st of June next, by which time it was probable he might recover his strength, and be able to travel on foot to Connaught. Nicholas Barnwall, of Turvey, and Bridget, his wife, Countess of Tirconnel, in regard of their great age and infirmity of body.

The transplantation of the Kilkenny submittees, as those of the Leinster army were called, that laid down their arms under the terms of the articles entered into on 12th May, 1652, had some features of peculiar hardship. The officers of the Parliament army engaged to really and truly mediate for them with the Parliament, that they might enjoy such moderate parts of their estates as should make the lives of those who should not retire in voluntary banishment to Spain, but live amongst the English, comfortable, and undertook that in the meantime they should enjoy such part of their estates as had not been disposed of; and under this latter clause the Commissioners for Ireland ordered them possession of their undisposed of estates till 1st April, 1653.

Part of Lord Trimleston's manor had been given *in custodium* to Mrs. Penelope Bayley, the widow of Colonel Bayley, by a special order of Lord Deputy Ireton, in 1650 ; but in May of 1652, for her greater security, she took a lease of them for one year from the state, which she let for the time to one Cusack, who assigned them to his brother-in-law, Lord Trimleston. When this lease expired, she renewed it for three years ; but Lord Trimleston, being in possession at the expira-

† $\frac{A}{6}$, p. 235.

tion of the first lease, contended he was entitled to hold them under the Kilkenny Articles, and bribed Mr. Bryan Darley, the surveyor, who was to put Mrs. Bayley in possession, by £4, Mrs. Bayley having given Mr. Darley £6. Lord Trimleston being thus in possession, Mrs. Bayley had to get an order to put him forth, and to have the surveyor arrested for the fraud.* When the order for transplantation issued in October, 1653, and Lord Trimleston and the other Kilkenny submittees were called on to transplant, Lord Trimleston on his own behalf and theirs pleaded that by the 6th article they expected the enjoyment of such remnant of their real estate as should make their lives comfortable amongst the English, and that this was not performed ; and that they were exempt from transplantation.   But the Commissioners for Ireland answered that the Act of Parliament overrode the articles, and that they must transplant to Connaught, where they would have one-third set out to them by the Loughrea Commissioners in some convenient place, with such houses and accommodation as might make their lives comfortable, and with due regard to the nature and goodness of the soil from whence they should remove.†   They then appealed to the Committee of Articles, at Westminster, who were of opinion that it would be a breach of faith to transplant them ; but the Commissioners enforced their view.   On 12th of April, 1655, they made their last effort, and got liberty to stay in their respective dwellings until the 1st of May, and their wives and children until the 20th.‡

These Kilkenny submittees were the lords and gentlemen of the Pale, the Barnwalls, the Nettervilles, Bellews, Plunkets and others.   They complained that the officers in possession of their estates were sheltering their tenants, and prayed that

---

* $\frac{A}{84}$, p. 408.   † $\frac{A}{8}$, p. 177.   ‡ $\frac{A}{6}$, p. 205.

they might be ordered to assist them in driving their cattle, and removing of their carriages to Connaught. But this was refused : all relation between landlord and tenant had ceased between them, but the transplantable tenants were ordered to be arrested.*

How strict was the imprisonment of the transplanted in Connaught may be judged, when it required a special order for Lord Trimleston, Sir Richard Barnwall, Mr. Patrick Netterville, and others, then dwelling in the suburbs of Athlone on the Connaught side, to pass and repass the bridge into the part of the town on the Leinster side on their business, and only on giving security not to pass without the line of the town without special leave of the governor.†

It has already been remarked that the descendants of those statesmen of Henry VIII.'s day, who were so full of schemes for confiscating the lands of the Irish, and transplanting or extirpating them, had to abandon their estates, and to transplant to Connaught. In Queen Elizabeth's reign there was no more deadly enemy to Ireland than Edmund Spenser ; he was secretary to Lord Grey de Wilton, all whose cruelties he justified. He deals with transplantation as if the Irish were beasts of the field, that might be driven from one province to another for the convenience of the English. One can scarce pity his lot, which was to see his castle of Kilcolman, late the abode of one of the Fitzgeralds, burned before his eyes with all it contained, including one of his infant children. The robber was thus robbed, the spoiler spoiled ; and he went down to his grave in darkness, in lodgings in London, banished by the Irish, who retook their former lands. By a retribution so common in Ireland, the grandson of this English settler had become Irish, and the very woes his ancestor had contrived for the Irish came to be inflicted on his descendant. Among

* $\frac{A}{6}$, p. 205.   † Ib., p. 346.

those seeking to be dispensed from transplantation to Connaught was William Spenser, whose grandfather was that Spenser who by his writings touching the reduction of the Irish to civility brought upon him the odium of that nation. That very estate near Fermoy which was confiscated from the Fitzgeralds, and conferred on him about seventy years before, is now confiscated anew, and set out among the soldiers of the Commonwealth army, and his grandson is ordered to transplant to Connaught as an Irishman. William Spenser appealed to Cromwell; and Cromwell, out of regard for the works of Edmund Spenser, his grandfather, endeavoured, but in vain, to save his lands for him.*

* " *Lord Protector to Commissioners for Affairs in Ireland.*
" *Whitehall, 27th March,* 1657.
" RIGHT TRUSTY AND WELL BELOVED,
        " A petition hath been exhibited unto us by William Spenser, setting forth that being but seaven years old att the beginning of the rebellion in Ireland, hee repaired with his mother to the Citty of Corke, and during the rebellion continued in the English quarters; that hee never bore arms, or acted against ye Commonwealth of England; that his grandfather, Edmund Spenser, and his father, were both Protestants, from whom an estate in lands in the barony of Fermoy, and county of Corke, descended to him, which during the rebellion yielded nothing towards his reliefe; that ye estate hath been lately given to the souldiers in satisfaction of their arrears, upon accompt of his professing the Popish religion, which since his coming to years of discretion hee hath, as hee professes, utterly renounced; that his grandfather was that Edmund Spenser, who by his writings touching the reduction of ye Irish to civility brought on him the odium of that nation, and for those works and his other good services Queen Elizabeth conferred on him y^t estate which the said William Spenser now claims. Wee have also been informed that ye gentleman is of a civill conversation, and that the extremitie his wants have brought him unto have not prevailed over him to put him upon indiscreet or evil practices for a livelihood. And if upon enquiry you shall find his case to be such, wee judge it just and reasonable, and do therefore desire and authorise you y^t hee bee forthwith restored to his estate, and that reprisall lands bee given

THE TROUBLES OF THE COMMISSIONERS FOR IRELAND.

Besides the complaints of the transplanting Irish, the Commissioners of Ireland had to meet and answer the petitions of their own officers. The Commissioners of Revenue found their returns affected by the transplantation, " it had so distracted and discomposed the people." Irish entrusted by their neighbours with collecting the assessment payable by the different baronies were escaping into Connaught with the balances, without passing their accounts.* Officers and Protestants prayed that they might not be deprived of their tenants and servants. Officers entrusted with clearing the towns of Irish, unwilling to be answerable for the consequences

to the souldiers elsewhere. In y[e] doing whereof our satisfaction will be the greater by the continuation of that estate to y[e] issue of his grandfather for whose eminent deserts and services to y[e] Commonwealth y[t] estate was first given to him.

" We rest, your loving friend,

" OLIVER, P."

Book of " Letters from the Lord Protector," p. 118, Record Tower, Dublin Castle.

* " The time for transplanting the Irish being at hand, and the ablest of the Irish inhabitants to remove thereupon, amongst which it is probable that the most of those persons who have been entrusted as commissioners, agents, or trustees for baronies will be included, who will some of them doubtless take the advantage to avoid accompting with the country for their receipts and collections before departure. . . . . We therefore desire you will take care to call all such of the Irish or others who have been entrusted with the receipt of publique moneys in your precinct, to account in convenient time before their transplanting. . . .

" Your affectionate friends,

" EDWARD ROBERTS. BENJAMIN WORSLEY.

" *Corke House, March 2nd,* 1654.

" *To the Commissioners of the Precinct of Limerick.*"

Records of late Auditor-General's Office, Custom House Buildings.

of literally executing the order, required categorical answers
from the government to their queries. Colonel Sadleir asks
whether any Irish Papist shall be permitted to live in the
town of Wexford ?   If any, whether all the seamen, boatmen,
and fishermen, or how many ?   How many packers and gillers
of herrings ?   How many coopers ?   How many masons and
carpenters ?   What shall be done with the Irishwomen.
which are Papists, who are married to Englishmen and Protestants ?   What shall be done with the Irishmen who are
turned Protestants, and come to hear the word of God ?*
The Commissioners at Loughrea troubled them even more.
They asked whether by Popish recusants of the Irish nation,
and therefore transplantable, might be understood those whose
fathers or mothers, or both, were English, only themselves born
in Ireland ?   Whether persons enlisted by their landlords,
being officers, though they were never in the field, nor marched
out of their country ?   Whether Papists that first served in
the rebel army, but then took service under the Commonwealth, if still on muster ?   Whether men marrying transplantable widows become themselves transplantable ?   Whether
the wives and children of those gone to Spain be transplantable, as well as those remaining behind in like condition with
themselves ?   What do the Commissioners for Ireland mean
by Irish widows of English extract ?   What course shall be
taken with those transplanted that set themselves down where
they choose, refusing to come to their assignments, contrary
to the 4th, 5th, 6th, and 7th instructions, which hinder the
Commissioners from giving any account either of the number
or quality of the transplanted persons, and also from dispersing
the septs according to instructions ?†

* $\frac{A}{85}$, p. 178.   † Ibid., p. 544.

THE FIRST ASPECT OF CONNAUGHT.

The difficulties of the government were increased by the reports arriving from Connaught from the earliest transplanters, to the families they left behind preparing to follow, who were thereby discouraged. They found the country a waste. The county of Clare was totally ruined, and deserted of inhabitants. Out of nine baronies, comprising 1300 ploughlands, not above 40 ploughlands at the most, lying in the barony of Bunratty, were inhabited in the month of June, 1653, except some few persons living for safety in garrisons.* Scarce a place to shelter in. The castles either sleighted by gunpowder, as dangerous to be left in the hands of the Irish ;† or occupied by the English soldiery, or by the ancient Irish proprietors, who looked upon the transplanters as enemies liable to supplant them, and therefore, encouraged their followers to give them rough reception.‡ Besides this, the Loughrea Commis-

* $\frac{A}{84}$, p. 205.

† " Upon reading the petition of Edmund Dogherty, mason, and the certificates of the Commissioners at Loughrea, setting forth that the said Edmond Dogherty is to receive the sum of £82 10s. 0d., for demolishing thirteene castles in yᵉ county of Clare, at £2 10s. 0d. each castle : ordered, &c.

" CHARLES FLEETWOOD, ROBERT GOODWIN.
" *Dublin,* 1*st January,* 1655."
Late Auditor-General's Records, vol. x., p. 188.

‡ " Whereas information hath been given unto this Board, that many of the Irish nation of the province of Connaught have offered several affronts and abuses to divers of the transplanted persons. . . . . . it is hereby ordered, that Sir C. Coote, Knt. and Bart., Lord President of Connaught, Colonel Ingoldsby, &c., or any two or more of them, be empowered upon proof made before them . . forthwith to transplant such Irish proprietors or others from their present habitations into some remote part of Connaught, that shall so menace or assault, &c., there to live.

" Dated at Athlone, 18th June, 1655." $\frac{A}{6}$, p. 346.

sioners gave some of the earliest transplanters assignments in the barony of Burren, in the county of Clare, one of the barrenest, where it was commonly said* there was not wood enough to hang a man, water enough to drown him, or earth enough to bury him.† They were therefore scared, like the first beasts too suddenly driven at a slaughter yard, communicating their terrors to the herd behind. The English officers, too, were not assisting to put them in possession of their assignments.‡ Ferrymen and toll-keepers were exacting tolls, contrary to the orders of government.§

* " Whitelock's Memorials," at the year 1651, p. 521.

†   " Council of Ireland to Loughrea Commissioners.

" Dublin Castle, 18th July, 1655.

" Being informed that you beginn to sett down persons in the baronies of Burren and Inchiqueen, which places being generally reputed and known to be sterill, wee fear it may much hinder the business of the transplantation, by disheartening those which shall come after, when they shall see such assignations made in the entrance of this work, &c." $\frac{A}{30}$, p. 82.

Grievances of the Transplanted in Clare.

" 2ndly. In regard it was the misfortune of your suppliants to be assigned on that part of yᵉ county of Clare that is most barren, unfertill, and waste, which yields no corn but oats (and that itself with much labour and husbandry), your suppliants pray that no sheaf or tax be exacted from them whence they remove.

" 3rdly. Whereas the several transplanted persons thither have withdrawne themselves with their cattle, as well back [across the Shannon] as into Connaught, and that have returned of late their substance in the book of the fourth part of the said county, may be forthwith forced to return back to the said county with their stocks, otherwise the remaining transplanted to be eased of their proportion of the charge for the future." 5th September, 1654. " Grievances of the transplanted inhabitants now in the county of Clare."

Order Book of the Council, Late Auditor-General's Office, Custom House Buildings, vol. vii.

‡ $\frac{A}{90}$, p. 745.   § $\frac{A}{5}$, p. 144.

FIRST YEAR OF THE TRANSPLANTATION.

But the progress of the transplantation during the first year was not rapid enough for the officers possessed by that land hunger characteristic of the Anglo-Saxon race. They complained of any delay being granted to the Irish as displeasing to God :—

" Letter from Dublin, May 31, 1654.

"We are somewhat in a confused posture yet with our transplantation : many are gone, but many others play ' loath to depart.' And many are dispensed with : as particularly one whole town, Cashel, towards which we had no great obligation upon us. But the Lord, who is a jealous God, and more knowing of, as well as jealous against their iniquity than we are, by a fire on the 23rd inst. hath burnt down the whole town in little more than a quarter of an hour, except some few houses that a few English lived in [having probably taken the best stone and slated ones], which were wonderfully preserved, being in the midst of the town, and the houses round each burnt to the ground, yet *they* preserved.

" The persons that got their dispensations from the transplantation died the day before the fire, of the plague, and none else long before nor since dead of the disease there."*

Six weeks later comes the following intelligence to London :—

" From Dublin, 12*th July,* 1654.

" The transplanting work moves on but slowly ; not above six score [families] from all provinces are yet removed into

---

* P. 3538, " Mercurius Politicus, comprising the summe of all Intelligence, with the Affairs and Designs now on foot in the three Nations of England, Ireland, and Scotland ; in Defence of the Commonwealth and the Information of the people. [Published weekly.] Licensed to be printed."

Connaught. The flood-gates being shut from transpórting [to Spain], and one vent stopt for sending away the souldiery, part of them Irish, they begin to break out into Torying, and the waters begin to rise again upon us."*

"From Dublin, August 24th, 1654.

"The work of transplanting is at a stand. The Tories flie out and increase. It is the nature of this people to be rebellious; and they have been so much the more disposed to it, having been highly exasperated by the transplanting work."†

The year closes, however, more satisfactorily :—

"From Dublin, December 21st, 1654.

"The transplantation is now far advanced, the men being gone for to prepare their new habitations in Connaught. Their wives and children and dependents have been and are packing away after them apace, and all are to be gone by the 1st of March next."‡

---

* P. 3636, "Mercurius Politicus," &c.   † P. 3732, ibid.

‡ P. 5048, ibid. They got a further short reprieve :—

"27th February, 1654–5.

"Whereas, by an order of 30th November last, it is declared that all persons in Ireland who are declared to be persons that ought to transplant themselves, their wives, children, and families into Connaught, at or before the 1st of March next, and should wilfully refuse or neglect to do so, should incur the penalties declared in and by the several acts, orders, instructions, and declarations in that behalf, more particularly in that of the 30th November above mentioned : the Lord Deputy and Council, taking into their serious consideration the immoderate and unusual fall of rain at this season of the year, and how much the deepness of the waies and weakness of cattle occasioned thereby may make their journeys more difficult and hazardous, especially to their wives and young children, with their breeding and young cattle : therefore, that all persons concerned may know (as it hath hitherto been in the hearts of those in authority over them, as hath been expressed in their proceedings towards them in this matter, to

SECOND AND FOLLOWING YEARS OF TRANSPLANTATION.

By the 1st March, 1654–5, the last of the Irish gentry and farmers were to be withdrawn across the Shannon. The temper of the officers and soldiers and other expectant planters

exercise all tenderness therein that is consistent with carrying on the work, withal to leave such as shall prove refractorie thereto without excuse), they do declare that the persons transplantable as above said and not dispensed with, as in and by that declaration of 30th November is held forth, do transplant themselves before the 1st day of March next, into the province of Connaught, according to former declarations, and address themselves to such as are there empowered for that purpose to take out their respective assignments of lands, and proceed to build and settle themselves there, and make provision for their families respectively. And it is further ordered, that such persons [i. e. husbands and heads of families] so transplanting themselves as aforesaid, their wives, children, and necessary servants, with their cattle, shall be permitted to continue at their present dwellings and holdings for such time as the Commander-in-Chief, with the Justices of Peace of each precinct, shall think fit to give lycense for under their hands and seals respectively, provided that the said persons themselves so to transplant as aforesaid do procure a certificate of the Commissioners in Connaught appointed to set them out lands there, that they have appeared before them, and are preparing for their families in Connaught, for want of which certificate, their wives, children, and servants remaining in the other three provinces, after the last day of March now next ensuing, are hereby declared out of protection. Provided also that not any lycense given by the Commander-in-Chief and Justices as aforesaid, to any of the wives, children, servants, or cattle belonging to any such persons shall extend for longer than the 20th May next at furthest, but are to be limited for less or more time within that space as they in their judgments (considering the conditions of the several persons so lycensed) shall think fitt.

" Dated at Dublin (as above),"

" Thomas Herbert, Clerk of the Council."

"Ordered by the Lord Deputy and Council that this declaration be forthwith printed."

British Museum, 806. i. 14.

may be judged by the following intelligence, all of which, like the foregoing, was written for publication in London :—

" *Athy, March* 4, 1654–5.

"I have only to acquaint you, that the time prescribed for the transplantation of the Irish proprietors, and those that have been in arms and abettors of the rebellion, being near at hand, the officers are resolved to fill the gaols and to seize them : by which this bloody people will know that they [the officers] are not degenerated from English principles; though I presume we shall be very tender of hanging any except leading men ; yet we shall make no scruple of sending them to the West Indies, where they will serve for planters, and help to plant the plantation that General Venables, it is hoped, hath reduced."*

The government, accordingly, pressed on the great work. They proceeded to seize and sell the crops of those families that delayed to transplant, and to apply the moneys arising from the sale for buying stores to relieve those that transplanted themselves according to the law.†

They issued the most threatening orders. They then ordered the general arrest of all transplantable persons untransplanted by a certain day,‡ under which men and women, all over the kingdom, were hauled out of their beds in the dead of

---

* P. 4530, " Mercurius Politicus," &c.

† Ibid., p. 4569.　　　　　　　　" *Monday, April 2nd*, 1655.

"The Lord Deputy and Council in Ireland have published a Declaration for making sale of the corn of such Irish proprietors and others that did not transplant themselves into Connaught according to the Declaration of 30th November last, for buying stores to relieve those that do transplant themselves according to the said Declaration."

" Perfect Proceedings of State Affairs, &c. (during the week between 29th March and 3rd April, 1655)."

‡ 19th March, 1654–5. General search for and arrest of all transplantable persons untransplanted, ordered, and courts martial appointed to try them. $\frac{A}{26}$, p. 75.

night to prison, till the gaols were choked,* and the Commissioners of Parliament for the affairs of Ireland were obliged to devise excuses to release them. But the aspect of Connaught was so terrible, that the wretched hunted nobility and gentry of Ireland still lingered. Death was necessary to make them move.

"*March 25th*, 1655.

"Daniel Fitzpatrick and another in Ireland [this was published in London for the satisfaction of the adventurers and other capitalists and speculators there] are condemned by the Commissioners in Kilkenny for refusing to transport themselves into Connaught, which makes the rest to hasten."

In the same month, with a view of making their movements quicker, a court martial, sitting in St. Patrick's Cathedral, Dublin, sentenced Mr. Edward Hetherington, of Kilnemanagh, to death. The Commissioners confirmed the sentence, and he was duly hanged on the 3rd of April, with placards on his breast and back, "For not transplanting."†

* "That pursuant to the said pretended act (27th September, 1653), some were put to death with inscriptions on their breasts and backs for non-transplantation. And for the more strict and effectual executing of the said pretended act, it was a frequent practice to make general restraint of all the Irish generally that were found out of the said province of Connaught, which were put in execution at one and the same time through all the other provinces, by troopers and souldiers dragging the poor people out of their beds in the dead time of the night, and bringing them in such troopes as there were not gaol room enough to contain them. Therefore some were put to death as aforesaid, others sold as slaves into America, others detained in prison till they were not able to put bread into their mouths, others (as partakers of the greatest favour that could be expected) sent to Connaught."

"The Roman Catholics of Ireland, their Answer to Proposals offered [to the Privy Council of England] in order to the Settlement of Ireland by the Commissioners from the Convention of Ireland in 1660." Carte MSS., Ireland, vol. vii., p. 6. Bodleian Library.

† "Upon reading the report of the court martial sitting in St.

Still the unfortunate gentry of Ireland would not obey the
law :—

"*Letter from Dublin*, 27th *July*, 1655.

"The business of transplanting is not yet finished. The
Irish, in many places, chuse death rather than remove from
their wonted habitations. But the state is resolved to see it
done."

But the spectacle of universal misery of the Irish nation,
and the evil consequences to the English planters themselves,
now called forth the book called " The Great Case of Transplantation in Ireland Discussed."* It was anonymous. But the

Patrick's Church, Dublin, touching one Edward Hetherington of Kilne-
mana, whom the said court found guilty of the breach of the Declaration
concerning transplantation of 30th November last, whereby it appears
that for the breach aforesaid, as also for that his disobedience to several
declarations for transplantation, he was found guilty by the court martial in July last (he being a person that had borne arms against the Commonwealth).   And likewise it did appear by an original examination
had from the High Court of Justice, by the positive oath of two Englishr-
men that in the year 1643 he was a Tory, and (with others) had
taken them prisoners near the Naas, and had confessed to them that he had
that day killed seven Englishmen, with many other circumstances likening
the truth thereof.   And that the said court have unanimously sentenced him to die as a spy, according to the penalties of the said declaration of the 30th November last.   Upon consideration had thereof, it is
thought fitt and ordered by this board, that the court martial do consider
their former proceedings ; and they are hereby empowered either to put
their former sentence of death against the said Hetherington into execution, or to reprieve him, as they shall judge most agreeable to justice.

"T. HERBERT, Clerk of the Council.
" *Dublin Castle*, 2nd *April*, 1655."
$\frac{A}{5}$, p. 114.

* " The Great Case of Transplantation in Ireland Discussed ; or, certain Considerations, wherein the many great Inconveniences in transplanting the Natives of Ireland generally out of the three Provinces of Leinster,
Ulster, and Munster, into the Province of Connaught are shown, humbly

author was Vincent Gookin, son of a planter of King James I.'s reign, then and long before resident in the county of Cork. He was one of the six members for Ireland returned to the first Commonwealth Parliament in 1653, called the Little Parliament.* He was elected by the people of Kinsale, and represented a large district in Munster.

Living among the Irish, he had as usual learned to love them. He had appreciated that hearty, affectionately loyal race of men, who seem to be fresh from nature's hand, and to belong to an earlier and uncorrupted world. His land hunger† had been appeased. He was possessed of considerable estates. He had tasted the free gaiety of a country that had escaped the feudal yoke.

Over the rest of Europe a thousand years of Roman and feudal slavery had divided society into conquerors and conquered, into gentlemen and serfs ; so that the lower classes are in many countries but emancipated villeins, exhibiting traces of their former serfish condition, in their brutal manners. Ireland escaped the feudal yoke, and hence perhaps it is, that the commonest Irishman has something in him of the gentleman.

tendered to every individual Member of Parliament, by a Wellwisher to the good of the Commonwealth of England." 4to. London : for J. C., 1655.

 * He also sat as one of the twenty-nine members for Ireland in the Parliament of 1654.

 † " The land hunger of the Anglo-Saxon race."—" The Times" newspaper. In another article of 29th November, 1861, on the Governor-General's throwing open the soil of India to English settlers, it says, " that the resolution of 17th October, 1861, appeals to one of the strongest passions in the human breast, the love of land. In most nations this feeling is strong, but in the British population the love of land [*of other peoples' land*] is powerful in the extreme. Our colonial wars are simply wars for land. We fight for land in New Zealand, at the Cape, and wherever we settle." Denied it at home, they are led or driven like buccaneers to make prey of it abroad.

Our author is an instance of the peculiar power possessed by Ireland, observed even by Giraldus, of enchanting strangers, who, he says, are scarce arrived before they are contaminated by the vices of the Irish.* These Circæan charms† are nothing else than the graces of a people not bowed or broken by the feudal yoke. Unless, indeed, it be the contrast presented between the life and gaiety of the Welsh, French, and Irish, and that dumbness, the characteristic, as the same Giraldus has observed, of men of Saxon and German stock.‡

His father, Sir Vincent Gookin, in 1634 published a pamphlet in Ireland, in the form of a letter to the Lord Deputy, being a bitter invective against the whole nation, Natives, Old English, New English, Papists, Protestants, and all, which so enraged all people against him, as they would have hanged him if they could.§ In his " Great Case of Transplantation Discussed," he objected that the soldiers lately disbanded (especially the private soldiers) had need of the Irish. They had

* " Topographia," chapter xxiv.—" How new-comers are stained with the same vices." Such are the only terms each Englishman employs, from the very first to the latest, to describe the habits of the Irish.

† " These were the Irish customs which the English colonies did embrace and use ; whereby they became degenerate, like those who had drunk of Circe's cup, and were turned into very beasts, and yet took such pleasure in their beastly manner of life, as they would not returne to their shape of men again." Sir John Davies, " Discovery why Ireland was never thoroughly subdued until the Reign of King James I.," p. 672.

‡ " Description of Wales," by Giraldus, chapter xv., "Their freedom and confidence in speaking."

§ Pp. 34-39, " Earl of Strafford's Letters," vol. i., folio.

Strange to find even Henry Cromwell, who had warred here as Colonel, and became afterwards Lieutenant-General and Lord Lieutenant, enchanted with the country :—

" Henry Cromwell to the Duke of Ormond.
" March 8, 1661-2.

" MAY IT PLEASE YOUR GRACE—The time of my protection expires apace. Nor is the expense of this towne [London] very suitable to my condi-

neither stock, nor money to buy stock, nor, for the most part, skill in husbandry. But by the labours of the Irish on their land, together with their own industry, they might maintain themselves, improve their lands, and by degrees inure themselves suitably to their new course of life.* Moreover, there were few of the Irish peasantry but were skilful in husbandry, and more exact than any English in the husbandry proper to the country ; few of the women but were skilful in dressing hemp and flax, and making woollen cloth. In every hundred men there were five or six masons and carpenters at least, and those more handy and ready in building ordinary houses, and much more skilful in supplying the defects of instruments and materials than English artificers.† They have always been known as uncommon masters of the art of overcoming difficulties by contrivances.

The transplantation would injure the revenue. It was paid out of corn which the Irish raised, living themselves on the

tion. It would be of great concernment to mee to knowe my doome [he was seeking to hold his Irish land], before I return into yᵉ country, and I suppose my businesse is now as ripe as ever it can be for a determination. Wherefore I humbly beg leave of your Grace to bee importunatt, that a period may bee putt to my languishings, and the great unsettlement of my relations. I neither expect nor desire to hold a foot of any restorable land, nor a foote more than what by the mercy of his Majesty's declaration is afforded mee. I onely entreat your Grace to save mee the vexation and hazard of solliciting and attendaunces in Ireland, and of contests with any person whatsoever *there*, where I wish above all other places to live though never so obscurely under your Grace's protection, to show how much your Grace's patience about my business hath obleiged. May it please your Grace, your Grace's most humble, most faithfull, and most obedient servant,

"HENRY CROMWELL."

Carte MSS. FF., p. 265, Bodleian Library.

* P. 16, "Great Case of Transplantation Discussed."
† P. 17, ibid.

roots and fruits of their gardens, and on the milk of their cows, goats, and sheep, and by selling their corn to the English they provided money for the "contribution."*

A considerable number of English had by this time already come over and scattered themselves over the country, purchasing farms, and buying stock. This early hope must be nipped in the bud. For, if the transplanting went forward, it would so multiply Tories, they could not live in the country,—and their stock could not live in towns,—and their improvements and buildings must be utterly lost, and themselves, when they least expected it, undone.† For many of the inhabitants of Ireland, who were then able to subsist on their gardens, unable to find subsistence in travelling to Connaught, or any immediate support when they reached that wasted province, would rather choose the hazard of Torying, than the danger of starving.‡ "The chiefest and eminentest of the nobility, and many of the gentry, had taken conditions from the King of Spain, and had transported forty thousand of the most active spirited men, most acquainted with the dangers and discipline of war.§ The priests were all banished. The remaining part of the whole nation was scarce one-sixth part of what they were at the beginning of the war, so great a devastation had God and man brought upon that land; and that handful of natives left were poor labourers, simple creatures, whose sole design was to live and maintain their families, the manner of which was so low that their design was rather to be pitied, than by any body feared or hindered.‖ Then there was the danger that in Connaught they would be under their chiefs, seated in a country furthest distant from England, with its coast most remote from the course of the English fleet, ready to receive aid from any

---

* P. 15, " Great Case of Transplantation Discussed."
† P. 17, ibid.   ‡ P. 20, ibid.   § Ibid., ibid.   ‖ P. 22, ibid.

foreign country. It was by these advantages the English in the late rebellion first lost Connaught, and last regained it."*

The taxation to maintain the army was so insupportable upon the people under protection, as to amount to a monthly diminution of their capital substance, and drove many husbandmen to such poverty that they had only the hard choice left of starving or turning Tories.† Their bands had been thus lately much increased; and the rigour of the Parliament in excepting them from mercy made them resist to the uttermost.‡ To all these objections was to be added the difficulty of enforcing the transplantation. "The Irish would say they could but find want and ruin at the worst if they stay, and why should they travel so far for that which will come home to them? Against transplantation the Irish have ('tis strange) as great a resentment as against loss of estate, yea, even death itself. But, supposing they should have a dram of rebellious blood in them, or be sullen and not go? can it be imagined that a whole nation will drive like geese at the wagging of a hat upon a stick"?§ And in conclusion it was asked, "When will this wild war be finished; Ireland planted; inhabitants disburthened; souldiers settled? The unsettling of a nation is easy work; the settling is not. The opportunity for it will not last always; it is now. The souldiers, exhausted with indefatigable labours, hope now for rest. It had been better if Ireland had been thrown into the sea before the first engagement on it, if it is never to be settled."‖

The publication of this work roused all the fury of the officers of the English army. It was just at the moment when one of the three great disbandings was about to take place, and lots to be cast and possession of their lands to be taken by the soldiery. They sent in petitions from various quarters.

---

* P. 26, " Great Case of Transplantation Discussed."
† P. 13, ibid. ‡ P. 25, ibid. § P. 26, ibid. ‖ Ibid.

"The Council of War at head quarters in Ireland" addressed
His Highness the Lord Protector, stating that the Parliament
had provided for their satisfaction in land and for the transplantation of the Irish, and that without such transplantation
your petitioners' lands cannot long be safely enjoyed by them
and their posterity." And they fell upon the author of the
book, including him amongst " some persons belonging to
Ireland," who endeavoured to obstruct them in their settlement upon the lands provided for them by Parliament, and
with plainly injuring the army, and unsettling the work of
English plantation in Ireland.* But, besides the odious charge
of being an Irishman, or of having "degendred" as Spenser
calls it, from being a " right Englishman," hating and despis-
ing the Irish and everything belonging to them but their lands,
they insinuated that he was bribed by them :—

" Dublin, February 16th, 1654–5.

" The Irish are troubled to hear of the dissolution of the
late Parliament, in whom they had great hopes ; but, blessed
be God! their hopes are prevented. There is a letter carrying on for maintaining of agents, of which I presume the gentleman that lately wrote the Case of Transplantation (thereby
abusing rulers) is to have a considerable share. The Irish are
much given that way, the sweetness of which makes some of
those that have lived long among them so much desire their
company; but assure yourself, that if they were in Connaught, Ireland would be a very good land, and soon all
planted."†

---

*   Numb. 26.

P. 4530, "Perfect Proceedings of State Affairs in England, Scotland, and Ireland, with the Transactions of other Nations, from Thursday,
March 15th, to Thursday, March 22nd, 1654-5. Entered into the Re-
gister's Book according to the Act for Printing. 4to. Printed at London
for Robert Ibbetson, dwelling in Smithfield, near Hosier-lane : 1654."

† P. 5136, " Mercurius Politicus," &c.

The Council of War sitting at Dublin plainly stated the real purpose of the transplantation.

From the officers in the country (as provincials are naturally more stupidly religious than people at head-quarters), came the following petition, in which is strangely mixed the Bible stuff they had crammed their heads and hardened their hearts with, and the true end in view,—the possession undisturbed of the lands they had seized from the gentry of Ireland :—

" The humble Petition of the Officers within the Precincts of Dublin, Catherlough, Wexford, and Kilkenny, in the behalf of themselves, their Souldiers, and other faithful English Protestants, to the Lord Deputy and Council of Ireland."

They pray that the original order of the Council of State in England, confirmed by Parliament September 27th, 1653, requiring the removal of all the Irish nation into Connaught, except boys of 14 and girls of 12, might be enforced: " For we humbly conceive [say they], that the proclamation for transplanting only the proprietors and such as have bin in arms will neither answer the end of safety nor what clse is aimed at thereby. For the first purpose of the transplantation is to prevent those of natural principles [i. e. of natural affections] becoming one with these Irish, as well in affinity as idolatry, as many thousands did, who came over in Queen Elizabeth's time, many of which have had a deep hand in all the late murthers and massacres. And shall we join in affinity [they ask] with the people of these abominations? Would not the Lord be angry with us till he consumes us, having said, ' The land which ye go to possess is an unclean land, because of the filthiness of the people that dwell therein. Ye shall not therefore give your sons to their daughters, nor take their daughters to your sons,' as it is in Ezra, ix. 11, 12, 14. ' Nay, ye shall surely root them out before you, lest they cause you to forsake the Lord your God,' Deut. vii., 2, 3, 4, 16, 18." . .

" 3rd. Thereby honest men will be encouraged to come and live amongst us, in reguard the other three provinces will be free of Tories when there is none left to harbour or relieve them . . .

" 4th. That malice or exasperation of spirit may be prevented that will arise in them against us when they see us enjoy their estates.

" 6th. You may thereby free many from being murthered by those whose relations were killed by their means [i. e. by the English] as instruments in the hand of the Lord, they being a people of such inveterate malice as to continue and labour to revenge themselves twenty or thirty years after an injury received which they cannot do when separated.

" 10th. You will thereby enlarge the liberties of the poor English who are confined within walls and garrisons, to their great impoverishment, in reguard that they are fain to house or barn their cattle, and to make use of barren land, whilst the Irish enjoy the benefit of the best land, orchards, and gardens in the country, and keep their cattle abroad both day and night, where they can and do conceal their cattle, which the English cannot do, who by that means will be liable to bear a greater proportion of contribution than the Irish; all which arguments and reasons we humbly submit to your honours' most serious consideration, desiring the Lord to direct and guide you therein, and what else may tend to the honour of God and comfort of this poor nation."*

Colonel Richard Lawrence, who seems to have been the leading member of the Committee of Transplantation formed on the 21st of November, 1653, published an answer.† He

---

* P. 5236, " Mercurius Politicus," &c.

† " The Interest of England in the Irish Transplantation stated; chiefly intended as an Answer to a scandalous, seditious Pamphlet, entitled, ' The Great Case of Transplantation in Ireland Discussed.' By a faithful Servant of the Commonwealth, Richard Lawrence." 4to, London : 1655.

said the true reason of the dislike of the Irish to transplant was that they looked to their national interest, and discerned that the transplantation laid the axe at the root of the tree of their future hopes of their recovering their lost ground;* and besides their unwillingness to quit the possession of their ancient inheritances, and to be settled upon other men's inheritances in Connaught, they foresaw, perhaps, that the Connaught proprietor might bid them such welcome as they would bid the soldier and adventurer upon their lands.†

Not only had Protestant statesmen of Ireland who were advised with on the matter, both at Westminster and in Ireland, recommended it, and several solemn meetings been held upon the business, but several godly ministers and other pious Christians had been desired to attend to seek the Lord together with them for direction in this work; and Colonel Lawrence did not remember that any of them had manifested dissatisfaction, or offered reasons against the work, though very many godly and judicious persons complained of its limitations and slow pace;‡ and he added, in conclusion, "If any rebellious consequences follow from the mooting of these objections by any Protestant friends of the Irish in such a nick of settlement, I doubt not but God would enable that authority yet in being to let out that dram of rebellious bloud, and cure that fit of sullenness their advocate speaks of."§

Accordingly, the state pressed on the great work. "They were resolved to see it done." Again and again they filled the gaols, threatening to execute the criminals.

Wholesale executions, however, for this crime, seem to have been thought inexpedient; but the government had no scruple, we see, to sending them to the West Indies. At the summer assizes of 1658 the numbers condemned to death in

* P. 19, "The Interest of England in the Irish Transplantation," &c.
† Ibid.   ‡ P. 9, ibid.   § P. 25, ibid.

the several counties for not transplanting were very great, but they were by the judges reprieved, and by his Excellency and the Council pardoned, but were, nevertheless, ordered to be transported into the Barbadoes, or some of the English plantations in America; and on the 26th of October, 1658, Sir Charles Coote, Knight and Baronet, President of Connaught, and Colonel Thomas Stubbers, Governor of Galway, were ordered to have a ship properly victualled to carry from 80 to 100 of these criminals,* and ready to sail with the first fair wind direct for the Indian Bridges in the Barbadoes.

* *" To the Rt. Hon. Sir Chas. Coote, Knight and Bart., Lord President of Connaught, and Coll. Thos. Sadleir, Governor of Galway, or either of them.*

" Council Chamber, Dublin Castle, 26th Oct., 1658.

" His Excellency and the Council having been pleased to pardon sundry persons who have been condemned at the assizes and general gaol delivery in the respective counties, and by the judges reprieved, have nevertheless thought fitt to order their transplantation into the Barbadoes, or some other of the English plantations in America, as also divers whose banishment hath been adjudged at the late assizes (pursuant to the Act of Attainder) for not transplanting, and conceiving Galway to be the fittest port, they request Sir C. Coote and Colonel Stubbers to deal with some merchant there about receiving them on board, and what may concern the fees expended in removing them from the prisons where they now are to Galway, the clothing them where needed, and having ready a properly victualled ship for such a number (which may be towards eighty or a hundred), and to set saile with the first faire wind directly for the Indian Bridges, the usual landing place in the Barbaboes, or other English plantation thereabouts in America, where he is within two days after arrival to set them ashore, to deliver them to the said merchant or merchants (who are to be at the charge and to have the disposal of them) shall direct, except the number of ten, who will be speedily designed to a person inhabiting in the Barbadoes; and by the time they have made arrangements with a merchant or merchants you will have a more particular account both as to the certain numbers to be sent from the gaols, and concerning a proper convoy for conveying them from garrison to garrison until they arrive at Galway." $\frac{A}{30}$, p. 338.

This was only the first batch of those sentenced at these assizes. By these means they continued to clear out the ancient gentry and farmers, and fix them in Connaught, where their condition is now to be considered.

THE CONDITION OF THE TRANSPLANTERS IN CONNAUGHT.

The cruelty of transplanting a nobleman like Lord Trimleston, for instance, with his stock of heavy cattle, from his rich grazing and fattening grounds in the county of Meath, to a fine sheep walk in the county of Galway—or John Talbot, of Malahide, from his castle in the best part of the county of Dublin to the wilds of Erris, in the county of Mayo, fit only for goats—induced the government to appoint a committee, of which Sir Charles Coote the younger, President of Connaught, was a member, to lay out certain baronies in Con-

"*26th January*, 1658-9.

Nathaniel Marks, High Sheriff of the Queen's County, is answered "that the convicts at the late assizes for not transplanting be secured in Mariboro' Castle until the gaol be made capable, pending the general returns of late convictions from all the judges of assize."— $\frac{A}{30}$, p. 355.

The following explains a passage in the letter of his Excellency and the Council given above:—

"*Council Chamber, Dublin Castle, 29th Nov.*, 1658.
"*To Mr. Edward Smyth.*

"SIR,—I have, by means of a friend of yours, the tenne men and two women hereunder named, ordered to be delivered to yourself or your assigns at the Indian Bridges or other port in the Barbadoes.

"These are only to signify to you the same, and that it is agreed with the merchant that you make discharge and payment for their passage, your friend here having taken care to defray their charge out of prison and conveyance on shippboard.

"THOMAS HERBERT, Clerk of the Council."
Ib., p. 343.

naught, to receive the inhabitants from certain counties in the
three other provinces, so that the transplanted might receive
suitable lands as near as might be in quantity and quality
to the places from whence they were removed.   Accordingly,
Sir Charles Coote furnished a scheme by which, for instance,
all the inhabitants of Ulster, except the Down and Antrim
Irish, were to be set down in various baronies in Mayo and
Galway.   They lay west of a line drawn due north from the
town of Galway, in which were comprised Erris and Conna-
mara, two of the wildest and barrenest districts in Ireland.
The committee probably thought it best suited the wild and
fierce nature of the Ulstermen, not reflecting nor caring, probably, that in the counties of Armagh, Tyrone, Monaghan,
and Cavan, there are some fine lands, the owners of which
must suffer great hardship in being set down amongst the
heath and rocks of Erris.   But these niceties could not, of
course, be attended to.   The Down and Antrim men, being of
ancient Scottish descent, originally from the Hebrides and
adjacent coast of Scotland, with some antagonism to the rest
of Ulster, were to be set down in the baronies of Clanmorris,
Carra, and Kilmaine, keeping them still divided from the other
Ulstermen.

To the Kildare, Meath, Queen's County, and Dublin Irish,
coming from the finest feeding and fattening lands in Ireland,
were assigned the barony of Boyle, comprising the famous
plains of Boyle, that fatten a bullock and a sheep to the acre;
and the baronies of Roscommon and Ballintubber, and the half
barony of Bellamo, in the county of Roscommon; and so of the
rest.*

But the transplanter's trials had only begun when he

---

* 12th Feb., 1655-6, " Proposal for effecting the better setting down
of the Irish transplanted into Connaught." $\frac{A}{24}$, p. 189.

reached Connaught. The officers employed had to be bribed by money if the poor transplanter had any money left, or by a secret promise that he would give him part of the lands allotted, if he got a good allotment, or speedy despatch.* Some of great rank, whose wives got longer dispensation or passes to return from Connaught, besieged the Council Board with their attendances, praying for special orders to the Loughrea Commissioners to give them and their families good assignments either of planted lands, i. e. having tenants yielding rents, or with a house upon it, or near a garrison. Thus Lady Margaret Talbot, who had already interested them by her sufferings and by being an Englishwoman, obtained from them an order that the Loughrea Commissioners should admit Sir Henry Talbot as tenant to 300 acres lying as contiguous as might be to the lands already allotted to him, in consideration of his many good services done to the English interest, and the great estate he lost in Leinster.† Having thus sped in her suit, they gave her twenty pounds in consideration of her distressed condition, to enable her to return to her husband and children in Connaught.‡

---

* "May 19, 1666. Sir James Cuffe claims as a Connaught purchaser. Brawn᷎ Byrne had a final settlement of 2000 acres. He contracted with Major Byrne for a certain sum of money, to let him have 200 acres, who afterwards conveyed to the claimant. Sir James Cuffe being one of the commissioners for setting out lands to the transplanted persons, the said Brawn Byrne alleged that the said contract was chiefly in consideration of obtaining his assistance to the procuring of the remainder of his 2000 acres to be set out to him, which was not done, he having never had more than these 200 acres." "Minute Book of the Court of Claims," p. 9, Office of the Crown and Hanaper.

† $\frac{A}{12}$, p. 154.

‡ "Ordered that James Standish, Esq., Receiver-General, &c. do out of the first public moneys that shall come into his hands issue forth and pay

Walter Cheevers, of Monkstown, descended from a family that came in with the Conquest* of Henry II., was possessed in 1641 of a large estate between Dublin and Kingstown. The ruins of his castle are still to be seen not far from the Salt-hill station of the Dublin and Kingstown railway. The Marquis of Ormond and Sir Maurice Eustace, by their report made to the King after the Restoration, certified that of their own knowledge he was very innocent of the rebellion.† But he was a Catholic and an Irishman (as that term was understood

unto the Lady Margaret Talbot, the wife of Sir Henry Talbot, the sum of £20, to enable her to returne to her husband and children in Connaught, and for the better reliefe of their distressed condition ; for payment whereof this (with the Lady Talbot's receipt) shall be a warrant.

"HENRY CROMWELL,   WM. STEELE, *Chancellor ;*

"ROBERT GOODWIN,   MILES THOMLINSON,

"W. BURY.

" *Council Chamber in Dublin, 20th March,* 1657."
Treasury Warrants, p. 142.

* John Cheevers, of Mayston, in the county of Meath, in his petition to the Lords Justices, sets forth that his ancestors have until the usurper's time enjoyed the lands granted unto them by King Henry II. on the Conquest. Vol. ii. p. 439, papers relating to the Act of Settlement ; Record Tower, Dublin Castle.

† "And very faithfull to our royal father of blessed memory ; and they saw no cause or reason why he should be evicted, as he hath long been, from the possession of his estate, more than that Colonel Edmund Ludlowe had obtained a grant of the same or most parte thereof from Oliver Cromwell. And therefore, &c.

"Given at White Hall, 22nd November, 1660, the 12th year of our reign. By His Majesty's command.

" EDWARD NICHOLAS.

" *To the Chief Baron, to the Sheriff of the County of Dublin,*
and all other our loving subjects whom it may concerne."

Book of King's Letters, Chief Remembrancer's Office, Court of Exchequer of Ireland.

in England), and had not shown that constant good affection to the Parliament of England that alone exempted the Irish from transplantation. He was, moreover, guilty of another crime (like the bear, who is often killed, not for what he has done, but for his skin)—he had a fine house and estate. This was granted by Cromwell to General Ludlow, one of the Commissioners of Parliament for the affairs of Ireland; and Mr. Cheevers was ordered to transplant, with his family, to Connaught. On the 16th December, 1653, he sent in to the Commissioners of Revenue of the precinct of Dublin the particulars required by government from all transplanters, by which may be seen the number of his family, and the extent of his stock and crop, and what tenants or friends proposed to accompany him to Connaught. The certificate is as follows :— viz :—" Walter Cheevers, of sanguine complexion, brown hair, and indifferent stature ; his wife, Alson Netterville, otherwise Cheevers, with five children, the eldest not above seven years old ; four women servants, and seven men servants, viz. Daniel Barry, tall stature, red beard, bald pate ; Thady Cullen, of small stature, browne haire, no haire on his face ; Morgan Cullen, of small stature, blind of one eye, with black haire ; Philip Birne, aged about forty years, black haire, low stature ; William Birne, tall stature, aged thirty-five years ; Patrick Corbally, aged forty years, red hair, middle stature. The said Walter doth manure twenty colpe of corn, and hath twenty cows, sixty sheep, thirty hoggs, two ploughs of garrans. The tenants willing to remove with him are Arthur Birne, of little stature, brown haire, aged thirty years ; Dudley Birne, middle stature, brown haire, aged twenty-five years—which tenants have a plough of garrans, twelve cows, forty sheep ; Martin McGuire, tall of stature, and redd haire, aged thirty years, hath six cows, four garrans, twenty sheepe ; Thos Eustace, lowe stature, browne haire, twenty-five years, hath ten cows, forty sheep, a plough of garrans, and ten hoggs.   The substance whereof we conceive to be true.

> " In witness whereof, we have hereunto set our hands and seals, the 19th day of December, 1653.
>
> " H. MARKHAM,   R. DOYLY,
> " THOˢ. HOOKER.   ISAAC DOBSON."*

When proceeding to Connaught, to obtain a Final Settlement there from the Commissioners sitting at Athlone, he took a letter to them from the state, directing them to assign him lands with a good house upon them, so as to enable him and his family to subsist and render his being there comfortable, in consideration that he had parted with a fair house and a considerable estate near Dublin,† of which they all probably had personal knowledge, as it is only natural to suppose they must have often dined at Monkstown Castle with their brother commissioner, General Edmund Ludlow.   But the Athlone Commissioners were either unable or unwilling to comply with the order ; for Mr. Cheevers had recourse again to government, complaining that he had not obtained the favour the government intended for him.‡   The truth was, it was found in July, 1657, that the lands in Connaught had fallen short to satisfy the decrees of the Athlone Commissioners, " except what was so remote and waste as to be useless ; and many Irish who (like Cheevers) had parted with considerable estates and convenient habitations, were thereby reduced to little better than a starving condition."   And, notwithstanding the Commissioners had contracted the three-mile line along the sea

---

* Book of Transplanters' Certificates, returned from the several precincts in the Province of Leinster, viz. Dublin, Wexford, Kilkenny, Carlow, Athy, Athlone, and Drogheda.   Records of the late Auditor-General's Office, Custom House Buildings.

† Letter from the Council, dated 27th August, 1656. $\frac{A}{30}$, p. 179.

‡ Ib., ib.

coast to one mile, and had given up to transplanters the lands about different garrisons, reserving only 500 acres around Clare Castle, 100 acres round Cahir na Mart (or Westport), 700 acres about Athlone, and lands of a mile compass about Carrigaholt, the government were informed there would still not be sufficient to satisfy the decrees given to the transplanted.*

Pierce Butler, Viscount Ikerrin, was the ancestor of the Earls of Carrick, a younger branch of the house of Ormond. He dwelt at Lismalin Park, in the barony of Ikerrin, in the county of Tipperary, contiguous to the county of Kilkenny, where the ruins of his ancient castle may still be seen on a hill side, overlooking a pleasant valley. Like the rest of his house, with the exception of the Earl of Ormond (who, being a king's ward, had been brought up, by order of the Court of Wards, a branch of the Court of Chancery, a Protestant), he was a Roman Catholic; and having, with the rest of his countrymen of that persuasion, taken the King's side against the Parliament, and been Lieutenant-General of the Leinster army, under Lord Mountgarret, he was included in the Decree of Confiscation pronounced by the Parliament of England, on the 12th August, 1650, against all who had not manifested their constant good affection to their interest. After the surrender of the Leinster Irish to the Parliament forces under the articles signed at Kilkenny on 12th May, 1650, he returned to the neighbourhood of Lismalin Park, and was there employed as tenant at will to the state, farming those lands that were so soon to pass to the conquerors, when the order of 14th October, 1653, was proclaimed, directing the Irish nation to transplant themselves into Connaught before the 1st of May following. On the 25th of January, 1654, he proceeded to Clonmel, and

* $\frac{A}{30}$, Letter of 27th July, 1657.

presented to the Commissioners of Revenue there the particulars of his family and establishment, their names, ages, and
descriptions, the extent of his stock and tillage, and the names
of those of his tenants and friends who were disposed to go
down with him into captivity in Connaught. By an abstract
of this certificate it appears that between his family and tenants
he had seventeen persons to accompany him.   He had already
tilled and cropped sixteen acres of winter corn ; he had four
cows, five garrans (or cart horses), twenty-four sheep, and
two swine ;* which he was to leave behind him in charge of
Lady Ikerrin, while he was to go forward into Connaught to
build a hut to shelter her and his daughters, who were to follow in autumn with the cows, sheep, swine, and household fur-
niture.   For on a general complaint that transplanters would
be great sufferers in their corn in ground, and other substance,
if they were not permitted to look after their harvest, they
obtained license for their wives and families to continue upon
their holdings until harvest came in (with a general provision
for all aged, decrepit, and sickly persons, that they might
not be put on hard things), which gave the government,
according to the usual practice of rulers, cause to praise themselves for their great mercy and kindness, because of this mo-
dification of their cruelty.† Lord Ikerrin, having fallen sick, as
the 1st of May, the time for transplanting, approached, got license
on account of his distemper to repair to the Bath in England
for six months, necessary, according to his physician's advice,
for the recovery of his health ; and Lady Ikerrin was dispensed
with from transplantation for two months from the 1st of May,
and her servants till the harvest was gathered in.‡   On his

* Book of Transplanters' Certificates of the precinct of Waterford. Records of the late Auditor-General's Office, Custom House Buildings.

† Lawrence, " Interest of England in the Irish Transplantation Stated,"
p. 7. London: 1655.

‡ Order of 24th April, 1654. $\frac{A}{85}$, p. 304.

return to Ireland some judgment may be formed of his poverty by an order of the Council of 27th November, 1654, by which Sergeant Mortimer (Sergeant at Arms attending the Council) was to pay the Lord Ikerrin £20 in consideration of his necessitous condition ; after which the said Lord Ikerrin was to acquiesce in the late order of this board for prosecuting his claim at Athlone, and not to expect any more money by order of this Council.* Lord Ikerrin, however, still evaded transplantation ; for in 1656 he went over to London, and in London found means to approach the Lord Protector, who, finding him in an extremely poor and miserable condition, without means to subsist in London, or to return back to Ireland, bestowed upon him some relief, and wrote to the Lord Deputy and Council of Ireland to allow him some proportion of his estate without transplanting him, or to provide some relief out of the revenue for him and his family : "For indeed," adds the Lord Protector, "he is a miserable object of pity; and we desire that care be taken of him, and that he be not suffered to perish for want of subsistence."† How this poor nobleman fared

---

* Volume of Treasury Warrants (No. 14). Late Auditor-General's Office, Custom House Buildings.

† "To the Right Hon. yᵉ Lord Deputy and Councell in Ireland.

"MY LORD AND GENTLEMEN,—We being informed by several persons, and also by certificates from several officers under our command in Ireland, that the Lord Viscount Ikerrin hath been of later times serviceable to suppress the Tories ; and we being very sensible of the extreame poor and miserable condition in which his lordship now is, even to the want of sustenance to support his life ; we could not but commisserate his sad and distressed condition by helping him to a little reliefe, without which he could neither subsist here nor returne back to Ireland; and therefore do earnestly desire you to take him into speedy consideration, by allowing him some reasonable proportion of his estate without transplanting him, or otherwise to make some provision for him and his family elsewhere, and to allow him some competent pension or money out of the revenue. Indeed he

after Cromwell's interference does not appear. But Lismalin had passed irrevocably to the soldiery, for it gave Sir William Petty opportunity of retorting upon his adversary Colonel Hierome Sankey, "his unhandsome dealings with his soldiers in the matter of Lismalin Park." No further payments appear made to Lord Ikerrin, and he probably soon sank under his misfortunes, for at the Restoration his grandson claimed the estate before the Commissoners of Claims.*

But even after getting an assignment the poor transplanter was not secure; the Commissioners by mistake or fraud might have given it to another: such was was the case of Maurice Viscount Roche, of Fermoy. His whole case well illustrates the misery of Ireland. Viscountess Roche, it appears, had been hanged by the sentence of one of those High Courts of Justice (or injustice) set up immediately after the surrender of the Irish in 1652, when victims were required to justify the former fury of the English, who had denounced all the Irish as murderers. She was condemned on the evidence of a strumpet for shooting a man with a pistol, whose name even was unknown to the witness; and though it was ready to be proved that Lady Roche was twenty miles distant from the spot, and that the sight of a pistol was enough to fright her from the

---

he is a miserable object of pity, and therefore we desire that care be taken of him, and that he be not suffered to perish for want of a subsistence:

"And rest, your loving friend,

"OLIVER, P.

$\frac{A}{28}$. "*Whitehall, 27th February,* 1657."

Book of Letters from the Lord Protector, Record Tower, Dublin Castle.

* "7th June, 1666, Viscount Ikerrin claims as an innocent Protestant; was born in 1639; was a student at Maudlin, Oxford, where he went to church; at Athlone went to church; Dean Blood administered the sacrament to him at St. Owen's Church, Dublin. Decree adjourned." Minute Book of Court of Claims, Hanaper Office, p. 43.

room.* Lord Roche was in 1654 dispossessed of his whole estate, having (as his petition sets forth) the charge of four young daughters unpreferred, to whose misery was added the loss of their mother by an unjust and illegal proceeding, for whose innocence he appealed to the best Protestant gentry and nobility of the county of Cork. Thenceforth Lord Roche and his children lived in a most disconsolate condition, destitute of all kind of subsistence (except what alms some good Christians in charity gave them), the consequence of which was, that one of his daughters fell sick and died for want of requisite accommodation either for her cure or diet. After ten months' attendance on those in authority at Dublin, all the succour he got was an order to the Loughrea Commissioners to set him out some lands there De Bene Esse.† With this order he was necessitated to travel on foot to Connaught, where he spent six months in attendance on the Commissioners at Athlone and Loughrea, and in these attendances and the prosecution ran himself £100 in debt. Yet at the last he had but an assignment of 2500 acres in the Owles in Connaught, and part in the remotest parts of Thomond, all waste and unprofitable; and from these he was evicted before he could receive any manner of profit, by others to whom the Commissioners had disposed of the same by Final Settlements, both before and after.‡

* "A Continuation of the Brief Narrative, and the Sufferings of the Irish under Cromwell," p. 7. Small 4to. London : 1660. [By Father Peter Walsh.]

† That, is temporarily, conditionally, for his present habitation and support, and to maintain his cows and other cattle, until he could prove at Athlone the extent of his estate confiscated, and his qualification, i. e. the class of his demerit or delinquency, or amount of want of affection for the Parliament of England.

‡ "The humble petition of Maurice Lord Viscount Roche, of Fermoy, to the Right Honourable the Lords Justices, March, 1661." Records of the late Auditor-General's Office, Custom House Buildings, vol. xvii., p. 112.

With such spectacles daily and hourly before their eyes, it is no wonder that the transplanted who could find means to fly, or were not tied by large families of children, sold their assignments for a mere trifle to the officers of government, and fled in horror and aversion from the scene, and embarked for Spain. Some went mad; others killed themselves ;* others lived on, and founded families there in their Final Settlements which subsist to this day, like some of the Talbots and the Cheevers ; and some laid their bones in Connaught, whose heirs got re-

* P. 19, " Threnodia Hiberno-Catholica, &c., &c. The Wail of the Irish Catholics : or, the Groans of the whole Clergy and People of the Kingdom of Ireland, in which is truly set forth an Epitome of the unheard of and transcendental Cruelties by which the Catholics of the Kingdom of Ireland are oppressed by the godless English under the Archtyrant Cromwell, the Usurper and Destroyer of the Three Realms of England, Ireland, and Scotland. By Friar Maurice Morison, of the Minors of Strict Observance ; Lecturer in Theology ; an Eye-witness of those Cruelties." Innsbruck. Printed by Michael Wagner : A. D., 1659. 12mo.

In the month of January, 1852, I went to see the lands of Kilsallaghan, lying near Saint Margaret's, seven miles north of Dublin, preparatory to bringing them to sale in the Incumbered Estates Court for the arrears of jointure of a kinswoman. It was church-time when I got there; and while waiting in a farmer's house till the service was over, as the church was on the lands attached to the ruined castle of Kilsallaghan, I asked the farmer's daughter if she knew who dwelt in the castle in old times, knowing very well that it had belonged to the Hores. She was quite aware of it; and on my asking if there was anything bearing the name of the family in the neighbourhood, she said there was Molly Hore's Cross up the road a bit. I was getting ready my note book to copy the inscription, when she informed me that it wasn't a stone cross, but a cross of the roads so named. I asked how it got the name ? She said, " When the orders came from Cromwell to put the people out, Molly Hore couldn't stand it, and she went into a stable they had down there, and hanged herself;" and they buried her, of course by the crowner's 'quest law, as a suicide, at the cross roads.

stored after the restoration of the monarchy,—as Lord Trimleston, on whose gravestone, within the ruins of the Abbey of Kilconnel that overlooks the fatal fields of Aughrim, may be still read the epitaph : " Here lies Mathew, Twelfth Lord Baron of Trimleston, one of the Transplanted."*

* Died at Monivea, in the county of Galway, 17th September, 1667. " Tour in Connaught," A. D., 1839, by Rev. Cæsar Otway, p. 145. 12mo. Dublin : Curry and Co.

PART III.

THE ADVENTURERS AND SOLDIERS.

———◆———

THE CIVIL SURVEY.

THE officers of the army (for the common soldiers had no voice in the matter) had now obtained their desires. The army, consisting of about 35,000 men, were to have their arrears satisfied in land at the Act rates, that is, to have 1000 acres plantation measure (equal to 1600 English measure) in Leinster, for every £600 of arrears—a like quantity in Munster for £450 of arrears,—a like quantity in Ulster for £300 arrears ; being at the rate of twelve shillings for the acre, plantation measure, in Leinster, eight shillings in Munster, and four shillings in Ulster.

The next step of the government was to take an account of what lands were forfeited, their extent and value. It was about Michaelmas Day, 1653, that the Commissioners for the affairs of Ireland received the instructions of the Parliament for the survey of the lands forfeited on account of the rebellion. Commissioners were immediately sent into every county in the three provinces, to take an account of the lands in the disposal of the government, which included not merely the lands forfeited by the Irish, but the Church and Crown lands.* They were to hold courts of survey, and to summon juries, and charge them, if necessary, to view and tread the metes and bounds of the premises ; and the Commissioners were to sum-

* $\frac{A}{90}$, p. 544.

mon and examine on oath all persons who could give evidence of the names of the late proprietor, of his conduct, and of the extent and value of his estate. Agents were to produce the rentals, and bailiffs to show the bounds ; and where they should find it impossible through the wastedness and depopulation of the county to inform themselves of the metes and bounds, and other certainties directed, they were to discover it as best they could.* It must have been painful to the owners of these estates and their families to see them valued before they had actually passed out of their hands, being only a preparation for their banishment, and for others to occupy their ancient hereditary seats, endeared to them by a thousand tender memories. But the Commissioners were enabled, by taking this inquiry before the proprietors were removed to Connaught, to obtain evidence not forthcoming two years later, when the Down Survey was executed, there being then in many places no persons remaining that knew the bounds, and families were obliged to be sent back from Connaught to show them to the surveyors.†

The purpose was to ascertain by the report of these Commissioners what was the amount of the fund applicable to the payment of the debt due to the adventurers, and to the army, and of the extent and value of the tithes and lands reserved to

* See a commission at full length in " Petty's History of the Down Survey," by Major T. A. Larcom, R. E., pp. 383–386. 4to. Dublin : 1851. Published for the Irish Archæological Society.

† " Whereas Mr. Henry Paris, late one of the Commissioners of Revenue of Clonmel, hath informed us that the transplantation hath been so effectually carried on in the county of Tipperary, and especially in the barony of Eliogarty, that no inhabitant of the Irish nation that knows the country is left in that barony, which may be a great prejudice to the Commonwealth, for want of information of the bounds of the respective territories and lands therein upon admeasurement ; it is therefore ordered, that it be referred to the Commissioners at Loughrea, to consider of four fitt and knowing persons of the Irish nation lately removed out of that barony into Connaught, and to return them with their families to reside in or near

the state ; so that the government might afterwards be enabled
to contract with skilled surveyors for an exact admeasurement
and maps of the lands, in order to a proper allotment of the
army's lands amongst the officers and soldiers, and that grants
and leases might be made with greater ease and security by
the government of the lands reserved to them, and that the assessments might be equally levied. This report was duly returned for all Ireland, and was called the Civil Survey.*

Having thus ascertained, by as near a computation as could
be made without actual admeasurement, the extent and value
of the lands seized from the former proprietors in each of the
three provinces on this side of the Shannon, a general council of officers next apportioned the amount of arrears to be
satisfied in each province. They then proceeded, like the adventurers, to draw the first or grand lot, to ascertain in which province each regiment of horse, foot, and dragoons was to be
satisfied its arrears. For on debate of the matter whether they
should take their lands by lot, or have them assigned to them
respectively by some competent authority, they resolved for
the former mode, declaring that they had rather take a lot upon
a barren mountain as a portion from the Lord, than a portion
in the most fruitful valley upon their own choice.†

their old habitations, for the due information of the surveyors appointed of
the respective bounds of each parcel of land admeasureable, and to continue there till further order.

                  " Thomas Herbert, Clerk of the Council.

" *Dublin*, 20*th December*, 1654." $\frac{A}{5}$, p. 54.

    * For a specimen, see " A Survey of the Half Barony of Rathdown, in
the County of Dublin, containing the parishes following, viz., Donnebrook,
Tannee, Kill, Monkstown, Killiny, Tully, White Church, Killternan, Kill-
gobbin, Rathmichael, and Connagh. By order of Charles Fleetwood,
Lord Deputy, October 4th, 1654." P. 528. " 2nd Desiderata Curiosa
Hibernica ; or, a Select Collection of State Papers," &c. 8vo. Dublin :
2 vols. 1772.

    † " Petty's Down Survey by Larcom," p. 91.

But when the officers in the Munster lot found that all the coarse mountain land in the baronies of Iveragh and Dunkerrin, in the county of Kerry (the neighbourhood of the Lakes of Killarney), considered by them " the refuse county" of Ireland, which they expected to have thrown in to them *gratis* as unprofitable, was counted as profitable (though ten, twenty, and thirty acres of it were sometimes counted for one*), they called the General Council of the Army together, and proposed to get rid of them. The Council, however, with a spice of humour, fixed them with these two coarse baronies, by reminding them of the pious intent upon which they had agreed to the lottery.†

THE DOWN SURVEY.

The officers of the army next agreed with the government to join them in contracting with Dr. William Petty, Physician to the Forces, to make accurate maps of the forfeited lands belonging respectively to the government and to the army, in the three several provinces of Leinster, Munster, and Ulster. Connaught was assigned to the Irish; and good maps of most of the lands in that province had been made about fifteen years before, by orders of Lord Strafford, when he intended the English plantation there, by which the government were enabled to set down the transplanted Irish there the more readily. It was characteristic of the period, that this great step in perfecting the scheme of plantation was consecrated with all the forms of religion, the articles being signed by Dr. Petty in the Council Chamber of Dublin Castle, on the 11th of December, 1654, in the presence of many of the chief officers of the army, after a solemn seeking of God, performed by Colonel Thomlinson, for a blessing upon the conclusion of so great a business.‡ Such is the account given by Dr. Petty, this able man being himself

---

* " Petty's Down Survey," by Larcom, p. 96.
† Ibid., p. 91.　　　　　‡ Ibid., p. 22.

all the while a freethinker, who laughed at the many different sects of that day, considering sects to be like worms and maggots in the guts of a commonwealth.* He was also of opinion that the gathering of churches might be termed "listing of soldiers."†

By his contract, Dr. Petty engaged to mark out upon the map the subdivision of the lands into so many parcels as might satisfy each man his particular arrears, thus showing each officer's and soldier's particular lot,‡ with an index of their names and position on the map. But this provision was afterwards dispensed with, as the army were not ready to subdivide at the time of the survey being taken, and the subdivisions were only returned by the officers in descriptive lists to the Chancery. These being sent at the Restoration to the Commissioners for executing the Act of Settlement, they remained amongst the documents they had had recourse to, and were destroyed in a great fire that burned down the Council Office, where they were then deposited, in the year 1711—an irreparable loss. Had they been marked in the Down Survey, there would have been seen regiment by regiment, troop by troop, and company by company, encamping almost on the lands they had conquered; for they were thus set down without intervals, and without picking or choosing, the lot of the first regiment ending where the lot of the second regiment began.

The field work of the survey was carried on by foot soldiers instructed by Dr. Petty, and selected by him as being hardy men, to whom such hardships as to wade through bogs and water, climb rocks, and fare and lodge hard, were familiar.§

* "Reflections on some Persons and Things in Ireland," p. 119. 12mo. London: 1660.

† Ibid., p. 92.

‡ "Articles of Agreement between the Surveyor-General and Dr. W. Petty," dated 11th December, 1654, Article 8. "Petty's Down Survey," by Larcom, p. 25.

§ Ibid., p. 17.

They were fittest, too, "to ruffle with" the rude spirits they were like to encounter, who might not see without a grudge their ancient inheritances, the only support of their wives and children, measured out before their eyes for strangers to occupy; and they must often when at work be in danger of a surprise by Tories. Some of the surveyors were captured by these bold and desperate outlaws, when the sending away of the forces for England and Scotland, about the beginning of the work, left him naked of the guards he had been promised.[*]

OF THE BOXING OF THE ARMY FOR LANDS.

Sir William Petty says, that as for the blood shed in the contest for these lands, God best knows who did occasion it; but upon the playing of the game or match the English won, and had, among other pretences, a gamester's right at least to their estates;[†] and like gamesters they proceeded to divide the spoil. The lands they had won were to be set out to the army by lot, and were to be so assigned to the different regiments in the several provinces, that the lands might be set out together without intervals, and without picking and choosing. Accordingly, it was ordered that the several regiments whose lots had fallen in any of the three provinces should be put into possession of their lands successively one after another, each regiment beginning to take their possession from the bounds of such places where the lots of the respective regiments preceding respectively ended.[‡] The regiments in each provincial lot cast lots to ascertain in what county and baronies each regiment

[*] "Articles of Agreement," ibid., pp. 123, 125.

[†] "The Political Anatomy of Ireland," 1672, by Sir W. Petty, p. 28, 1st vol. "Tracts and Treatises relating to Ireland," by Alexander Thom and Sons. 2 vols. 8vo. Dublin: 1861.

[‡] Pp. 64, 65, "Petty's Down Survey," by Major Thomas A. Larcom, Irish Archæological Society's Publication. 4to. Dublin: 1851.

should be satisfied. A lot or ticket was then made for every
troop or company, containing the names of the several officers
and soldiers of the troop or company, the arrears due to each,
and the number of acres due to the entire troop or company.*
These lots or tickets were prepared on papers of equal size, and
sealed with wax wafers or glue, so as one might not be distinguished from the other without opening them. They were
then to be put in a box, out of which they were to be drawn as
lots, to distinguish in which of the baronies the proportion of
land due to each company was to fall.†

The lands in the several baronies having been already arranged by the Surveyor-General in a fixed sequence, called a
file or string of contiguity,‡ the Commissioners for setting out

---

* " Ordered, that the officers of the army now at head quarters do consider how the lotts of the party now to be disbanded may be drawn most
equally. 20th August, 1655." $\frac{A}{5}$, p. 223.

" Ordered, that the Surveyor-General do prepare lotts for each regiment,
and for each company and troope of each regiment, inserting the name of
each regiment, troope, and company in the lotts, that the troopes and
companies may know who are to begin, and in what manner they are to
proceed successively to take their satisfaction." Ib., p. 224.

† Boxing was a term in common use in that day : thus, " Waste lands
and undisposed of may be lett to any English well affected, not exceeding
three years, without putting yᵉ same to yᵉ box, rendering such reasonable
rent, &c.   Dated at Cork, 7th of July, 1652.
                                    " MILES CORBETT.   JOHN JONES."

Order Book of Council, vol. vii., Landed Estates Record Office.

Again—" Or, if they [discovered forfeitures] may bee sett out at un-
equall rates, whether there shall bee a free and open boxing for them indifferently, as whereby one that has received his clear satisfaction in Munster
may box for the dubiouse lands of Ulster?" " Petty's Down Survey," by
Larcom, p. 200.

‡ " Your petitioners propound that every barony may be reduced,

the lands to the particular regiment proceeded on the day appointed to the place of drawing, generally some town nearest to the chief baronies, and there in the presence of the officers and soldiers of the regiment drew the lots for the first barony. They were directed to draw out only one lot at once, and, opening it, to read it aloud in the hearing of all persons present, and then to file the lot on the file of that barony, entering the same in their record, fairly and distinctly, before another lot was drawn ; and so to proceed, lot by lot, until as many lots were drawn as contained all the number of acres in the barony in the disposal of the Commonwealth, according to the survey,* with a copy of which they came provided. As soon as the lot was drawn, all persons into whose shares the barony fell were to deliver up their debentures upon the spot, in order that they might be cancelled ; but each man received in exchange a certificate, stating the fact of the debenture having been delivered up, and declaring the amount of arrears in the debenture, and the number of acres to be set out in the barony to satisfy it.†

---

as to the several denominations comprehended therein, into one continued file or string of contiguity." "Petty's Down Survey," by Larcom, p. 239.

"*Monday*, 10*th December*, 1666.

"The three regiments claym for lands in the county of Kerry, sett out to them in satisfaction for their arrears. . . . . The claymants produce a string whereby the lands were sett out. . . . . Mr. Petty swears that the paper signed was the original, written by himself and Sir W. Petty,—that these strings had as much force as injunctions,—that they took possession under them." Minute Book of Court of Claims, p. 3. Hanaper Office.

* The Civil Survey.

† The proceedings thus described are set out in "A Commission for yᵉ Setting out Lands in yᵉ County of Corke to yᵉ Disbanded Forces in lieu of their Arrears. *Dated at Dublin, yᵉ* 10*th day of January*, 1653-4." $\frac{A}{81}$, p. 31.

Thus Lord Broghill, Colonel Phaire, and others, were appointed Commissioners, on 10th January, 1654, to set out lands in the baronies of Fermoy, Duhallo, Condon, Orrery, and other baronies in the county of Cork, to satisfy arrears due to the officers and soldiers of the regiments, troops, and companies named in a schedule annexed to the commission, amounting to £60,611, 8s. 6d., which required 75,735 acres, 2 roods, to satisfy them,—lands in the county of Cork being rated by the army, as between themselves, at £800 per thousand acres. The Commissioners were to fix a time and place for drawing lots, of which they were to give seven days' previous notice at least, in Cork, Mallow, Youghal, and Bandon.   They were directed by the commission to begin to draw out the lots for the barony of Fermoy, and so lot by lot, until all the land in the barony was exhausted; and if the number of acres in the lots drawn for any barony should exceed the amount of land in the barony, the defect was to be supplied out of the adjacent barony,—the particular parish or townland where to begin the supply having been appointed before drawing the first lots, in order to avoid controversy or imputation.   The officers and soldiers who fell to be satisfied in any one barony or allotment were immediately to take possession ; and, having subdivided it between them, were to send up the subdivision, with each man's lot described by such bounds and other certainties as it could be known to the Commissioners of Revenue of the precinct.* Upon getting possession, the half pay of the officers and soldiers ceased.   But, in addition to the original list of those to be satisfied by the Commissioners, additional lists were constantly sent down of soldiers whom they were to admit to re-

---

* " A Commission for yᵉ setting out Lands in yᵉ County of Corke to the Disbanded Forces in lieu of their Arrears." $\frac{A}{81}$, p. 31.

ceive their satisfaction as if they had been in the original lists.*

OF THE EQUALIZING OF COUNTIES AND BARONIES.

The state gave all the forfeited lands to the army at the Adventurers' or Act Rates; but the several regiments composing each provincial lot were unwilling to cast the regimental lots, or lots to ascertain in what counties and baronies within the province the several regiments were to be satisfied their arrears, without some regard to the value of lands. They thought it too desperate a hazard for a regiment to cast a lot and find itself paid off with 10,000 acres of land in the mountains of Kerry, while the next regiment received 10,000 acres in the rich pastures of Tipperary or Limerick as of equal value, though the army received all the Munster lands from the state at £450 per 1000 acres. Accordingly, they equalized or set an approximate or more real value on the lands in the several

* " A list of several persons of Captain Lewis Jones's troop of horse that desire satisfaction for their arrears in the county of Sleigo :—

	£	s	d.	A.	R.	P.
Corporal John Jones, ...	43	19	0	97	3	24
Alexander Irwin, ...	22	14	4	45	1	24
Christopher Jones, ...	21	15	8	43	2	0
Richard Jones, ...	20	8	2	40	3	8
James Hugh, ...	21	3	5	42	1	8
Quarter-Master Nicholas Goulding, . .	232	14	9	465	1	24
Pence excluded, total is	£367	13	0	735	1	8

" These are to certify that the arrears of the above persons are stated, and amounts to the several sums according to their names respectively annexed, for which proportions of land are required at the rate of £500 for 1000 acres; as is likewise to their sums affixed, which amounts in the whole for the said £367 13s. 0d. to the sum of 735A. 1R. 8P.   30th March, 1655.   "WILLIAM DIGGES.

" To Major W. Shepherd, Major John King, and the other Commissioners for setting out lands in the county of Sleigo, that they be added to the list of those to be satisfied there, and be permitted to draw lots as if they had been named in the original list." $\frac{A}{85}$. p. 220.

counties and baronies, when casting lots for lands in discharge of their pay. Thus the regiments in the Munster lot valued the barony of Glaneroughty, containing the mountain land of Kerry, at £250 per thousand acres ; but the barony of Clanwilliam, containing the Golden Vale of Tipperary, at £1100 per thousand acres.*

THE COUNTIES AS VALUED BY THE ARMY.

In the following list will be seen the valuation of the several counties by the army, to make them more equal among themselves, preparatory to casting the first " Grand" or " Provincial Lot," to determine in what province each regiment was to be satisfied its arrears.

" Dublin, the 21st November, 1653.

" *A Particular of the Rates of the severall Counties in the Provinces of Leinster, Munster, and Ulster, as they were agreed to by the Generall Council of Officers to be settled upon each of the said Counties respectively, in order to the setting out of Lands for the satisfaction of the Arrears of them that are disbanded, until the pleasure of the Parliament shall be further known therein, or a more exact account had of the quantity of Forfeited Lands in Ireland ; viz. :*

FOR EVERY THOUSAND ACRES IN THE PROVINCE OF LEINSTER.

Rates in the Act.	Counties.	New Rates.
£ 600	Wicklow.	Six hundred pounds.
600	Longford.	Six hundred pounds.
600	King's County.	Six hundred pounds.
600	Waxford.	Nine hundred pounds.
600	Catherlo.	Eleven hundred pounds.
600	Kildare.	Thirteen hundred pounds.
600	Kilkenny.	Eleven hundred pounds.
600	Queen's County.	Nine hundred pounds.
600	West Meath.	Nine hundred pounds.
600	Meath.	Thirteen hundred pounds.
600	Dublin.	Fifteen hundred pounds.
	The barony of Athirdee in the county of Louth, twelve hundred pounds ; the rest of the county being reserved wholly for the Adventurers.	

* $\frac{A}{84}$, p. 354. Order dated 28th July, 1653.

FOR EVERY THOUSAND ACRES IN THE PROVINCE OF MUNSTER.

Rates in the Act.	Counties.	New Rates.
£ 450	Cork.	Eight hundred pounds.
450	Waterford.	Eight hundred pounds.
450	Tipperary.	One thousand pounds.
450	Limerick.	Eleven hundred pounds.
450	Kerry.	Four hundred and fifty pounds.

FOR EVERY THOUSAND ACRES IN THE PROVINCE OF ULSTER. *

Rates in the Act.	Counties.	New Rates.
£ 200	Antrim.	Five hundred and twenty pounds.
200	Armagh.	Four hundred and sixty pounds.
200	Tirone.	Four hundred pounds.
200	Fermanagh.	Four hundred and twenty pounds.
200	Donegal.	Four hundred pounds.
200	Londonderry.	Four hundred and fifty pounds.
200	Cavan.	Four hundred pounds.
200	Monaghan.	Four hundred and twenty pounds.
200	Down	Five hundred and twenty pounds.

For every thousand acres in the baronies of Sligo, Five hundred pounds.

VALUATION OF THE BARONIES.

The lots for provinces having been cast, the officers of the several regiments in each provincial lot, before lotting for counties, valued the different baronies in their lot.

In the following list, which only concerns some one of the three general assignments of lands made to the army in September, 1655, and July and November, 1656,† and is unfortunately incomplete, will be found not only the equalization of the several baronies, but the names of the different captains, troops, and companies, to whom they were to be set out in succession.

* From an original printed Declaration, small folio of six pages, in the library of Charles Haliday, Esq., of Monkstown Park, Monkstown. "Dublin: by William Bladen: A.D. 1653."

† "Petty's Down Survey," by Larcom, p. 174.

Names of the Counties where the Disbanded are to be satisfied.	The Names of the Regiments out of which the Disbanded are reduced.	Names of the particular Troopes and Companies that are Disbanded.
Wexford.	Lord Henry Cromwell's Regiment of Horse. Lieutenant-Generall Ludlow's Regiment of Horse. Colonell Daniel Abbott's Regiment of Dragoons. Sir Hardress Waller's Regiment. Lord President's Regiment. Colonell Phair's Regiment. Loose Companies.	Captain Barrington. His owne Troope. Captain Ivorie's. Captain Nunn's. Captain Clayploe. Captain Packenham. Captain Holmes. Captain Candler. Captain Wilkinson. Captain Collis. Captain Cartrett. Captain Morgan. Major Cuppage. Captain Highgate. Major Shepherd. Captain Skinner. Supernumeraries of the Lord Henry Cromwell's Regiment to be added to this Lott.
West Meath and East Meath.	Colonell Ingoldsby's Regiment. Generall Venables' Regiment. Colonell Axtell's Regiment. Colonell Clarke's Regiment. Loose Companies.	His owne Troope. Captain Napper. Captain Cambell. Captain Wrenn. Captain Gibbons. Lieutenant-Colonell Pinchion. Captain Bromwell. Captain Cornock. Captain Gardiner. Captain Talbott. Captain Disney. Captain Waltham. Supernumeraries of the Lord President's Regiment of Horse.
Kilkenny and Queen's Co.	Colonell Stubbers.	His owne Company. Captain Burrell. Captain Helsham. Captain Lynocks. Captain Garrett. Captain Mathews. Captain Pennyfather. Captain Richards.

The Names of the Baronies that are to be set out to the Disbanded in succession.	The Rates of the severall Baronies.
Forth.	£800 per thousand acres.
Bargy.	700 per thousand acres.
Shilmalier,	600 per thousand acres.
Bantry.	600 per thousand acres.
Delvin.	£800 per thousand acres.
Half Fore.	800 per thousand acres.
Corkerrie, }	600 per thousand acres.
Moygoise.	
Kells.	650 per thousand acres.
Ferbill.	800 per thousand acres.
Moyfenrath.	1000 per thousand acres.
Clonlonan. }	600 per thousand acres.
Moycashel.	
Kilcoursie.	
Liberties of Kilkenny.	£800 per thousand acres.
Upper Ossory.	500 per thousand acres.

Names of the Counties where the Disbanded are to be satisfied.	The Names of the Regiments out of which the Disbanded are reduced.	Names of the particular Troopes and Companies that are Disbanded.
Limerick and Kerry.	Lord President of Connaught's Regiment. Colonell Richard Lawrence.	Colonell Chidley Coote. Colonell Richard Coote. Major Ormsby. Major King. Captain St. George. The Lord President of Connaught, his owne arrears, and the Supernumeraries of his owne Troope. The Supernumeraries of the Lord Broghill's Troope. Captain Mould. Lieutenant-Colonell Jones. Captain Eudes. Supernumeraries of the Life Guard, Generall Officers and Traine.
Tipperary and Waterford.	Colonell Prettie's Regiment. Colonell Sadler's Regiment. Loose Company.	Captain William Bolton. Captain Alland; each of them to have thirty out of their respective Troopes to place with them if they can gain so many to be free thereunto. Captain Thomas. Captain Nicholls and Major Brereton. Major Richardson. Supernumeraries of Colonell Prettie's Regiment to be added to this Lott.
Cork.	Loose Company. Lord Protector's Foot. Colonell Hewson. Loose Companies.	Captain Dutton. Captain Seagrave. Captain Pelham. Captain Turner. Captain Hinchman. Captain Jordan. Captain Markham. Major Walters. Supernumeraries of Commissary-General Reynolds, and Colonell Sankeys.

'he Names of the Baronies that are to be set out to the Disbanded in succession.	The Rates of the severall Baronies.
Coshlea.	£600 per thousand acres.
Small County.	800 per thousand acres.
Coshma.	700 per thousand acres.
Iracht I Connor.	350 per thousand acres.
Clannoris.	350 per thousand acres.
Corkaguiny.	250 per thousand acres.
Glanerought.	250 per thousand acres.
Clanwilliam.	1100 per thousand acres.
Gualtier and Middlethird.	£500 per thousand acres.
	350 per thousand acres.
Kinalea, and Kerricurrihie.	£570 per thousand acres.

PROVINCE OF ULSTER.*

Names of the Counties where the Disbanded are to be satisfied.	The Names of the Regiments out of which the Disbanded are reduced.	Names of the particular Troopes and Companies that are Disbanded.
Tirone.	Lord Deputy's Regiment.	Captain Morris. Supernumeraries of the Lord Deputy's Regiment of Horse. [*The rest is wanting*].

OF THE EQUALIZING OF THE LANDS IN THE LOT OF A TROOP OR COMPANY.

Thus the different regiments provided for some degree of equality in value as between themselves. But as the lands to satisfy each troop or company were set out by lot in a gross sum to the troop or company after the rate set upon the county or barony, without regard being had to the different and unequal value of the lands in themselves, it would necessarily follow that if a subdivision were not made in proportion to the real difference, some would have lands of a much greater value than others. It was therefore provided that the different regiments, troops, and companies, should nominate out of themselves persons to subdivide and set out the lands fallen to the regiment, troop, or company, according to their true and real value.† Accordingly, after the troops or companies were assigned a barony, the officers of the troop or company proceeded to rate the lands at their exact value, before casting lots or proceeding to divide them by agreement amongst the troop

* $\frac{A}{81}$, p. 136.   † "Petty's Down Survey," by Larcom, p. 278.

or company. Thus the generals of the army, the gentlemen of the life guard, and officers of the train (the artillery of that day), having received the Liberties of Limerick, as a supply, in case their lot of the barony of Clanwilliam in the county of Limerick should prove insufficient to satisfy their arrears, the Liberties being valued at the rate of £1500 per thousand acres, they particularly and distinctly equalized the several towns and seats belonging to the Liberties, according to the respective goodness, quality, and condition of the land, and according to the nature of the improvements in each of them, and set a value upon the particular places, in order to make the lots then about to be cast equal among themselves.*

SALE OF DEBENTURES BY THE COMMON SOLDIERS TO THEIR OFFICERS.

In the interval between the surrender of the principal Irish armies, in 1652, and the perfecting of the scheme for setting out the lands in Ireland, which was not published till Michaelmas, 1653, the distresses of the men, and even officers, for want of payment of their arrears, became very great. To raise moneys for their subsistence, they were found to be selling their debentures, the poor soldiers' dearly earned wages, at inconsiderable sums, thus depriving themselves of a future comfortable subsistence intended for them by those in authority, who would never have given out the lands at such low rates, but in tenderness to the soldiery, and in order to plant the country with those poor creatures whom the Lord had preserved in hardships and dangers, that they might enjoy the fruits of their labour.† Debentures were accordingly forbidden by the act to be sold until the soldiers were actually

* $\frac{A}{81}$, p. 168.

† " Order, dated 28th July, 1653." $\frac{A}{84}$, p. 354.

in possession of their several allotments.* But the prohibition
seems to have been unheeded, and practically void, because of
the general desire of the men to sell, and of the officers to
purchase ; for it appears by the claims sent in at the Restoration
to the Commissioners for executing the Act of Settlement
(still subsisting†) as well as the many deeds of assignment in
private custody, signed by all or nearly all the privates of
different troops and companies, that the men conveyed their
rights to their officers.‡ The government themselves were
obliged to license the sale of them. Thus Lieutenant Goul-
burn got liberty, on 23rd of November, 1653, for him and his
three servants to make sale of their debentures for their pre-

---

* Act for the Satisfaction of the Adventurers for Lands in Ireland
and Arrears due to the Soldiery there, &c. Section 3, Scobell's "Acts and
Ordinances."

† "Lists of Claims," among the Records of the late Auditor-General
and Surveyor-General's Offices, in the custody of William Henry Hardinge,
Esq., Landed Estates Record Office, Custom House Buildings.

‡ SOLDIERS' ASSIGNMENT OF THEIR DEBENTURES TO THEIR OFFICER.

"KNOW ALL MEN by these presents, that wee, John Kingfoot, Thomas
Etherett, Thomas Goodg, Ambrose Bayley, John Thomas, Lawrence Scott,
Richard Gumbleton, Henry Frampton, Richard Boxley, Benjamin Fox,
Thomas Right, John Piner, John Samon, William Yelding, Tobias Burt,
John Lewis, Thomas Smith, Thomas Padle, John Jones, John Cads, John
Davis, James Blow, William Hill, Evan ap Lewis, Thomas Dalton, William
Johnson, Henry Fidey, Vincent Watkins, Gregory Bolton, Robert Rutter,
William Weaver, Robert ap Richard, George Symes, and Robert Davis,
Souldiers in Lieutenant-Colonell Richard Steephens's Company, of the late
regiment of foote belonging to Colonell Daniell Axtell, in consideration of
one hundred and thirty six pounds to us and every of us, respectively and
proportionably in hand paid by Arnold Thomas, Ensigne to the said company, by these presents do grant, assign, bargaine and sell to the said
Arnold Thomas, his heirs, and assigns, ALL our right, interest, and estate
in anie parcels of land, of what nature and qualitie it shall happen, and of
what number of acres they shall happen to be and amount unto, lying and

sent necessities, notwithstanding the late printed declaration inhibiting the sale.* Often the government were obliged to advance money from the treasury on security of the debenture as in the case of distressed widows of men or officers whose husbands had been killed in the service, often "slaine by the Toryes," leaving them a great charge of small children behind, and their distress increased by the great cost of coming to Dublin in hopes of possession of their lands, and long attendance there about taking out their husbands' debentures. In such cases small sums were ordered to be paid to enable them to return to their children, the advance to be endorsed on the

being within the dominion of Ireland, which are to be assigned and ascertained unto us in recompense of our services under the Parliament and Commonwealth of England in our service heare in Ireland, together with our severall debentures, with the sums therein mentioned to be due unto us, and to be satisfied out of the forfeited lands of delinquents by the Commissioners appointed for stating accompts, TO HAVE AND TO HOLD to the said Arnold Thomas, his heirs, and assigns, to be held of the chief lords of the fee by services thereupon due and of right accustomed for ever. And wee have constituted and in our places severally put our well beloved friend, Richard Woods, late Marshall to the said Colonell Richard Axtell's regiment, our true and lawfull atturney, to enter and take possession for us and in our names of all such parcells of land wherever they shall fall, happen, or be assigned by lott or otherwise, within the dominion of Ireland; and after such possession so taken, them and everie of them for us and in our names peaceable possession thereof to the aforesaid Arnold Thomas to deliver, according to the tenor of these presents. In witness whereof, wee have hereunto put our hands and seals, this 26th day of June, 1656." Copied from the original, in the possession of Joseph Hanly, Esq., 25, Lower Gardiner-street.

The deed is above a yard in length, though little more than six inches in width; and the thirty-six seals, being attached by parchment labels, give it something of the appearance of a fringed window vallance. Three only of the soldiers sign their names; all the rest, as well as the attesting witnesses, are marksmen.

* Dated 28th July, 1653. $\frac{A}{84}$, p. 354.

debenture, so that it might be defalked thereout when lands should be given in satisfaction of the debenture.† At last de-

---

* "Upon consideration had of the low and necessitous condition of Dorothy Arthur, widow ordered that Mr. Standish, Receiver-General, do out of the first publique moneys, &c., pay unto the said Dorothy Arthur £4 0s. 0d., yᵉ same to be on accompt of yᵉ moneys due upon yᵉ said Widdow Arthur's debenter, and to be endorsed on yᵉ same, that it may be defalked thereout when lands shall be given in satisfaction thereof. 10*th January*, 1654.

"Chaˢ. Fleetwood,   Miles Corbet,   Matᵗʰ. Thomlinson."

Order Book of Council, p. 209.   Late Auditor-General's Records, Custom House Buildings, vol. x.

To Jane Weare, widow of Lieutenant Arthur Weare, "who has a debenter for £190, the arrears of her husband accrued before 1648, and has been at great cost coming to Dublin in hopes of possession of her lands, to enable her to return to her children, to be defalked out of her debentur, £6 13s. 4d., *Oct*. 29, 1654." Ib., p. 41.

"Upon reading the peticon of Elice Morton, and consideracon had thereupon, and of her present necessitous condicon by reason of her husband's death, who was in yᵉ Parliament's service, and slaine by yᵉ Toryes, leaving her a greate charge of small children behinde, as also by reason of her long attendance att this place about taking out her husband's debenters whereby she hath suffered much poverty and want;" ordered Twenty Shillings.   *January* 8, 1654-5.

"Charles Fleetwood,   Miles Corbet,   Robert Goodwin." Ib. p. 208.

"Upon consideration had of the petition of Jane Platt, widdow, it appearing that her husband, Ensign George Platt, decᵈ. was about two years since slaine in the Commonwealth's service, leaving the petitioner in a poor distressed and helpless condition, with three small children depending on her for maintenance; it is ordered that J. Standish, Esq., do, &c. pay unto Mr. T. Edwards, in trust for the said Jane Platt, the sum of £32, the same to be in full satisfaction of her debenture, which is to be delivered up to be cancelled.   *Dublin, June* 11, 1655."   Ibid., p. 92.

bentures were freely and openly sold ;* and there were regular debenture brokers, and a market rate, and prohibitions (of course eluded) against buying under eight shillings in the pound. And Dr. Petty prides himself upon always buying from the regular debenture brokers, and never at first hand from the necessitous soldier (though trepanners were sent to entrap him into purchasing); while officers were notoriously guilty of buying of their own poor soldiers remaining under their command, "whom we may well conceive frightable into any bargain, by what aweings or other means may be left to consideration."†

In this manner a considerable part of the debentures were sold before the assignments of lands; and when the disbanding and assignment of lands took place, the common soldiers who had not parted with their debentures, refused in many instances to plant.

On the 1st of September, 1655, was to take place the first and largest of the three great disbandings of the army, and the assignment of lands to them for their arrears of pay,‡ the two years which had elapsed since the passing of the act of 27th September, 1653, for their satisfaction in land, having been consumed by surveys, and the contest of the officers with the government as to the quantity of land applicable to their immediate payment. The different regiments of the army, which had been for three years garrisoning towns or posts of strength, tilling fields in the neighbourhood of their garrisons as part of

---

* " Anno 1653, debentures were freely and openly sold for 4s. and 5s. per pound." Petty's 'Political Anatomy of Ireland," p. 26.

† Petty's " Reflections upon some Persons and Things in Ireland," &c. pp. 34—36. 12mo., London : 1660.

‡ Petty's " History of the Down Survey," by Major T. A. Larcom, p. 174.

their pay,* were now to march under command of their officers to the different counties in which each regiment was to be satisfied its arrears, there to cast lots, to determine in what baronies the several troops and companies should sit down.

In 1649 the English army were mutinous at being ordered on service into Ireland, denying the right of the government to send them out of England ;† and in 1653 the common soldiers do not seem to have been too well satisfied with the plan, originating with the officers, that the arrears of the army should be satisfied in Irish lands. The state in Ireland were fully aware of the temper of the common men ; and the anxiety of the Lord Deputy is evident in the tone of his circular letter, addressed to each commanding officer of the several troops and companies to be disbanded on the 1st September, 1655 :—

---

* " Petition of the officers within the precincts of Dublin, Catherlough, Wexford, and Kilkenny on behalf of themselves and other faithful English Protestants, Feb. 1654–5." P. 62, *supra*, and p. 16.

† It was in April, 1649, that four regiments of horse, and four of foot, out of fourteen regiments of the army of England, were ordered by the Parliament for service in Ireland. The officers, knowing the temper of the men, called a council of the army ; and the council, after a solemn seeking of God by prayer, cast lots which regiments of the old army should go. Fourteen paper lots were prepared, ten of the papers being blank, and four of them with " Ireland" written on them ; and all being put into a hat, and shuffled together, they were drawn out by a child, who gave to a n officer of each regiment in the lot the lot of that regiment ; and being drawn in this inoffensive way, it was pretended that no regiment could take exception to it.[a] The army, however, was mutinous ; and it required the presence of old Colonel Skippen, then in the House of Commons, and many other influences, to appease it. Once embarked, however, others easily followed, and Cromwell's successes brought numbers to his standards. In December, 1649, " we hear by letters from York of a rendez-vous of Colonel Lilburn's party that are marching for Ireland, about a hundred old blades, stout men, and well horsed, ready for the service."[b]

[a] Whitelock's " Memorials," p. 397 b.   [b] Ib., 434.

" Dublin Castle, 20 *Aug*^t. 1655.

" SIR,—In pursuance of his Highness's command, the council here with myself and chief officers of the army having concluded about disbanding part of the army in order to lessening the present charge, it is fit that your troope be one. And accordingly I desire you would march such as are willing to plant of them, into the barony of Shelmaliere in the county of Wexford, at or before the 1st day of September, where you shall be put into possession of your lands for your arrears, according to the rates agreed on by the committee and agents. As also you shall have upon the place wherein you are so much money as shall answer the present three months arrear due to you and your men, but to continue no longer the pay of the army than upon the muster of this August. The sooner you march your men the better ; thereby you will be enabled to make provision for the winter." After some sweetening hints that they will be perhaps paid hereafter as a militia, he concludes :—

" And great is your mercy, that after all your hardships and difficulties you may sit down, and, if the Lord give his blessing, may reape some fruits of your past services. Do not think it a blemish or underrating of your past services that you are now disbanded ; but look upon it as of the Lord's appointing, and with cheerfulness submit thereunto ; and the blessing of the Lord be upon you all, and keep you in His fear, and give you hearts to observe your past experience of signal appearances. And that this fear may be seen in your hearts, and that you may be kept from the sins and pollutions which God hath so eminently witnessed against in those whose possessions you are to take up, is the desire of him who is

" Your very affectionate friend to love and serve you,*

"CHARLES FLEETWOOD."

* " Mercurius Politicus," p. 5582.

The newswriters for the state, who always represent the disposition of people actually to be what the government wishes it should be, described the soldiers as quite content with being disbanded :—

"*Dublin, September 5th,* 1655.

" I have little to add to my last besides the enclosed. My Lord Deputy* takes shipping for England to-morrow, and the officers and souldiers are all marcht (that were disbanded) to their lots in the counties of Wexford, Lymerick, Eastmeath, Westmeath, &c. They are generally fully content ; I never saw a business of the kind go on with less repining, so great have our blessings been under the government of him who is departing from us. Our loss will be your gain ; it will be your mercy to make better use of such a mercy as he is than we have done. We doubt not but God will furnish him that shall succeed, viz. the Lord Henry Cromwell, with a spirit fit to his work, which in this nation is much, and requires much of the Lord's assistance, as he hath found to his comfort that is now leaving us. The several Commissioners for setting out land to the disbanded officers and souldiers are hasted out of town, that the souldiers may be speedily settled, and comfortably lie down on their portions, which is so much the more to be accepted, in that they are not at the will of their cruel enemies to seek their bread at their hands ; but having by the blessing of God obtained their peace, they may sit down in the enjoyment of their enemies fields and houses which they planted not, nor built not; they have no reason to repent their services, considering how great an issue God hath given."†

The Commissioners, however, gave a different account

---

* Fleetwood, who had married Bridget, Oliver's eldest daughter, widow of Major-General Ireton.

† P. 5620, " Mercurius Politicus."

from the spot. They informed the government that divers officers and soldiers of the regiments and companies of foot appointed to be disbanded, when they appeared before them,
would not sit down upon their lands, notwithstanding the encouragement offered by a new suit of clothes,* and one month's
half-pay ;† and notwithstanding the government promised to

"29 *August*, 1656.

" Upon consideration had of the petition of John Fforsett for self and
other disbanded soldiers, praying satisfaction of cloth allowed to others disbanded at the same time, which they have not yet received ; ordered that
it be referred to the Auditor-General of his Highness's Court of Exchequer
to examine the truth of what is suggested in the within petition ; and if
they find the same to be true, and within the rule, to prepare orders for the
same, as formerly for others in like cases.

"THOMAS HERBERT, Clerk of the Council."

†   " *At the Castle of Kilkenny, this* 21*st September*, 1655.

" *The Lord Deputy and Council to the Commissioners appointed to set
out Lands to the Disbanded in the County of Cork.*

" GENTLEMEN,—We hope that before this time you have proceeded in
the setting out of lands to the disbanded officers and souldiers according to
your instructions. And whereas upon the petition of several of the said
disbanded, with the advice of the cheif officers and soldiers, one month's half
pay was ordered for their subsistence till they should be actually settled
in possession of lands for their arrears ; and having had consideration how
the said half pay should be regularly issued to the disbanded ; it is thought
fit and ordered that you do forthwith send to the Auditor-General of the
Army a particular and distinct list of the non-commissioned officers and
souldiers to whom you have set out lands, taking care that none be in the
lists but such as were lately actually disbanded, and included in the muster
of August last, because the benefits of the said half pay is only to extend
to such, and is to issue on your certificate aforesaid.

"THOMAS HERBERT, Clerk of the Council.

$\frac{A}{30}$, p. 94.

" The like letter, *verbatim*, was sent to Waterford, Wexford, Kilkenny, East and West Meath, Limerick, and Kerry." Ibid.

consider of their demand that a sufficient number of Irish labourers, husbandmen, and servants might be allowed to stay amongst them until they should be better enabled to plant without them.*

It was the officers only, in point of fact, that promoted the design of taking land for their arrears ; and some even of them seem to have shared the discontent of the common men, as Lieutenant-Colonel Scott was arrested for agitating the disbanded companies sitting down in the county of Wexford, in September, 1655, by treasonable words against his Highness, tending to mutiny and distemper.† In Ireland the common men found no beer, no cheese ; they had no ploughs nor horses, nor money to buy them. The Irish were for the most part transplanted, or had betaken themselves to the woods and mountains as Tories.

But beyond all other wants was felt that imperious want, the want of women. They were forbidden under heavy penalties to take Irish girls for wives. For any amours with them during their service in the army they were severely flogged ;‡ and as

* $\frac{A}{5}$, p. 245.   † $\frac{A}{5}$, p. 243.

‡   "*June* 15, 1655.
           "*By the Court Marshall.*

" Whereas, by a court marshall this day held at Whitehall, Hugh Powell, souldier in Captain Lieutenant Hoare's Company, of Collonel Huson's regiment, was convicted and found guilty of fornication, within the third article of warre, and for the same was adjudged to be whipped on the bare back with a whipcord lash, and have forty stripes while he is led through the four companies of the Irish forces before Whitehall, at the time of the parade on Munday next, and twenty stripes more after that at Putney, while hee is led through those of the Irish party that quarter there, neer the Widow Nashe's house there ; You are hereby required to cause the said sentence of the court marshall to bee put in execution with effect ; and the chief officers present with the said Irish companys at the time of the parade at Whitehall, on the said Munday, as also the chief officers present with those of the Irish party quartering at Putney, are hereby

the soldiers always pretended that the Irish girls they married
were converts to English religion, Ireton forbade all intermarriages, unless the girls first passed an examination into the

desired to draw the said companies into two single files, to the end the said
Hugh Powell may bee led through and receive his punishment accordingly.

"Signed in the name and by the order of the said Court,

"THOS. MARGETS, *Advocate.*

" *To the Marshall General of the Army, or his Deputies.*"

P. 4795, "Mercurius Politicus."

" *Dublin Castle*, 17 *March*, 1653-4.

"Upon the information of Colonel Solomon Richards, that Captain
William Williamson is now prisoner in Dublin upon suspicion of committing fornication with a woman in the county of Tipperary, during the time
of his service there ; and that the said Colonel has entered into a recogni-
zance to prosecute the said Captain for the misdemeanour and offence aforesaid ; and forsomuch as the said offence is alleged to have been committed
within the precinct of Clonmel as aforesaid ; it is ordered that the said Captain Williamson be sent forthwith in safe custody from Dublin to Clonmel,
there to be secured by the said Colonel Richards, and the rest of the Commissioners for administration of justice there in order to his tryal ; and that
the recognizances be delivered to the said Colonel Richards to be cancelled :
whereof all whom it may concern are to take notice.

"CHARLES FLEETWOOD, MILES CORBET, JOHN JONES."
$\frac{A}{85}$, p. 187.

July 16, 1655 : William Sword, a foot soldier in Lieutenant-Colonel
Venables' own company, belonging to Ireland, for like offence was adjudged
"to be whippt at the limbers of a piece of ordnance in Windsor, from the
Castle gate to the Churchyard gate, in the High Street, and back again,
with a whipcord lash." "Mercurius Politicus," p. 4797.

But what were these to the punishment of high treason denounced
by the Statute of Kilkenny (40 Ed. 3, sec. 2, A. D. 1367) against any Englishman who should make alliance with an Irishwoman by marriage,
concubinage, or amour ? "The court doth award that thou shalt be had
from hence to the place from whence thou diddest come, and so
drawne upon an hurdle [or sledge] to the place of execution ; and there

real state of their hearts before a board of military saints, under penalty, if the soldiers marrying were dragoons, of being reduced to foot soldiers—if foot soldiers, to pioneers—without hope in either case of promotion.* After being disbanded, if

to be hanged, and let down alive, and thy privie parts cut off, and thy entrals taken out and burned in thy sight ; then thy head to be cut offe, and thy body devided in foure parts, and to be disposed of at Her Majestie's pleasure." (Sentence on William Parry, LL. D., at Westminster, 25th February, 1584-5, for High Treason. " State Trials," vol. i., p. 128.) See similar sentences upon fifteen regicides on 16th October, 1660 (ibid., vol. ii., p. 401). Nor was the disembowelling alive a mere form of words. " When the executioner began his tremendous office on Babington, one of the Gunpowder Treason conspirators, the spirit of this haughty and heroic man cried out amidst the agony, ' *Parce mihi, Domine Jesu !*' Spare me, Lord Jesus" (D'Israeli's "Curiosities of Literature," vol. iii., p. 102.) At the execution of Mr. Green, in 1642, a lady knelt and held the poor gentleman's head fast beneath her hands ; and while the executioner ripped up his belly, and laid the flaps on both sides, the poor sufferer was so present to himself, that he made the sign of the cross with one hand. Meanwhile his face sweated, blood issued from his mouth, ears, and eyes ; and his forehead burned with so much heat, that she could scarce endure her hand upon it (note, ibid.).

And the Irish are to be called barbarous for not having had punishments like those of the "just and honourable law of England !" (Sir J. Davies' "Discoverie," p. 665). By which law also women in England were to be stripped and flogged in public by men, till the year 1817, and privately in prison till 1820.

* " *By the Deputy Generall of Ireland.*

" Whereas divers officers and souldiers of the army doe daily intermarry with the women of this nation who are Papists, or who onely for some corrupt or carnall ends (as it is to be feared) pretend to bee otherwise, and who, while remaining in, or not being really brought off from those false ways in which they have or doe walk, are declared by the Lord to be a people of his wrath. And though a reall change in the blinde deluded people of this nation were to be wished and ought to be endeavoured by all good people (it being the joy and delight of any that God hath brought home to himselfe to see the like worke upon others hearts

they married any of these attractive but "idolatrous" daughters of Erin, they were liable to have them taken from them, or to march after them to Connaught if they could not do without them.

COMMON SOLDIERS CHEATED OF THEIR LOTS OF LAND BY THEIR OFFICERS.

But even if the soldier had not sold his debenture to his officer, and was willing to plant, he was sometimes cheated by him of his lot. For, on coming down to look for possession, the poor soldier would be shown a bog or other piece of coarse land, and the officer would tell him that was the lot set out to him, and by that means bought the good land which really was the poor man's at the price of the bog.* In such cases

also, which frame of spirit I trust all Christians in this army have towardes that people) ; yet that none be left to their own misguided judgments in things where usually blinded affection makes them take any pretence for a reall worke of God on the heart, I think fitt to let all know that if any officer or souldier of this army shall marry with any women of this nation that are Papists, or have lately been such, and whose change of religion is not, or cannot be judged (by fitt persons, such as shall be appointed for that end) to flow from a reall worke of God upon their hearts, convincing them of the falsehood of their owne ways, and goodness and truth of that way they turn to, or that from any circumstance accompanying that action it shall be judged to be but from carnall ends that they have made this change, I say that any officer who marries any such shall hereby be held uncapable of command or trust in this army, and for any soldier, &c., [as above], unlesse God doe by a change wrought upon them with whom they have married take off this reproach. *Given at Waterford*, 1*st May*, 1651.

" IRETON."

" Severall Proceedings in Parliament from 17th to 24th July, 1651," p. 1458.

* " Reflections upon some Persons and Things in Ireland, by Letters to and from Dr. Petty, with Sir Hierome Sankey's Speech in Parliament," p. 114. 12mo. London : 1660.

one can easily conceive how the man might be willing to take a horse in exchange, and a few shillings in his pocket to ride home with; and that thus the traditions, so common in Ireland, like that of the White Horse of the Peppers, that the price of such and such an estate was a white horse, have their foundations in fact. A barrel of beer is said to have been the consideration paid to the soldiers of his troop by Captain Bassett, for their lands, which formed part of those set out to the Lord Deputy Fleetwood's own troope, described in the map now exhibited.* Thus the scheme of an extensive plantation of English yeomanry in Ireland, ready at all times to furnish a stout military population to recruit the forces in England, or to turn out in arms to defend their own interest against the Irish or any foreign force coming to their aid, so often attempted before in the course of the century, again failed. The former schemes, however, were better contrived, being plans for regular colonization; but the Cromwellian design was wild in the extreme, for of all bodies an army is the worst to colonize with. What chance would there be of a colony, if at this day a regiment of cavalry or infantry were marched into the wilds of Ireland and there disbanded, and told to plant?†

* The map, copied from one in possession of Major Waring of Waringstown, is entitled "Part of the Barony of Lower Evagh, in the County of Down, and Part of Toome Barony, in the County of Antrim; fallen by Lott to Captain Bassett's [   ]." The map is a transcript of the Down Survey; but it gives particulars not found in that Survey, inasmuch as there are in the several parishes of Magheralin, Donaghcloney, and Tullylish, in the county of Down, the following entries on the map :—
" Part of yᵉ parish set forth to yᵉ Lord Deputy Fleetwood, his own Troope." It is evidently one of those maps which Dr. Petty was bound by the ninth article of his contract to furnish to every officer and soldier, to demonstrate his several proportion ; provided that no map be required of any proportion less than one thousand acres. Petty's " Down Survey," by Major T. A. Larcom, p. 26.

† Harington, author of " Oceana," is said to have by his writings in-

ATTEMPTS OF THE OFFICERS TO TAKE UNFAIR ADVANTAGES OF ONE ANOTHER IN THE SETTING OUT OF LANDS.

The opportunity for the officers to obtain unfair advantages seems to have been principally in the setting out of the lands. The surveyors either left out lands from the lot,—sometimes in favour of an influential officer, not of the troop or company, who had got possession of land under a lease *in custodium* from the state, and who hoped by holding longer possession to get

fluenced Cromwell to this step. "That empire follows the balance of property in land, whether lodged in one, in a few, or in many hands, he was the first that ever made out. Some despised his discovery, alledging it was plain to every man's capacity : as if his highest merit did not consist in making it so. But a third sort sought to rob him of the glory of this invention ; for, our author having lent one of them a part of his papers, he published a small piece to the same purpose, entitled ' A Letter from an Officer of the Army in Ireland,' &c. Major Wildman was reputed the author by some, and Henry Nevill by others." " Oceana, and other Works of James Harington, Esq.," by J. Toland. Folio, p. xviii. Third Edition. London : 1747.

" We have a memorable instance of foresight in Harington, who, born nearly two centuries before 1789, foretold the French Revolution. His words are :—' Look you to it ; where there is tumbling and tossing upon the bed of sickness, it must end in death or recovery. Though the people of the world, in the dregs of the Gothic Empire, be yet tumbling upon the bed of sickness, they cannot die : nor is there any recovery for them but by Ancient Prudence,[a] whence of necessity it must come to pass that this drug be better known. If France, Italy, and Spain, were not all

[a] " Harington in all his works employs the words Ancient Prudence to express the destruction of the Gothic feudal law of primogeniture, and the replacing of it by the ancient prudence of equality. What he says of Great Britain being a province of France if she does not adopt the Ancient Prudence, is a powerful reason for her to destroy the feudal law of primogeniture, and to cease to weaken herself by persisting to keep her distant possessions. Note by General Arthur C. O'Connor."

" Monopoly the Cause of All Evil," by Arthur Condorcet O'Connor. 3 volumes, imperial 8vo. Firmin Didot. Paris and London : 1848.

a grant of it in fee—or, if an officer got a lot he did not relish, he endeavoured to throw out the coarse land, and encroach at the expense of his neighbours.

Colonel Le Hunte was captain of Cromwell's life or body guard of horse, a most influential person. He was in possession by lease from the state of some of the rich lands in the suburbs of New Ross, at the time when Major Samuel Shepherd's company was to be set down with the disbanded party in the county of Wexford, the lot of the Major's company falling near the town and liberties of Ross.

The lots ought in due course to be set out without interval ; but the surveyors left out 1500 acres of this fine land, pretending partly that it was on lease to Colonel Le Hunte, and partly that some of it was burgess land belonging to the town. Major Shepherd had influence enough to get Colonel Le Hunte's lease suspended; and by an inquisition from the Exchequer got it found that the land was not corporation land, but forfeited land, and he recovered it for his company.*

Colonel Warden having obtained an order of the Council Board to be satisfied his arrears in the barony of Gowran, in

---

sick, all corrupted together, there would be none of them so : for the sick would not be able to withstand the sound, nor the sound to preserve their health without curing of the sick. The first of these nations (which if you stay her leisure in my mind will be France) that recovers the health of Ancient Prudence shall certainly govern the world. For what did Italy when she had it ? And as you were under her sway, so shall you in like case be reduced to a province. I do not speak at random. Italy in the consulship of Lucius Emilius Papus, and Caius Attilius Regulus, armed upon the Gallic tumult that then happened, of herself, and without the aid of foreign auxiliaries, 70,000 horse, and 700,000 foot. But as Italy is the least of those countries in extent, so is France now the most populous." P. 353, vol. iii.

* $\frac{A}{12}$, p. 75.

the county of Kilkenny, the lands of Jackstown, Kilbeg, and Kilmarry were assigned to him by the Commissioners for setting out lands ; but by leaving out all the coarse lands in his lot, he encroached into Columkill, and made up his pretended want out of the best part of Columkill, in the lot of Quartermaster Hugh Farr.*

Similar to this was one of the charges against Dr. Petty, that he reserved or withheld out of the strings of lands, when handing them to the Commissioners to be set out to different regiments, several choice places, under pretence that they were encumbered or doubtful, for the benefit either of himself or friends. Sir Jerome Sankey imputed to him some underhand dealing in this way with the Liberties of Limerick. The Liberties of Limerick would appear to have been considered the very choicest lands for disposal among the army, and to have been reserved for the gentlemen of the life guard, and officers of the train, evidently two of the most influential corps in the army. Captain Winkworth, having obtained an order for this coveted district, presented it to Dr. Petty, who simply told him that the lands were reserved, and that he could not have his debenture satisfied. Out of this incident, Sir Jerome Sankey founded the charge in Parliament, of which Sir W. Petty gives a graphic sketch, that well illustrates the picture of these conquerors quarrelling among themselves over their prey. After a whole string of other charges, " Why then, Mr. Speaker (said Sir Jerome), there's Captain Winkworth : Captain Winkworth came with an order for the Liberties of Limerick; but the Doctor said, ' Captain, will you sell? will you sell ?' ' No,' said the Captain, ' it is the price of my blood.' Then said the Doctor, ' 'Tis bravely said : why then, my noble Captain, the Liberties of Limerick are meat for your master,' meaning the Lord Deputy ;"† Sankey's cause of quarrel with

---

* $\frac{A}{12}$, p. 71.   † Petty's "Down Survey," by Larcom, p. 299.

Dr. Petty being that he stopped Sankey's unrighteous order for rejecting three thousand acres fallen to him by lot, and enabling him arbitrarily to elect the same quantity in its stead,* thus rejecting at his pleasure what God had predetermined for his lot.†

OF THE DISTRIBUTION BY THE ADVENTURERS OF THEIR ALLOTMENTS.

Matters are usually badly managed from a distance ; and as the Committee of Adventurers directed their affairs in Ireland from Grocers' Hall in London, the business could scarce fail to become entangled.

Their mode of proceeding was to quarter and sub-quarter baronies (without regard to the quantity of forfeited land in each barony), sometimes by a north and south line crossed by an east and west line, sometimes by parallel lines running east and west, or north and south, sometimes by diagonal lines, the rule being (in order to preserve denominations entire) that on whatever side of the quartering line the greatest part of a denomination fell, the whole was to be reputed to lie entirely on that side ; which rule was also applicable to sub-quarterings.‡   But, instead of first reducing the townlands into one continued file or string of contiguity of "*neat*" lands, setting aside for a time encumbered or "*dubiose*" lands, that so it might be known with certainty from the first to the last disposable denomination in what order of priority each should be disposed of, the managers in London gave assignments on the

---

* Petty's "Reflections on some Persons and Things in Ireland," &c., p. 69.

† Ibid., p. 85.

‡ Petty's " Down Survey, by Larcom," p. 238.

different quarters and subquarters without proper oversight.*
Not knowing accurately what quantities of forfeited land
were in each quarter and subquarter, they overloaded some,
which thereby became deficient to answer the claims. Some
baronies, for like want of information (or perhaps from misdeal-
ing) were redundant. In some, lands set down as forfeited

* ADVENTURER'S CERTIFICATE.

" To ALL TO WHOM THESE PRESENTS SHALL COME, GREETING,—
Whereas, by an ordinance made by His Highness the Lord Protector by
and with the advice and consent of his Council, bearing date the 6th August, 1654, entitled an Ordinance appointing a Committee of Adventurers
for Lands in Ireland, for determining differences among the said Adventurers, Wee, Sir Thomas Dacres, Sir John Clotworthy, Alderman Thomas
Andrews, Alderman John Fowke, Alderman Samuel Avery, Thomas
Ayers, John Blackett, Senior, William Webb, William Hawking, Charles
Lloyd, George Almery, Thomas Barnardiston, John Greensmith, Lawrence
Bromeswold, Thomas Brightwell, Deputie Hutchinson [with many others],
or anie eleven or more of us, are authorised to settle a method for determining by lott how many and which of the adventurers proportions falling
within one and the same particular barony wherein the escheated lands
shall fall short of the allotment shall be continued and laid out in such barony, or how much thereof; and which of the said adventurers shall take
his proportion or how much thereof elsewhere, according to the Act of Parliament made on that behalf. And also to settle a method by lott for ascertaining the subdivisions of adventurers proportions that shall continue
in all and everie the severall baronies according to the respective allotments. Now WEE DO HEREBY CERTIFY that the barony of Eliogarty, in
the county of Tipperary, in the province of Munster in Ireland, being
equally and indifferently divided into four quarters, that is to say, North
East, No. 1 ; South East, No. 2 ; South West, No. 3 ; and North West,
No. 4 ; Ellen Milborne, wife of John Milborne, of the parish of St. Cle-
ment Danes, in the county Middlesex, Bitt Maker, upon a lott made according to the method by us sett down, by virtue of the said ordinance, and duly
drawne in her behalfe, is to have to her and her heirs and assigns for ever
two hundred and twenty-two acres, three roods, and thirty perches of
meddow, arrable land, and profitable pasture, Irish measure, which amounts
to 359 acres, 3 roods, 31 perches, English measure ; and all the woods,

were found to be not forfeited, or were restored to delinquent Protestants.

The consequences were painful: some had too much; others, too little, or none at all. Some were found to have satisfactions consisting of several townlands in length from one extremity to another, more than three times the breadth. Others had townlands not contiguous.* They had, in fact, skipped over coarse townlands, instead of proceeding regularly in the line of progression. Others had taken bites as it were out of several townlands, whereas, in making satisfaction, more than two denominations should never be cut:† for as, the next preceding satisfaction might not exactly have exhausted the last denomination, the following satisfaction might of course have to begin with a broken one, and for the same reason end with one; so much cutting might be necessary, but not more.

boggs, loughs, waters, fishings, and barren mountains, cast in over and above, together with the houses and edifices thereon, and in her said lott contained in the North West quarter, No. 4, of the same baronie, if the same be there to be had, the numbers one, two, and three, being first satisfied, beginning her said measure for the same with the rest of the adventurers for the said quarter of such forfeited and profitable lands as aforesaid, where No. 3 shall end, in what part of the said four quarters soever of the said baronie the same shall happen to be; and soe measuring from thenceforward until she and they shall have her and their full proportion of lands lying most contiguously together in that quarter of the same baronie if the same be there to be had: and in case of deficiency of forfeited and profitable lands for satisfaction of the said Ellen Milborne and the rest of the adventurers in the said quarter in the residue of the said barony, the Nos. 1, 2, and 3, being first satisfied, then she and they are to have satisfaction for the same, or so much thereof as shall be so wanting elsewhere: in witness whereof, wee have hereunto sett our hands and seals, this 26th day of March, 1654."

Attached are eleven seals. I am indebted to the kindness of Mr. Joseph Hanly for the use of this instrument.

* Petty's "Down Survey," by Larcom, p. 241.

† Ibid., ib.

The deficient adventurers looked to the county of Louth, allotted by the act for a supply in case of deficiency of the ten
half counties, and even threatened to come upon the four reserved counties, the government reserve ; while the army,
which had only received lands to the amount of twelve shillings and three pence per pound of their arrears and were
eager for more, were also looking for Louth, and insisted that,
if Dr. Petty were employed to overhaul the adventurers' proceedings, they would be found to have had lands sufficient.
Petty was accordingly, with the assent of the adventurers, directed to arrange the whole ; and some light is thrown on the
mode of distributing the lands to the army by his proceedings
in this business. He formed two parallel lists of deficient and
redundant baronies, the first deficient barony to be repaired
out of the first redundant, and so downward, till all were satisfied, and at the end it would be found if Louth were free for the
army.

The several denominations in each barony were to be made
into one continued file or string of contiguity, and so be set
out, and these strings to be arranged by three several artists,
from whom the priority of the lots of the adventurers were care-
fully withheld ; and, when made, one of the strings was to be
chosen by lot, as the only rule in the matter of succession,—
provisions to prevent any charges of partiality.

And these same artists were to determine by what line every
townland should be cut in cases where there might be occasion
for cutting, for making up a just number of acres answering to
each lot or debt*—a very necessary provision for Dr. Petty's
safety ; for he had found in the case of the soldiers, that when
the surveyor did not lay the house and orchard on the right

* Petty's " Down Survey," by Larcom, where, in chapter xvi., pp.
227-256, these proceedings are set forth.

side of the line, the party disappointed was sure to say Dr. Petty employed incompetent surveyors.

The priority of the certificates or order of succession in which they should be satisfied, like as the succession of the debentures, was also fixed beforehand—in spite of which, in the soldiers' case, if they fell upon coarse land, better land being behind, it was said Dr. Petty had overcharged the lot, and stuffed in his own friends :* if better lands were before, then debentures were not equally and impartially fixed.†

THE REPLANTING OF IRELAND.

IRELAND being now divided between the adventurers, the English army, and the government, who may all be considered as new purchasers of their several portions, the great opportunity so long looked for had arrived for improving the country, and rendering it as fruitful, prosperous, and flourishing, as the mother country of England.

The original design of the Parliament was to leave untransplanted of the Irish, besides boys and girls entertained as servants in English families, only a few who had never been in arms, to serve as husbandmen and herdsmen to the English, and thus to impose upon the new planters the necessity to bring tenants from England. However, having regard to the difficulty of this perfect and absolute English plantation, the Commissioners for the Affairs of Ireland resolved to divide Ireland into three districts or divisions,—one of them to be a pure Irish plantation; another, a pure English plantation, to consist wholly of English (not excluding, however, Dutch, Swiss, and Germans, or other foreigners, provided they were

---

* Petty's " Reflections on some Persons and Things in Ireland," p. 113.
† Ibid, ib., p. 115.

opposed to the Irish); the third, a mixed plantation of English landlords and masters, with a permission to take Irish tenants and servants, but only such as were without the rule of transplantation.*

Connaught, as bounded by the River Shannon, including the county of Clare, had been already appointed by Parliament for the habitation of the Irish nation. The reason of this selection was, its peculiar suitableness for the purpose of imprisonment. It is, in fact, an island surrounded (all but ten miles) by the Shannon and the sea, and the whole river easily made into one line with the sea by the erection of three or four forts between Jamestown, at the head waters of the Shannon, and Sligo, the northern port of Connaught. On the eastern side of the kingdom was to be found, it was observed, a similar scope of land rendered nearly an island by the Boyne, the Barrow, and the sea. These two rivers, rising within four or five miles of one another in the Bog of Allen, and flowing respectively north and south, make their issue to the sea,— the one at Drogheda, and the other at Waterford,—the distance between the head waters being, at the period of the Commonwealth settlement of Ireland, an impassable bog, or continued fastness, and no passage but through such passes as could be easily secured ; and the two rivers in winter overflowed, and in summer the few fords upon them, readily spoiled or guarded.† In Henry VIII.'s day, this pass between their head waters was considered the door of the English Pale (of which O'Connor, as dwelling next to it, was by the Irish called their key),‡ and was closed by building the four castles of Kinnefad, Castlejordan, Ballinure, and Kishavann.§ It

---

* " The Great Interest of England in the well Planting of Ireland with English People Discussed," p. 21. By Colonel Richard Lawrence.

† Ibid., p. 26.

‡ " State Papers of Henry VIII. (Ireland)," vol. i. p. 325.

§ Ibid., vol. ii., p. 241.

was now proposed that this well-secured district should become
a pure English plantation, or what might more properly perhaps have been called an anti-Irish plantation, to consist altogether of English (or foreigners who were Protestants), without a single Irish tenant or servant permitted.* It was only
the revival of a scheme of Richard II.'s day, who made all the
Irish engage to transplant from it, and find new homes for themselves by plundering their own countrymen west of the River
Barrow.† It was also among the projects for the new planting of Ireland in Henry VIII.'s day after Thomas Fitzgerald's
rebellion. The Earl of Surrey, when Lord Lieutenant of Ireland, discussed with Henry VIII. the plan of planting it with
foreigners, as English in sufficient numbers were not then to
be had. He suggested, however, the danger, if Spaniards,
Flemings, Almains, or any other nation save the king's natural subjects were planted there, that they might retain their
allegiance to their foreign sovereign.‡ Religion had not in
1520 created a difference between the Irish and other nations ;
but now, in 1653, there were foreign nations to be found, who,
agreeing with the English in religion, might always be trusted
to continue enemies of the Irish, and might be invited to form
part of this plantation.§ Being nearest to the succour of Eng-

* " Great Interest of England in the well Planting of Ireland with
English People Discussed," p. 21.

† Sir John Davies, " Discovery why Ireland was never thoroughly
subdued until the Reign of King James I.," p. 615.

‡ " State Papers of Henry VIII. (Ireland)," vol. i. p. 79.

§ " The expectation of this day is the hope of Israel . . . . I look also
somewhat upon the hopefull appearance of replanting Ireland shortly, not
only by the adventurers, but haply by the calling in of exiled Bohemians
and other Protestants also, and haply by the invitation of some well-
affected out of the Low Countries."

" Ireland's Natural History, written by Gerard Boate, and now published by Samuel Hartlib, Esq., dedicated to his Excellency Oliver Crom-

land, being coasted on the east by the sea, and to be rendered defensible on the land side by a few forts upon the banks of the rivers, the plantation might easily secure itself in case of any rising of the Irish inhabitants of the two other districts.* The third, or mixed plantation, was to be in the territories lying in the middle of Ireland, between the Irish plantation of Connaught and the pure English plantation enclosed by the Barrow and the Boyne. In this mixed plantation no transplantable persons were to be taken as tenants or servants, and only such Irish as should be in each case specially authorized by the state. The landlords were to be bound to make them speak English within a limited time, and their children were to be taught no Irish; they were to observe the manners of the English in their habit and deportment wherein the English exceeded them. Their children were to be brought up under English Protestant schoolmasters; they were to attend the public preaching of Protestant ministers; they were to abandon their Irish names of Teig, and Dermot, and the like, and to call themselves by the significance of such names in English; and for the future were to name their children with English names, especially omitting the (O') and (M'); and, lastly, should build their houses with chimneys as English in like capacity do, and demean themselves in their lodging and other deportments accordingly.†

well, Captain Generall, and to the Right Hon[ble] Charles Fleetwood, Commander in Chief (under him) of all the Forces in Ireland." Dedication, p. 6. 4to. London: 1652.

By the Act of 27th September, 1653, all foreign Protestants were made as free of Ireland as the natives of England. " Act for Satisfaction of Adventurers and Soldiers," p. 366, Petty's " Down Survey," by Larcom.

* " The Great Interest of England in the well Planting of Ireland with English," p. 26.

† Ibid., p. 39.

OF ENGLISH PLANTERS INVITED BACK BY THE GOVERNMENT FROM
AMERICA.

Ireland was now like an empty hive, prepared to receive its
new swarm.* One of the earliest efforts of the government
towards replanting the parts reserved to themselves was, to
turn towards the lately expatriated English in America. In
the early part of the year 1651, when the country, by their
own description to the Council of State, was a scene of un-
paralleled waste and ruin, the Commissioners for Ireland
affectionately urged Mr. Harrison, then a minister of the Gospel in New England, to come over to Ireland, which he would
find experimentally was a comfortable seed plot (so they said)
for his labours. On his return to New England, it was hoped
he might encourage those whose hearts the Lord should stir
up to look back again towards their native country, to return
and plant in Ireland. There they should have freedom of
worship, and the [mundane] advantages of convenient lands,
fit for husbandry, in healthful air, near to maritime towns or secure places, with such encouragement from the state as should
demonstrate that it was their chief care to plant Ireland with a
godly seed and generation.† Mr. Harrison was unable to come;
but some movement appears to have been made towards a
plantation from America, as proposals were received in January,
1655, for the planting of the town of Sligo and lands thereabouts, with families from New England; and lands on the Mile
line, together with the two little islands called Oyster Island
and Coney Island (containing 200 acres), were leased for one
year, from 10th of April, 1655, for the use of such English

---

* "The Great Interest of England in the Well Planting of Ireland
with English People," p. 3.

† "Letter of the Commissioners for the Affairs of Ireland," dated from
Dublin, September 18th, 1651. $\frac{A}{2}$.

families as should come from New England in America, in order to their transplantation.*

In 1656, several families, arriving from New England at Limerick, had the excise of tobacco brought with them for the use of themselves and families remitted ;† and other families in May and July of that year, who had come over from New England to plant, were received as tenants of state lands near Garristown, in the county of Dublin, about fifteen miles north of the capital.‡

And who knows but the time may yet come for the government of England to turn to the lately expatriated nation of Irish which peoples the northern, southern, and western States of America, and the more distant territories of Australia, and invite them " to look back again towards their native country," by changing the policy of near seven hundred years, and framing laws to promote the acquisition of Irish lands, not by English capitalists, but by the sons of Ireland ?

Were some court to be again erected for the sale of lands in Ireland, offering as many millions of acres as were set up for sale by the late Encumbered Estates Court, and were due security given to the Irish, the Irish would probably be seen hastening in fleets over the Pacific and Atlantic Oceans, armed with American and Australian gold, to purchase back the land of their fathers. For there be many who (like Doctor

---

* $\frac{A}{5}$, p. 78 ; p. 125, ib. † $\frac{A}{10}$, p. 227.

‡ " Order on the petition of John Stone to become tenant to the state for 40 or 50 acres at Garristown, he being desirous to settle himself with the families that came over from New England to plant in this country, 5th May, 1656." $\frac{A}{12}$, p. 9.

" Order to let to John Barker (late come from New England, and now desirous to plant here) 30 acres of the lands of Garristown, for the term of one year, paying only contribution for the same, in case they find the said Barker is willing to inhabit the same, and not to assign it to another. *Council Chamber, Dublin, 30th July,* 1656." Ibid., p. 187.

Petty) had rather live on their ancient patrimonies near home, enjoy their old tried friends, and breathe their native air, than to cross oceans and pass to new climates, and have a partnership in the rich mines of Potosi.*

PROCEEDINGS OF THE ADVENTURERS IN REPLANTING.

The adventurers, if their presence and activity may be judged of by their proceedings against the Irish, came over after their delays,—so much complained of by the Commissioners for the Affairs of Ireland—in 1656, and 1659. It is probable they found great difficulties interposed by the officers of the army, their rivals as planters, who had been for some years in possession of the country, and had familiarized themselves with its ways and inhabitants. And there is reason to think that many of the Irish proprietors, who had been hitherto left in possession of their lands in the adventurers' baronies, or lingered there during the adventurers' delay in coming over, got countenance from the officers. The latter had some reason to wish them to stay ; for they bore part of the assessment on account of their tillage and their cattle, and it fell heavier as the numbers to share the burden grew fewer. Even the poor wandering Ulster creaghts became objects to entice into a neighbourhood on this account ; and in the orders of the Council for forcing them to give up that barbarous mode of life, wandering up and down with their families and herds of cattle, in order to fix them to tillage, inquiries were often directed to know by whose encouragement they came to the other provinces.† Consequently the officers may not have been very willing to drive off the Irish proprietors occupying the adventurers' lands in their neighbourhood. Thus William Wallace,

---

* " Reflections on some Persons and Things in Ireland," preface, p. 3 ; and ibid., p. 183. 12mo. London: 1660.

† $\frac{A}{10}$, p. 161.

agent for the adventurers entitled to the barony of Duleek, in the county of Meath, adjoining the town of Drogheda, in April, 1657, complained that there were Popish proprietors still remaining in the barony, and prayed that they might be transplanted into Connaught according to the proclamation. It was referred by the Council to two justices of the peace of the county of Meath to examine the allegations, and, if true, to put the declaration into due and speedy execution for removing them into Connaught.* The M'Coughlan's Country, formed in the reign of James I. into the barony of Garrycastle, in the King's County, was in the neighbourhood of Banagher, the navel of Ireland. The agent of one of the adventurers, whose lot had fallen in the barony of Garrycastle,† complained to the

* $\frac{A}{12}$, p. 335.

† The barony of Garrycastle, in the King's County, in the province of Leinster [as divided among the adventurers, A. D. 1655:—]

North Quarter, No. 1.

	ACRES.
The Lord Wenman, ...	600
Mr. Samuel Roles, ...	1000
Mr. John Roles, ...	450
Mr. Parker, ...	600
John Sadler, ...	100
Richard Quiney, ...	100
Benjamin Banister, ...	100
Henry Hanwell, ...	100
	3050

South Middle Quarter, No. 3.

	ACRES.
Mr. Gregory Clements, ...	3000
Mr. Botterill, ...	50
	3050

North Middle, No. 2.

	ACRES.
Mr. John Sweetinge, ...	400

Council, that this adventurer, Gregory Clements by name, had been kept out of possession for two years by Mrs. Mary Coughlan.* She had delivered the possession to others, officers probably, who connived at her attempt. She had evidently created a powerful interest, which she was able still to exert ; for even after this complaint made, instead of being ordered instantly to transplant, the case was referred for perusal of papers and records to the Commissioners sitting at Athlone ; and she subsequently got dispensed for six months, under the suggestion the better to provide a settlement for herself and family in Connaught.

But women are always hard to deal with in cases of ejectment, and two others gave the adventurers equal trouble as Mrs. Coughlan—the one Lady Thurles, the other Lady Dunsany. The Viscountess Thurles was the Earl of Ormond's mother. The castle and town of Thurles, with 4000 acres adjacent, was her dower land. There she had dwelt since the breaking out of the war of 1641, and had given her powerful protection to many English who fled to her friendly shelter.

North Middle, No. 2, continued.

	ACRES.
Mr. Humphry Markworth, ...	1700
Mr. John Marriott, ...	225
Mr. Hevingham, ...	600
Mr. James Cocks, ...	100
Mr. John Blenkhorne, ...	50
	3075

South, No. 4.

	ACRES.
Mr. Pye, ...	1000
Mr. Gregory Clements, ...	2000
Mrs. Mary Fountaine, ...	2210
	3210

From Joseph Hanly, Esq., 27, Lower Gardiner-street.

* $\frac{A}{12}$, p. 335.   † Ibid., p. 69.

From 1643 to 1646 she had advanced considerable sums to the relief of the English army—£300 at one time, and £500 at another, and many other sums. When Major Peisley was forced to yield his neighbouring garrison of Archerstown to the Irish forces, and he and others of his company were wounded and much spent out and weakened, she invited him and his whole company to her house, and entertained them for many weeks, and sent them to the English garrison of Doneraile, well cured, and refreshed with supplies of moneys and provisions. But all this could not save her. She was an Irish Papist; for Lord Ormond was the only Protestant of his family, by the accident of being made a king's ward on his father's death, and brought up in the family of Doctor Abbott, Archbishop of Canterbury ; and, though she had shown much good affection, she had dwelt in the enemy's quarters. She therefore fell short of a constant good affection ; and forfeit her dower lands she must, and by rule transplant to Connaught.* The barony of Eliogarty had fallen to the adventurers ; and Mr. John Gunn, their agent, claimed the lands in the possession of the Lady Thurles, " a Popish recusant and transplantable," and urged her removal †. The lands the adventurers obtained. It was not in the power of the Commissioners to refuse them ; but Lady Thurles' personal transplantation was dispensed with from time to time; and she probably dwelt with the Countess of Ormond (who continued possessed of her property, though her husband's the Earl's was confiscated), till her son returned with increased honours and power at the Restoration.

Other adventurers, whose lots had fallen in the barony of Skreen, in the county of Meath, were anxious to plant and commence the improvement of that neighbourhood. In their lot

---

* " Book of the Proceedings at the Mallow Commission, 18th July, 1656." Record Tower, Dublin Castle.

† $\frac{A}{12}$, p. 45.

lay the castle and lands late the estate of Lord Dunsany. In 1655 they had sent their agents over to Ireland, and on the 13th July in that year proceeded to the castle of Dunsany, accompanied by the high constable and sheriff of the county, bearing the order of the Council, and demanded entrance and possession of the place for the adventurers. But the Lord of Dunsany's lady denied the possession unless she were forcibly carried thence. There was a pause; probably the sheriff was friendly, and advised a delay—a report to the principals, perhaps, in London or Bristol. Next year they came themselves, Hans Graham and others; and on the 4th July, 1656, the high constable with his force was ordered peremptorily to put the adventurers into the quiet possession of the castle; and Major Stanley, justice of the peace, was ordered to keep the peace there, whilst poor Lady Dunsany should be removed by main force from her home by the high constable and his men.*

But if rank and title and English blood could not save high-born ladies from being thrust from their homes by the adventurers, they were not likely to treat the Irish with much consideration. John Pitts, of Devonshire, adventurer, cast a lot in London, which fell to be satisfied in the county of Tipperary. Mr. Pitts came over in February, 1656, with his certificates; and, having presented them to the registrars of forfeited lands, got an order to the being put into possession of a parcel of land in the barony of Iffa and Offa, in the neighbourhood of Clonmel. Under this order he made a formal entry upon his fine rich lands of Tipperary, and then returned into England for the bringing over his family, for the planting and setting down upon his lot. On the 12th June, 1656, he came over in order to the taking up his abode in Tipperary; but was kept out of his lot by " the insolency of that Irish

----

* $\frac{A}{12}$, p. 124.

rebel [so he reported to the Commissioners for Ireland] that
formerly held the lands," who showed some delay in turning
out with his wife and daughters, to make way for him, Mr.
Pitts and his establishment, from Devonshire. Mr. Pitts had
recourse to the Council Board; and Richard Le Hunte, high
sheriff of Tipperary, was thereupon directed to call all parties
before him, and if it should appear that the said rebel, Philip
O'Neale, one of the sons of Hugh O'Neale,* was a proprietor of
that or other parcel of land, that he should take care to secure the
body of the said Philip, for his not transplanting according to
the rule in the Act of Parliament, in order that such proceedings might be had as should be agreeable to justice, and that
the adventurer be put into possession of the lands according to
law.†

That the law in this case meant the will of the strongest,
and the administering of justice meant the enforcing of that will,
was probably the reflection of Philip O'Neale in his prison
hours, and afterwards as he took his way with his weeping wife
and daughters to Connaught: his love for English law was
probably not much increased. What protection it afforded to
Mr. Pitts is not recorded; his safety (if safety he enjoyed)
must have been secured by some other sanction than respect
for the law and constitution of England.

THE PROCEEDINGS OF THE OFFICERS IN REPLANTING.

It might at first be supposed that the officers would prove
harder masters than the adventurers. But the officers had

---

* It need scarcely be mentioned that this was not the historical Hugh
O'Neil, who warred against Queen Elizabeth. He was simply some pro-
prietor of land dwelling near Clonmel, and his son Philip a rebel like the
Earl of Ormond and Lord Dunsany.

† $\frac{A}{12}$, p. 108.

been in Ireland near six years before the adventurers began
to come over in any numbers to take possession of their lots,
and had by that time contracted ties with the Irish in many
ways. After the surrender of the Irish armies, the gentry, who
had almost all been officers, returned to their former neighbourhood, pending the final resolutions of the Parliament concerning
their fate, and took to the tillage of their ancient inheritances for
their support. Between the English officers who occupied their
mansions as military posts or under *custodiums* (i. e. orders for
temporary possession by the state), and the families of the
former owners, many friendships must have been formed. The
late proprietor and the officer had probably been often engaged in conflict ; but now that the war was over, it would
only the more dispose them to intercourse. Many of the
officers were single men ; they must have invited the family
from the offices to the house, and the officer would scarce
fail to become a conquest to some of his fair captives. Just as
Strongbow and his followers, captivated by Irishwomen, took
wives of the native race, so did the captains and lieutenants
of Cromwell's army intermarry with the Irish, and that too
long before peace had been proclaimed between the armies.
Ireton, Lord Deputy and Commander-in-Chief in 1651, had to
forbid the banns ; his officers and soldiers were taking Irish
wives ; he forbade any such marriage to any of them, under
pain of being cashiered.* In 1652, amongst the first plans for
paying the army their arrears in land, it was suggested there
should be a law that any officers or soldiers marrying Irishwomen
should lose their commands, forfeit their arrears, and be made
incapable to inherit lands in Ireland.† No such provision, however, was introduced into the Act, because it provided against
this danger more effectually by ordering the women to trans-

---

* $\frac{A}{84}$, p. 341 ; and p. 106, n., *ante*. † $\frac{A}{2}$, p. 286.

plant, together with the whole nation, to Connaught. Those in authority, however, ought never to have let the English officers and soldiers come in contact with the Irishwomen, or have ordered another army of young Englishwomen over, if they did not intend this provision to be nugatory.

Planted in a wasted country amongst the former owners and their families, with little to do but to make love, and no lips to make love to but Irish, love or marriage must follow between them as necessarily as a geometrical conclusion follows from the premises. For there were but few who (in the language of a Cromwellian patriot),

> ——" rather than turne
> From English principles, would sooner burne;
> And rather than marrie an Irish wife,
> Would batchellers remain for tearme of life."*

The strongest proof of the frequency of these intermarriages are the various orders putting in force the provisions of Ireton's proclamation over officers still in the service.† Over those who were disbanded and set down on their lots they had no control, and these formed a very large proportion of the army. Thus connected with the Irish, they began to protect

---

* " The Moderate Cavalier ; or, the Soldier's Description of Ireland. A Book fitt for all Protestants Houses in Ireland." 4to. Printed [at Cork, apparently], 1675.

† Commissioners of the Revenue of the precinct of Galway to examine what civil or other officers within that precinct are married to Irish Papists, and to certify their names and employments, respectively, forthwith to the Commissioners of the Commonwealth. *January,* 1654. $\frac{A}{85}$, p. 28.

" Whereas we are informed that William Moreton, now clerk to the Commissioners of Revenue at Wexford hath maried a Papist (contrary to the tenor of the declaration in that behalf), whereby he hath made himself incapable of continuing in his said employment ; and forasmuch as there is recommended to us one Rowland Samuell, that hath a charge of

them—the surest way of learning to like them ; for, as we hate
those we have injured, so we love those we have benefited.
Accordingly it has been remarked of English statesmen who
have been placed over the Irish, that they are ever afterwards
found to be their defenders. The officers, too, seem to have
quickly relished the freedom and easy animation of Irish life
that forms so great a contrast to the character of those countries where the feudal system has prevailed,—a charm which
enchants men with Ireland, converting strangers, as Giraldus

wife and family, that is a person able and faithful to officiate in his stead ;
it is ordered that the said William Moreton be dismissed his said employment from the date hereof, and that the said Rowland Samuell do serve the
said place in his room. *Dublin*, 14*th July*, 1654.

"CHARLES. FLEETWOOD,   MILES CORBET."

$\frac{A}{82}$, p. 499.

About forty years after the Cromwellian Settlement, and just seven
years after the Battle of the Boyne, the following was written : " We cannot so much wonder at this [the quick " degenerating" of the English of
Ireland], when we consider how many there are of the children of Oliver's
soldiers in Ireland who cannot speak one word of English.   And (which is
strange) the same may be said of some of the children of King William's
soldiers who came but t'other day into the country. This misfortune is owing
to the marrying Irishwomen for want of English, who come not over in so
great numbers as are requisite.   'Tis sure that no Englishman in Ireland
knows what his children may be as things are now ; they cannot well live in
the country without growing Irish ; for none take such care as Sir Jerome
Alexander [second Justice of the Common Pleas in Ireland from 1661 to
his death in 1670], who left his estate to his daughter, but made the gift void
if she married any Irishman ;" Sir Jerome including in this term "any lord
of Ireland, any archbishop, bishop, prelate, any baronet, knight, esquire, or
gentleman of an Irish extraction or descent, born and bred in Ireland, or
having his relations and means of subsistence there," and expressly, of
course, any " Papist." " True way to render Ireland Happy and Secure ; or,
a Discourse wherein 'tis shown that 'tis the Interest both of England and
Ireland to encourage Foreign Protestants to plant in Ireland ; in a Letter
to the Hon. Robert Molesworth." 4to. Dublin. Andrew Crook : 1697.

had remarked, to the ways of the Irish almost as soon as they are planted here.*

They also we may be sure, soon learned to prefer the hearty courtesy of their Irish tenants and labourers to the churlish manners of the Anglo-Saxon clowns. But the adventurers differed much from the officers; they were merchants and traders, full of all the ignorant prejudices of the English against the Irish, knowing no tie between man and man but interest or necessity, and unaccustomed to the management of land and tenants, which is a kind of statesmanship.

The officers immediately upon obtaining a lease or *custodium* from the state (pending the preparation of the law that gave them land for their arrears), took the Irish as tenants for want of English; for in a country where lands were to be had for the asking, no one would come from a better country to a worse, to labour as a servant or tenant on another man's lands when he might till or pasture his own. As the impossibility of getting English tenants grew more evident, and the urgent want

---

* It is not a little curious to find Irish harpers in their houses within five years of their planting. In 1663 the army lately planted in Ireland formed a plot to seize the Castle of Dublin, and to overthrow the government, being discontented at the proceedings of the Court of Claims. Amongst the vast mass of intelligence furnished to the Duke of Ormond, then Lord Lieutenant, is the following conversation between Colonel Edward Warren and an Irish harper :—

" Colonel Edward Warren, being at Rathmolyon in the barony of Moyfenragh, in the county of Meath, discoursing with Richard Malone, a blind harper, aged thirty-six years, asked him how many governments he remembered in his tyme? Malone answered that he remembered several, naming the several alterations during these twenty-one years. Whereunto the said Warren answered, that before it were long he might add one more government to the rest." Carte MSS., Bodleian Library, vol. G. G., p. 389. Endorsed in the Duke's hand : " Concerning Colonel Edward Warren." Warren was executed with Major Alexander Jephson, 15th July, 1663. Their dying speeches are given, ibid., vol. vii., Ireland, pp. 248, 249.

of tillage increased, the officers in Limerick, Cork, Kerry, and various counties, got general orders, giving dispensations from the necessity of planting with English tenants, and liberty to take Irish, provided they were not proprietors or swordmen. But the proprietors who had established friendships with their conquerors secretly became tenants under them to parts of their former estates, ensuring thereby the connivance of their new landlords against their transplantation.

On the 1st June, 1655, the Commissioners for the Affairs of Ireland (Fleetwood, Lord Deputy, one of them), being then at Limerick, discovered this fraud, and issued a peremptory order revoking all former dispensations for English proprietors to plant with Irish tenants ; and they enjoined upon the Governor of Limerick and all other officers the removing of the proprietors thus sheltered and their families into Connaught, on or before that day three weeks.* But, happily, all penal laws against a nation are difficult of execution. The officers still connived with many of the poor Irish gentry, and sheltered them, which caused Fleetwood, then Commander of the Parliament forces in Ireland, upon his return to Dublin, and within a fortnight after the prescribed limit for their removal was expired, to thunder forth from Dublin Castle a severe reprimand to all officers thus offending. Their neglect to search for and apprehend the transplantable proprietors was denounced as a great dishonour and breach of discipline of the army ; and their entertaining any of them as tenants was declared a hindrance to the planting of Ireland with English Protestants. " I do therefore [the order continued] hereby order and declare, that if any officer or soldier under my command shall offend by neglect of his duty in searching for and apprehending all such persons as by the declaration of 30th November, 1654, are to trans-

* $\frac{A}{6}$, p. 173.

plant themselves into Connaught ; or by entertaining them as tenants on his lands, or as servants under him, he shall be punished by the articles of war as negligent of his duty, according to the demerit of such his neglect."*

OF THE FIVE COUNTIES.

But, to turn to that district included within the Boyne and the Barrow, on the east coast of Ireland, which was to be a pure English plantation, to counterbalance the Irish one on the west, encircled by the Shannon and the sea, and to become a new English pale—here, if anywhere, would be established that model of English life and manners, the great object of all the inhuman laws enacted for so many ages by the government. But first a word upon the extent of the district. It was contracted to narrower limits. Upon consideration that the land lying north of Dublin, between the Liffey and the Boyne, was the ancient residence of the English,—the best tillage and grazing land in the kingdom, and one level plain from Dublin to Dundalk, without any fastnesses for Irish to harbour in,—it was not thought necessary to keep that part within the scheme, and so much of the original plan was abandoned. It was now confined to that part of the county of Dublin lying south of the River Liffey, with the counties of Wicklow, Wexford, Kildare and Carlow. Thenceforth the territory was known as the Five Counties south of the Liffey and within the Barrow, or (shortly) the Five Counties. On 17th July, 1654, it was ordered that all this territory should be wholly transplanted of Irish Papists by the 1st of May, 1655, on pain of being taken as spies, and proceeded with before a court martial.

* " Book of Printed Declarations of the Commissioners for the Affairs of Ireland" (formerly belonging to General Fleetwood). British Museum, 806 h. 14
—————
24.

The English proprietors, many of them officers who had received lands in the counties of Wicklow and Wexford for their arrears, fearing to be deprived of their tenants and servants, and left without means to till their lands or save their crops, presented petitions to the government against the measure, as the time for carrying out the order approached. Mr. Annesly, who brought up the petitions, was directed to be present at a meeting of the Council on 19th February, 1655, to offer what he conceived to be material in their support.* He urged that the English and Protestant proprietors and planters in the Five Counties were necessitated to employ Irish in their tillage and husbandry, to make some profit of their lands, which had long lain waste by the rebellion. After several debates he obtained an order of reference to Sir Hardress Waller, Colonel Axtell, Colonel Lawrence, and others, to consider what parts should be totally cleared of Irish ; in what parts should be allowed such Irish tenants as, being neither proprietors nor swordmen, might be dispensed from transplantation ; and how the rest might be laid waste ; and how the towns and villages where such Irish should be suffered to inhabit might be disposed of with most security and least offence to the neighbouring English.† The order, however, was not withdrawn ; for on the 21st May, 1655, the clearing was suspended until 1st August following, in order that the proprietors might have time to provide themselves with English and Protestant tenants, and in the meantime might have tenants and servants to reap their harvest. But English tenants and servants were not to be had, and the officers and the other planters were loth to lose their Irish ones : they connived at their stay beyond the 1st of August, and finally got liberty to keep a selection of them approved by Commissioners specially appointed by the State, on some very stringent conditions. The proprietor was to engage that such

* $\frac{A}{5}$, p. 37. 　　　　　　　　　† $\frac{A}{5}$, p. 95.

tenants and servants as he should be permitted to retain should become Protestants (and Protestants of whose real conversion the government could be satisfied) in six months; and as evidence of their candid and genuine compliance with being instructed in the true Protestant religion, they were to come to the meeting-house to hear the Word every Lord's Day, if within four miles; upon every other Lord's Day, if within six miles; if further, once a month. Their children were to learn the catechism in the English tongue, without book, which the minister should teach.* But the government seem to have forgotten the naming of the children with English names, instead of Dermot and Teig; and the chimneys, and the English deportment in houses, lodging, and manners, wherein the English exceeded them.† But probably there was about as much use in the one as the other. The landlords wanted their labour, and not English piety or Anglo-Saxon elegance. For though the letter of one of the officers remains, requesting the prayers of their friends, that now they had come to possess houses they had not built, and vineyards they had not planted, they might not forget the Lord and his goodness to them in the day of their distress‡, one that knew them well a few years later said, he had hunted with them, diced with them, drunk with them, and fought with them, but had never prayed with them ;§ and another, that an Irish Protestant was a man who never went to church, and hated a Papist.

* "Book of Printed Declarations by the Commissioners for the Affairs of Ireland." British Museum, $\frac{806\ h.\ 14}{24}$.

† P. 119, supra.

‡ Letter of Colonel William Allen, Adjutant-General of the Army, and Commissioner of Cromwell's Court of Claims in Ireland, in the year 1653. "History of the King's Inns, by Bartholomew Duhigg," p. 179. 8vo: Dublin.

§ "Civil Wars of Ireland." By W. Cooke Taylor, LL.D., vol. ii., p. 64, n. 3. Two vols. 12mo. London: 1830.

OF THE RE-INHABITING OF THE TOWNS BY NEW ENGLISH, BY
THE ORDERS OF THE GOVERNMENT.

The government, by the Act of 26th September, 1653, for
satisfying the adventurers, the army, and the public creditors,
reserved all the forfeited property in cities and boroughs for
themselves. In the early part of the war, in hopes to induce
merchants and traders, English and foreign (provided they
were Protestant), to whom houses in seaport towns were
more useful than lands, to advance funds, the Parliament of
England offered the principal seaport towns in Ireland for
sale: Limerick, with 12,000 acres contiguous, for £30,000,
and a rent of £625 payable to the State ; Waterford, with
1500 acres contiguous, at the same rate ; Galway, with 10,000
acres, for £7500, and a rent of £520 ; Wexford, with 6000
acres, for £5000, and a rent of £156 4s. 4d.* But this offer,
though tempting, found no bidders : all these towns were still
in the possession of the Irish, and merchants of all others are
least inclined to buy the bear's skin before the bear be dead.
The cities and towns, accordingly, fell into the hands of the
Parliament of England, with all their inhabitants, the population being almost entirely of English descent.†

The Parliament, having them at its mercy, on the surrender
of the Irish forces in 1652, determined to clear all the cities and
towns of Ireland of their ancient population, and to repeople
them from England. Orders had at various times been issued,
between 1652 and 1656, to clear the towns. In 1654, by order

---

* Ordinance of 14th July, 1643. " Scobell's Act and Ordinances,"
p. 47.

† Take Waterford :—" This sea-town hath no naturall Irish in it, nor
would admit any in during these troubles." " News from Dublin," 9th
June, 1647, " Perfect Diurnall of Passages in Parliament," p. 1629.

of the Committee of Transplantation, no Irish or Papists were to be allowed in the city of Kilkenny after the 1st of May, except necessary labourers and artificers, not exceeding forty, and these to be persons not within the rule of transplantation.*

On the 8th of July in the same year the Governor of Clonmel was authorized to grant dispensations to forty-three persons, in a list annexed, or as many of them as he should think fit, being artificers and workmen, to stay for such time as he might judge convenient, the whole time not to exceed the 25th March, 1655.† On 5th June, 1654, the Governor of Dublin was authorized to grant licenses to such inhabitants to continue in the city (notwithstanding the declaration for all Irish to quit) as he should judge convenient, the licenses to contain the name, age, colour of hair, countenance, and stature of every such person; and the license not to exceed twenty days, and the cause of their stay to be inserted in each license.‡ Petitions went up from the old native inhabitants of Limerick,§ from the fishermen of Limerick ;‖ from the Mayor and inhabitants of Cashel,¶ who were all ordered to transplant ; but, notwithstanding these orders, many of them still clung about the towns, sheltered by the English, who found the benefit of their services.

Whilst the gentry were hurried off from their mansions and demesnes, which the officers and soldiers were in haste to enjoy, and were obliged to transplant to such pittance of land as should be assigned to them in Connaught, the population of the towns who lived by trade or labour, such as apothecaries, basketmakers, butchers, bakers, carpenters, chandlers, copoers, harnessmakers, masons, shoemakers, and tailors, con-

* $\frac{A}{85}$, p. 157.   † Ib., p. 479.   ‡ Ib., p. 430.

§ Ib., p. 244.   ‖ Ib., p. 363.   ¶ Ib., p. 247.

tinued to reside upon their holdings and make themselves useful to their new masters. Applications were frequently made
in favour of some who were found particularly useful. Thus
on the 20th March, 1654, on the certificate of Colonel W.
Leigh and other officers within the precinct of Waterford,
Dr. Richard Madden was dispensed with from transplantation
into Connaught ; but as to his desire of residing in Waterford,
it was referred to Colonel Lawrence, the governor there, to
consider if he conceived it fit his request should be granted.*
On the 12th September, 1656, application was made to the
Commissioners for the Affairs of Ireland on behalf of Dr.
Anthony Mulshinogue, whose good affection to the English
by his faithful advice and assistance in his profession was
proved on the trial of the qualifications of the ancient natives
of Cork, by the certificate of Sir W. Fenton and Major-General Jephson, and several other persons of quality in the county
of Cork, who prayed for his dispensation from transplantation,
desiring that his residence among them might be permitted,
being destitute of physicians of his ability. Dr. Mulshinogue
was spared from transplantation, and was permitted to follow
his practice in those parts, but not to dwell in any garrison
there.†

Yet the officers, when they first arrived, vented their
calumnies (according to the national custom) against the
Irish physicians,—writing to their friends in England in
1651, that for want of a sufficient number of English doctors
for the army, they were obliged to put themselves in the hands
of Irish, "which was more [so they maliciously said] than the
adventures in the field."‡ Testimony to the worth and integrity of this profession, however, came at the very same time, as
if to confute these calumnies, from Colonel Hewson, Governor

* $\frac{A}{85}$, p. 184.　　　　　　　† $\frac{A}{12}$, p. 223.

‡ "Whitelock's Memorials," January, 1650-1, p. 436.

of Dublin, one of the most religious men in the army (as appears by the amount of Bible quotations in his letters), and therefore fullest of hatred against the Irish. The last Papist that dared to meet his eye in Dublin was a chirurgeon, a peaceable man.* Similar calumnies followed the poor Irish midwives : imputations against their want of skill are mixed with suggestions of danger to Englishwomen in labour, and children in the birth, " from the evil disposition and disaffection, as might be presumed," of the Irish midwives. And Dr. Petty and others were ordered to consider of the evil, and propose a remedy.† And when an English midwife arrived in Dublin, all officers, civil and military, were ordered for her encouragement to be aiding and assisting her in the performance of her duty.‡

---

*   " 19 *June*, 1651.
" Mr. Winter, a godly man, came with the Commissioners, and they flock to hear him with great desire ; besides, there is in Dublin, since January last, about 750 Papists forsaken their priests and the masse, and attends the public ordinances, I having appointed Mr. Chambers, a minister, to instruct them at his own house once a week. They all repaire to him with much affection, and desireth satisfaction. And though Dublin hath formerly swarmed with Papists, I know none (now) there, but one who is a chirurgeon, and a peaceable man. It is much hoped the glad tidings of salvation will be acceptable in Ireland, and that this savage people may see the salvation of God ; which that the Lord may accomplish shall be the desire of
" Your loving friend,
" JOHN HEWSON."
" Severall Proceedings in Parliament, from 26th of June to 3rd day of July, 1651," p. 1412.

† $\frac{A}{5}$, p. 317.

‡ " *By the Commissioners of Parliament for the Affairs of Ireland.*
" Whereas we are informed by divers persons of repute and godliness, that Mrs. Jane Preswick hath through the blessing of God been very successful within Dublin and parts about, through the carefull and skillfull

But, whilst private interest protected some, it effected the banishment of others. Thus on the 10th October, 1656, on the petition of William Hartley, and others, all Popish shoemakers were to be searched for by the mayor and sheriffs of Dublin, and none allowed to inhabit in Dublin or the suburbs, but to be ordered to withdraw and conform to the proclamation

discharge of her midwife's duty, and instrumental to helpe sundry poore women who needed her helpe, which hathe abounded to the comfourte and preservation of many English women, who (being come into a strange country) had otherwise been destitute of due helpe, and necessitated to expose their lives to the mercy of Irish midwives, ignorant in the profession, and bearing little good will to any of the English nation, which being duly considered, we thought fitt to evidence this our acceptance thereof, and willingness that a person so eminently qualified for publique good and so well reported of for piety and knowledge in her art should receive encouragement and protection suitable to her well deserving ; and knowing that works of this nature contract envy from some and discouragement from others, either for publique prejudice or for lucre's sake ; and taking notice through divers examinations and depositions extant, that this Mrs. Preswick hath of late received divers publique affronts, and that violence hath been used by some evil disposed persons, to her great horror and discouragement, whereby she hath lost opportunities of giving desired helpe to women in labour of child birth, and through those affrights is become timorous, and consequently less able to exercise the midwife's function, much to the dissatisfaction of divers ; these are therefore to signify our abhorrence of such evill, and to declare that in case any person (of what degree or relation so ever) shall contrary to law and good conscience offer any affront or violence for the future to the said Mrs. Preswick, *alias* Beere, in her daily going up and down to perform her publique trust and office of midwife as aforesaid, such persons are to expect a severe proceeding with according to law. And all justices of the peace, officers civil and military, and others concerned, are to take notice, and be ayding and assisting to her in the performance of her duty as aforesaid. *Dublin, 23rd May,* 1655.

" Thomas Herbert, Clerk of the Council."

$\frac{A}{5}$, p. 166.

made in the case.* And on 3rd of April, 1657, on the petition of the Protestant coopers of Dublin, it was referred to the mayor and sheriffs as to the truth of the allegations, and they were to report to the Council Board why the Irish coopers therein mentioned had not been removed, according to the former orders and declarations of their board for that purpose.†

General orders for the arrest of all transplantables untransplanted were also made from time to time, and crowds of inhabitants were arrested,—and others fled, some to creep back again when the storm had blown over. In the year 1656 there was a printed declaration published, ordering all the Irish and Papists to withdraw to a distance of two miles from all walled towns or garrisons before the 26th of May in that year, which seems to have been executed with more rigour than usual ; for on the 2nd of August the Mayor of Dublin was directed to report the progress made, probably because many transplantable persons, owners of houses in the city, still lingering in Dublin, were found on the 18th July to have refused to give up their houses to the new English lessees of the State. On 24th October the Mayor was directed to take effectual means to remove all that might be then dwelling in the city, and all places within the line, within forty-eight hours after publication of the order.‡ And on 19th November a list of the names of all not removing was returned to the Council, with the view of ordering them for trial by court martial.

About this time, probably, the English began to come over in greater numbers, with a view to trade. On 15th May, 1655, it was ordered on the petition of the Protestant inhabitants of the city of Kilkenny, that " for the better encouragement of an English plantation in the city and liberties," all the houses and lands lately belonging to the Irish, and now in the posses-

* $\frac{A}{12}$, p. 227. † Ib., p. 337. ‡ $\frac{A}{5}$, p. 264.

sion of the State, should be thenceforth demised to English and
Protestants, and none others ; that no English merchants or
traders should drive any trade or merchandize in the city or
liberties by Irish agents or servants ; and that all Irish should
quit Kilkenny within twenty days, except such artificers as any
four justices of the peace should for the convenience of that
corporation license to stay for any period not exceeding one
year.* Private interest, however, still interfered with the execution of the law. The officers sheltered merchants who acted as
their factors in trade.   Public creditors who got an order to be
satisfied a large debt by confiscated houses, extending down
whole streets,† were only too willing to keep the poor Irish
occupants ; or they let them secretly to others, as there were
no English ones to be had.

The government, however, though baffled, still kept the
great work in view. On 31st December, 1656, finding that
divers Irish transplantable into Connaught had not only neglected to remove, but had continued to reside, or had intruded
themselves into sundry cities, walled towns, and garrisons
throughout this nation, they issued several special orders, directed to the governors of the several cities, towns, and garrisons in the three provinces, to send up lists of the names of
all such persons, in order probably to the arrest and trial of
some of them at the assizes, where numbers were often found
guilty of not transplanting, and transported to the Barbadoes.

After the summer assizes of 1658, Sir Charles Coote, Lord
President of Connaught, and Colonel Sadleir, Governor of Galway, were directed to treat with Colonel Stubbers or other
merchants, about having a properly victualled ship for eighty
or one hundred prisoners ready to sail with the first fair wind
to the Indian Bridges, the usual landing place in the Barbadoes,

---

* $\frac{A}{6}$, p. 367.   † $\frac{A}{81}$, p. 292.

or other English plantations thereabouts in America.* These were proprietors who had been sentenced to death for not transplanting, but had been pardoned by his Excellency.† At Barbadoes the prisoners were to be delivered to certain merchants (who were to pay the cost of their transportation), all except ten, who were to be consigned to a person to be speedily named.‡ This was a Mr. Edward Smyth, a merchant resident at the Barbadoes. His lot, however, was afterwards increased to twelve, ten men and two women; and upon receiving them at the Indian Bridges, or elsewhere in that island, he was to pay Colonel Stubbers four pounds per man for transportation and victuals.§

The consequence of clearing the towns of their inhabitants was to leave them ruinous: the few English were not enough to occupy them, and the deserted houses fell down, or were pulled down to use the timber for firing. Lord Inchiquin, President of Munster, was charged in 1647 with having given houses in the city of Cork, and farms in the suburbs, to his own menial servants, as barbers, grooms, and others. His answer was, that upon the expelling of the Irish out of Cork, it was to the benefit of the State that he should place any persons in the houses on the sole condition of upholding them, which otherwise, being waste and uninhabited, would have fallen to the ground; and though by this means many of the houses were preserved, yet for want of inhabitants about three thousand good houses in Cork, and as many in Youghal, had been destroyed by the soldiers, finding them empty, and for want of firing in their guards.‖

For such a scene of desolation as the cities and towns of Ireland presented at this period, recourse must be had to the

---

* $\frac{A}{10}$, p. 244. † $\frac{A}{30}$, p. 338. ‡ Ib., ib. § Ib., p. 343.

‖ Pp. 5, 6, " Articles humbly presented to the House of Commons against Murrough O'Brien, Lord Baron of Inchiquin, and Lord President

records of antiquity; and there, in the ruined state of the towns of Sicily, when rescued by Timoleon from the tyranny of the Carthaginians, there is to be found a parallel. Syracuse, when taken, was found comparatively destitute of inhabitants. So little frequented was the market place, that it produced grass enough for the horses to pasture on, and for the grooms to lie in by them as they grazed. The other cities were deserts, full of deer and wild boars; and such as had this use for it hunted them in the suburbs round the walls.* And such was the case in Ireland. On the 20th December, 1652, a public hunt by the assembled inhabitants of the barony of Castleknock was ordered by the State of the numerous wolves lying in the wood of the ward, only six miles north of Dublin.†

But this desolation was, as usual, only preparatory to the improvement of Ireland. On the 4th of March, 1657, the Commissioners for the Affairs of Ireland pressed upon the government in England the improved condition of affairs, and that the towns were now ready for the English, and urging them to make it public in that country that they had been cleared of Irish, as appears by the following letter :—

" *To Secretary Thurloe.*

" *Dublin Castle, 4th March,* 1656–7.

"Right Honourable,—The Council, having lately taken into their most serious consideration what may be most for the security of this country, and the encouragement of the English to come over and plant here, did think fitt that all Popish recusants, as wel proprietors as others, whose habitations is in any port-towns, walled-towns, or garrisons, and who did not

of Munster, subscribed by Lord Broghill and Sir Arthur Loftus; with a clear Answer thereto made. By Richard Gething, Secretary to the Lord President." Small 4to. London : 1647.

* Plutarch, Life of Timoleon.

† $\frac{A}{82}$, p. 492.

before the 15th September, 1643 (being the time mentioned in
the act of 1653 for the encouragement of adventurers and soldiers), and ever since profess the Protestant religion, should
remove themselves and their families out of all such places,
and two miles at the least distant therefrom, before 20th May
next; and being desirous that the English people may take
notice, that by this means there will be both security and conveniency of habitation for such as shall be willing to come over
as planters, they have commanded me to send you the enclosed declaration, and to desire you that you will take some
course, whereby it may be made known unto the people for
their encouragement to come over and plant in this country.

" Your humble servant,
" THOMAS HERBERT, Clerk of the Council."*

But the government took other measures to inhabit the
towns.   By the act for satisfying the adventurers and soldiers,
any of them were at liberty to purchase any of the houses
lately belonging to the Irish in any cities or walled towns, at
the rate of six years' purchase, and to get a free grant of any
vacant places and waste grounds within them on condition of
building.   It was in house property in towns that the Parliament paid off many public debts.   Thus a debt of £3697 10s.
of moneys disbursed by Captain John Arthur was satisfied in
forfeited houses in the town of Wexford. And just as in setting
out lands to the disbanded soldiery the lands were to be set
out without intervals, and without picking and choosing, so
Captain Arthur was bound to make his choice at which end or
other part of the town to begin his satisfaction, taking the
houses and proceeding orderly on both sides of the street, until his due proportion should be reached. Commencing with
the house of Robert Wilkinson, in the parish of Selsker, returned in the Civil Survey as lately belonging to one James

* $\frac{A}{30}$, p. 246.
L

Stafford, an Irish Papist, a list of 200 houses in long enumeration, with the names of their late Irish possessors, and their annual value, was set out to him in satisfaction of his debt.*

The town of Galway, the last fortress of the Irish, surrendered to Ludlow on the 20th March, 1652, on articles securing the inhabitants their residence within the town, and the enjoyment of their houses and estates. The taxation was soon so great, that many of the townspeople quitted their habitations, and removed their cattle, unable to endure it.† Consequently the contribution fell the heavier on the remaining inhabitants. This tax was collected from them every Saturday by sound of trumpet; and if not instantly paid, the soldiery rushed into the house, and seized what they could lay hands on. The sound of this trumpet, every returning Saturday, shook their souls with terror, like the trumpet of the day of judgment.‡ On the 15th March, 1653, the Commissioners for Ireland, remarking upon the disaffection thus exhibited, confiscated the houses of those that had deserted the town. Those that fled were wise in time. On 23rd July, 1655, all the Irish were directed to quit the town by the 1st of November following, the owners of houses, however, to receive compensation at eight years' purchase; in default, the soldiers were to drive them out.§ On 30th October this order was executed. All the inhabitants, except the sick and bedrid, were at once banished, to provide accommodation for such English Protestants whose integrity to the State should entitle them to be trusted in a place of such importance; and Sir Charles Coote on the 7th November received the thanks of the government for clearing the town, with a request that he would remove

---

* $\frac{A}{81}$, p. 292.   † $\frac{A}{82}$, p. 704.

‡ Contemporary account in Hardiman's "History of Galway," p. 134.

§ Ibid., p. 136.

the sick and bedrid as soon as the season might permit, and take care that the houses while empty were not spoiled by the soldiery.* The town was thus made ready for the English.

There was a large debt of £10,000 due to Liverpool for their loss and suffering for the good cause. The eminent deservings and losses of the city of Gloucester also had induced the Parliament to order them £10,000, to be satisfied in forfeited lands in Ireland. The Commissioners of Ireland now offered forfeited houses in Galway, rated at ten years' purchase, to the inhabitants of Liverpool and Gloucester, to satisfy their respective debts, and they were both to arrange about the planting of it with English Protestants. To induce them to accept the proposal, the Commissioners enlarged upon the advantages of Galway. It lay open for trade with Spain, the Straits, the West Indies, and other places; no town or port in the three nations, London excepted, was more considerable. It had many noble uniform buildings of marble, though many of the houses had become ruinous by reason of the war, and the waste done by the impoverished English dwelling there. No Irish were permitted to live in the city, nor within three miles of it. If it were only properly inhabited by English, it might have a more hopeful gain by trade, than when it was in the hands of the Irish that lived there.† There was never a better opportunity of undertaking a plantation and settling manufacturers there than the present, and they suggested that it might become another Derry.

But it is a comparatively easy thing to unsettle a nation or ruin a town, but not so easy to resettle either when ruined.‡ And Galway, once frequented by ships with cargoes

* Hardiman's "History of Galway," p. 137, n.

† $\frac{A}{30}$, p. 255; ibid., p. 315.

‡ "The Great Case of Transplantation Discussed," p. 26. 4to. London: 1655.

of French and Spanish wines, to supply the wassailings of the
O'Neils and O'Donels, the O'Garas and the O'Kanes, her
marble palaces handed over to strangers, and her gallant sons
and dark-eyed daughters banished, remains for 200 years a
ruin ; her splendid port empty, while her " hungry air" in 1862
becomes the mock of the official stranger.

CONCLUSION.

THE THREE BURDENSOME BEASTS.

———◆———

DESOLATION OF IRELAND.

IRELAND, in the language of Scripture, now lay void as a wilderness. Five-sixths of her people had perished. Women and children were found daily perishing in ditches, starved. The bodies of many wandering orphans,* whose fathers had embarked for Spain, and whose mothers had died of famine, were preyed upon by wolves. In the years 1652 and 1653, the plague and famine had swept away whole countries, that a man might travel twenty or thirty miles and not see a living creature. Man, beast, and bird were all dead, or had quit those desolate places. The troopers would tell stories of the place where they saw a smoke, it was so rare to see either smoke by day, or fire or candle by night. If two or three cabins were met with, there were found there none but aged men, with women and children; and they, in the words of the

---

* "Upon serious consideration had of the great multitudes of poore swarming in all parts of this nacion, occasioned by the devastation of the country, and by the habits of licentiousness and idleness which the generality of the people have acquired in the time of this rebellion; insomuch that frequently some are found feeding on carrion and weeds,—some starved in the highways, and many times poor children who lost their parents, or have been deserted by them, are found exposed to, and some of them fed upon, by ravening wolves and other beasts and birds of prey." "Printed Declaration of the Council, 12th of May, 1653." $\frac{A}{84}$, p. 138.

prophet, "become as a bottle in the smoke ; their skins black like an oven, because of the terrible famine." They were seen to pluck stinking carrion out of a ditch, black and rotten; and were said to have even taken corpses out of the grave to eat. A party of horse hunting for Tories on a dark night discovered a light; they thought it was a fire which the Tories usually made in those waste counties to dress their food and warm themselves; drawing near, they found it a ruined cabin, and, besetting it round, some alighted and peeped in at the window. There they saw a great fire of wood, and sitting round about it a company of miserable old women and children, and betwixt them and the fire a dead corpse lay broiling, which as the fire roasted, they cut off collops and ate.* Such was the depopulation of Ireland, that great part of it, it was believed, must lie waste many years,—much of it for many ages.† But these great wastes were haunted by three burdensome beasts, that troubled the comfort of the English. In the first united Parliament of the Three Kingdoms, at Westminster, in 1657, Major Morgan, member for the county of Wicklow, deprecated the taxation proposed for Ireland, by showing that the country was in ruins ; and, besides the cost of rebuilding the churches, courthouses, and markethouses, they were under a very heavy charge for public rewards, paid for the destruction of three beasts. "We have three beasts to destroy (said Major Morgan), that lay burthens upon us. The first is the wolf, on whom we lay five pounds a head if a dog, and ten pounds if a bitch. The second beast is a priest, on whose head we lay ten pounds,

---

* The description of an eye-witness—" The Interest of Ireland in its Trade and Wealth stated," Part 2nd, p. 86. 12mo. Dublin : 1682. By Colonel Richard Lawrence.

† " The Interest of England in the well Planting of Ireland with English," p. 31. Small 4to. Dublin : 1656. By Colonel Richard Lawrence.

—if he be eminent, more. The third beast is a Tory, on whose head, if he be a public Tory, we lay twenty pounds ; and forty shillings on a private Tory. Your army cannot catch them : the Irish bring them in ; brothers and cousins cut one another's throats."*

FIRST BURDENSOME BEAST, THE WOLF.

When the Great Jehovah in his inscrutable wisdom directed the sons of Israel to return to the land of Canaan, where they had been humbly and hospitably entertained for many years, and charged them to kill all the inhabitants without mercy, and divide their ancient inheritances by lot, he warned them against destroying them too suddenly. "Thou shalt smite them, and utterly destroy them ; but thou must not consume them at once, lest the beasts of the field increase upon thee."† In Ireland, from too rapidly exterminating the people, the wolves multiplied in the great scopes of land lying waste and deserted in all parts of the country, and increased till they became so serious a public nuisance, by destroying the sheep and cattle of the English, that various measures had to be taken against them. Ireland had of old been celebrated for her wolf dogs, which, with her equally celebrated hawks, were considered fit presents for kings. The officers quitting for Spain in 1652, proud of their dogs, were found to be taking them with them ; but the tide waiters at the different ports, now crowded with these departing exiles, were directed to seize the dogs, on account of the increasing number of the wolves, and send them to the public huntsman of the precinct.‡

Public hunts were regularly organized, and deer toil brought over from England, and kept in the public store for setting

---

* " Burton's Parliamentary Diary," 10th June, 1657.

† Deuteronomy, chapter 7th.

‡ $\frac{A}{82}$, p. 202.

up while driving the woods with hounds and horn for these destructive beasts of prey.* Irishmen were occasionally employed, and furnished with passes to go with guns to kill them in particular districts, as in the county of Wicklow.† This curse, one of the consequences of the great desolation, the government charged upon the priests. For if the priests had not been in Ireland, the troubles would not have arisen, nor the English have come, nor have made the country almost a ruinous heap, nor would the wolves have so increased.‡ By a similar process of reasoning it is proved that it is the Irish that have caused the ruin, the plundering, and desolation of the country from the days of the first invasion for so many ages.

By a printed declaration of 29th June, 1653, republished on 1st July, 1656, the commanders of the various districts

---

* " Whereas some money hath been issued on account to Colonel Daniel Abbott and others, for providing of toyles for taking of wolves, which have been brought over for publique use; and understanding that part thereof is at present at Greenhill, near Kilcullen; ordered that Captain Tomlins, Comptroller of the Traine, do forthwith take care that the said toyles and other materials thereto belonging be brought from Greenhill, or any other place, and laid into the publique stores, and there kept until further direction shall be given concerning the same. *Dated at Dublin*, 29*th August*, 1659.

$\frac{A}{17}$, p. 45.   " Thoˢ. Herbert, Clerk of the Council."

† " Ordered that Richard Toole, with Morris M‘William his servant, with their two fowling pieces, and half a pound of powder and bullet proportionable, be permitted to pass quietly from Dublin into the counties of Kildare, Wicklow, and Dublin, for the killing of wolves. To continue for the space of two months from the date of the order. *Dublin*, 1 *November*, 1652." $\frac{A}{82}$ p. 454.

‡ " Declaration of the Lord Lieutenant of Ireland (Cromwell) in answer to the Declaration of the Irish Prelates and Clergy in a Conventicle at Clonmacnoise. Printed at Corke, and now reprinted at London. Ed. Griffin, at the Old Bayley, March 21, 1650."

were to appoint days and times for hunting the wolf ; and persons destroying wolves and bringing their heads to the Commissioners of the Revenue of the precinct were to receive for the head of a bitch wolf, £6; of a dog wolf, £5; for the head of every cub that preyed by himself, 40s. ; and for the head of every sucking cub, 10s.* The assessments on several counties to reimburse the treasury for these advances became, as appears from Major Morgan's speech, a serious charge. In corroboration it appears that in March, 1655, there was due from the precinct of Galway £243 5s. 4d. for rewards paid on this account. But the most curious evidence of their numbers is that lands lying only nine miles north of Dublin were leased by the State in the year 1653, under conditions of keeping a hunting establishment with a pack of wolf hounds for killing the wolves, part of the rent to be discounted in wolves' heads, at the rate in the declaration of 29th June, 1653. Under this lease Captain Edward Piers was to have all the State lands in the barony of Dunboyne in the county of Meath, valued at £543 8s. 8d., at a rent greater by £100 a year than they then yielded in rent and contribution, for five years from 1st of May following, on the terms of maintaining at Dublin and Dunboyne three wolf dogs, two English mastiffs, a pack of hounds of sixteen couple (three whereof to hunt the wolf only), a knowing huntsman and two men, and one boy. Captain Piers was to bring to the Commissioners of Revenue at Dublin a stipulated number of wolf heads in the first year, and a diminishing number every year ; but for every wolf head whereby he fell short of the stipulated number £5 was to be defalked from his salary.‡

---

* $\frac{A}{84}$, p. 255. Republished 7th July, 1656.—" Book of Printed Declarations of the Commissioners for the Affairs of Ireland." British Museum.

† $\frac{A}{30}$, p. 30.   ‡ $\frac{A}{82}$, p. 686.

SECOND BURDENSOME BEAST, A PRIEST.

On the 8th December, 1641, both Houses of Parliament in England passed a joint declaration, in anwer to the demand of the Irish for the free exercise of their religion, that they never would give their assent to any toleration of the Popish religion in Ireland, or in any other of His Majesty's dominions.* Cromwell's manifesto, too, cannot be forgotten, that where the Parliament of England had power the mass should not be allowed of.† Pym had previously boasted that they would not leave a priest in Ireland.‡ Such a measure was the proper complement of the Declaration; for what could priests be about but spreading their religion if they staid? For them, during the war, there was no mercy; when any forces surrendered upon terms, priests were always excepted; priests were thenceforth out of protection, to be treated as enemies that had not surrendered. Twenty pounds was offered for their discovery, and to harbour them was death.§ This obliged them to fly,

* 4th " Rushworth's Collections," p. 455.

† " Declaration of the Lord Lieutenant of Ireland, in answer to the Acts of the Popish Clergy at Clonmacnoise. Printed at Cork, and reprinted in London. March, 1650." 4to.

‡ " Nalson's Historical Collections."

§   " INTELLIGENCE FROM IRELAND.

" *Dublin*, 11 *November*, 1650.

" SIR,—You will hear from Waterford more certain news, and from Munster, than from hence. The Toryes are very busye in these parts, and it is probable they will increase; for all the Papists are to be turned out of this city; and for the Jesuits, priests, fryers, munks, and nunnes, 20ˡⁱ will be given to any that can bring certain intelligence where any of them are. And whosoever doth harbour or conceal any one of them is to forfeit life and estate.

" Your humble servant,

" EVANS VAUGHAN."

" Several Proceedings in Parliament from 21st to 28th November, 1650," p. 912.

and to hide until they heard of some body of swordmen being ready to sail for Spain. Thereupon it was their custom to get the officers commanding to apply for leave to transport them together with his troops.* Occasionally they would apply for protection, while waiting to transport themselves of their own accord.†

To be proscribed, however, was nothing but what they were used to from the days of Queen Elizabeth. There were statutes in force making the exercise of their religion death.‡ Yet, as Spenser remarked, they faced all penalties in per-

---

* Colonel Teelin, who has licence to transport one thousand Irish for the service of the King of Spain, to have liberty to take away all priests in Ireland that send in their names. 26 *January*, 1654. $\frac{A}{83}$, p. 85.

Colonel Edmund O'Dwyer being licensed to transport 3500 Irish, for the service of the Prince de Conde; ordered that he be permitted to enlist and transport such priests, Jesuits, and other persons in Popish orders, who are still in Ireland, and shall give in their names. *4th November*, 1653.

$\frac{A}{84}$, p. 112.

† "Whereas John Barnewall, priest, is desirous, in conformity with the late Declaration of the said Commissioners of Parliament, to depart this nation into some of the parts beyond the seas in America; and in order thereto has desired some time to be granted to him for making provision for his voyage; ordered that he be permitted to reside in this nation till the 7th of April next, he acting nothing to the prejudice of the Commonwealth, nor exercising his priestly function in the interim: provided the said John Barnewall do at the expiration of the term abovesaid depart this nation, according to the intention of the said proclamation. *Dated at Dublin, the* 7 *February*, 1653."

$\frac{A}{82}$, p. 585.

"Ordered that the Mayor of Dublin be desired forthwith to press a fitt and able vessel in this port for the transportation of such a number of the Popish clergy as are to go with Lieutenant-General Farrell for Spain. *Dublin*, 19*th February*, 1652-3." $\frac{A}{82}$, p. 639.

‡ Ibid., p. 585.

formance of their duties. They spared not to come out of
Spain, from Rome, and from Rheims, by long toil and dangerous travelling to Ireland, where they knew the peril of death
awaited them, and no reward but to draw the people unto the
Church of Rome.* These laws occasionally slept; but were
revived by proclamation when the fears or anger of the government or people of England were aroused, as by the
Powder Plot, though the Irish had no part in it. And then
the priests had to fly to the woods or mountains, or to disguise
themselves as gentlemen, soldiers, carters, or labourers. They
had no fear that any of the Irish would betray them for all
the large rewards offered. But pregnant women, and others,
hastening on foot out of the Protestant parts towards those
places where priests were known to be harboured, was frequently the cause of their being apprehended. In this way
Connor O'Dovan, Bishop of Down, was tracked, taken, and
committed prisoner to the Castle of Dublin, in 1611.† Bar-
naby Rich at this very time represents a student of Trinity
College as meeting a priest, his acquaintance, in the streets of
Waterford : he asks the priest what means his ruffling suit of
apparel, his gilt rapier, and dagger hanging by his side, more
gentleman-like than priest-like ? He accounts for his disguise
by the proclamation of 1605, forbidding a priest to remain in
the realm.‡

---

* "Spenser's View of Ireland," p. 584.

† P. 340, " Analecta sacra nova et mira de Rebus Catholicorum in
Hiberniâ, pro Fide et Religione Gestis, divisa in tres Partes. . . . Collec-
tore et Relatore T. N.   Philadelpho, Coloniæ, 1617." 12mo, p. 581.
(By Rothe, R. C. Bishop of Ossory.)

‡ P. 1, " A Catholic Conference between Sir Tady Mac Marall, a
Popish Priest of Waterford, and Patrick Plaine, a Young Student of Trinity
College, by Dublin. Wherein is delivered the manner of Execution that
was used upon a Popish Bishop and a Popish Priest that for several matters

There were many parts of the country, however, where it was no easy thing to drag a priest from his hiding place. The government, therefore, on the 6th January, 1653, issued orders that all priests and friars who should be willing to transport themselves, and should give due notice of their intention, should have liberty, within twenty days from the date of the order, to proceed to the waterside without molestation, and sail thence with the first ship; but after that time every priest remaining in Ireland should be arrested and dealt with as the government should think fit; and five pounds would be paid to any person lodging a priest in gaol.* It was under this provision that the heavy burdens complained of by Major Morgan were incurred. The numbers of priests lodged in gaol, and the frequency of the rewards, attest the activity of the pursuit. Such orders as the following are abundant:—10th August, 1657— Five pounds, on the certificate of Major Thomas Stanley, to Thomas Gregson, Evan Powel, and Samuel Ally (being three soldiers of Colonel Abbot's regiment of Dragoons), for the arrest of Donogh Hagerty, a Popish priest, by them taken and now secured in the county gaol of Clonmel;† to be equally distributed between them. To Arthur Spunner, Robert Pierce, and John Bruen, five pounds, to be divided equally among them, for the good service by them performed in apprehending and bringing before the Right Honourable the Lord Chief Justice Pepys, the 21st of January last (1657), one Edmund Duin, a Popish priest.‡ To Lieut. Edward Wood, on the certificate of William St. George, Esq., J.P., of the county of Cavan,

---

of Treason were executed at Dublin the 1st of February last, A. D. 1611. By Barnabie Rych, Gent., Servant to the King's Most Excellent Majesty." 12mo. London: 1612.

* $\frac{A}{82}$, p. 635; $\frac{A}{90}$, p. 396.

† Treasury Orders, p. 9. ‡ Ibid., p. 120.

dated 6th November, 1658, twenty-five pounds, for five priests and friars by him apprehended, viz.: Thomas McKernan, Turlough O'Gowan, Hugh McGeown, Turlough Fitzsymons, who upon examination confessed themselves to be both priests and friars.* 13th April, 1657. To Sergeant Humphry Gibbs, and Corporal Thomas Hill (of Colonel Leigh's company), ten pounds, for apprehending two Popish priests (viz., Maurice Prendergast, and Edmund Fahy), who were secured in the gaol of Waterford ; and being afterward arraigned, were both of them adjudged to be and accordingly were transported into foreign parts.†

In prison their condition may be realized by such orders as the following:—" 4th August, 1654. Ordered, on the petition of Roger Begs, priest, now prisoner in Dublin, setting forth his miserable condition by being nine months in prison, and desiring liberty to go among his friends into the country for some relief; that he be released upon giving sufficient security that within four months he do transport himself to foreign parts, beyond the seas, never to return, and that during that time he do not exercise any part of his priestly functions, nor move from where he shall choose to reside in, above five miles, without permission.‡   Ordered, same date, on the petition of William Shiel, priest, that the said William Shiel being old, lame, and weak, and not able to travel without crutches, he be permitted to reside in Connaught where the Governor of Athlone shall see fitting, provided, however, he do not remove one mile beyond the appointed place without licence, nor use his priestly function."§

At first the place of transportation was Spain. Thus:—" 1st of February, 1653. Ordered that the Governor of Dublin take

---

* Treasury Orders, p. 300.   † Ibid.

‡ $\frac{A}{4}$, p. 364.   § $\frac{A}{82}$, p. 513.

effectual course whereby the priests now in the several prisons of Dublin be forthwith shipped with the party going for Spain ; and that they be delivered to the officers on shipboard for that purpose : care to be taken that under the colour of exportation they be not permitted to go into the country."*

" 29*th May*, 1654. Upon reading the petition of the Popish priests now in the jails of Dublin ; ordered, that the Governor of Dublin take security of such persons as shall undertake the transportation of them, that they shall with the first opportunity be shipped for some parts in amity with the Commonwealth, provided the five pounds for each of the said priests due to the persons that took them, pursuant to the tenor of a declaration dated 6th January, 1653, be first paid or secured."†

But no orders could keep them from ministering to their flocks. Of this there are many instances. 4th January, 1655, there was paid to Captain Thomas Shepherd the sum of five pounds, pursuant to the declaration of 6th May, 1653, for a party of his company that on 27th November last took a priest, with his appurtenances, in the house of one Owen Birne, of Cool-ne-Kishin, near Old Leighlin, in the county of Catherlogh, which said priest, together with Birne, the man of the house, were brought prisoners to Dublin.‡ On the 8th of the same month, Richard and Thomas Tuite, Edmund and George Barnwell, and William Fitzsimons, all names belonging to what would now be called the Catholic gentry, maintained the castle of Baltrasna, in the county of Meath, in defence and rescue of a priest supposed to have repaired thither to say mass. For this they were arrested, and their

* $\frac{A}{82}$, p. 629.   † $\frac{A}{85}$, p. 418.

‡ $\frac{A}{10}$, p. 7.   Orders of Council, Late Auditor-General's Records, Custom House Buildings, vol. x., p. 204.

goods seized. To these Cornet Greatrex and his soldiers laid claim, on the ground of a forcible entry of the said castle, kept against them with arms and ammunition by such who maintained a priest in his idolatrous worship, in opposition to the declaration of the State in that behalf.*

As it had now been manifest from many years' experience, (to use the language of the Commissioners of Parliament for the Affairs of Ireland), that Popish priests held it to be their duty to estrange the minds and affections of the people from the authority and government of the English Commonwealth† (which it must therefore be supposed would otherwise have been so warmly bestowed upon it by the Irish), and that no ordinary admonition could withhold them, though they thus exposed their lives to danger, and threatened to ruin this miserable nation, the Commissioners for Ireland began to transport them to Barbadoes, to prevent them from returning to their own and their people's destruction.‡   On 8th December, 1655, in a letter from the Commissioners to the Governor of Barbadoes, advising him of the approach of a ship with a cargo of proprietors deprived of their lands, and then seized for not transplanting, or banished for having no visible means of support (though the charity of the Irish never yet failed such victims of the law, whether of high or low degree), they add that amongst them were three priests; and the Commis-

---

* $\frac{A}{6}$, p. 45; ibid., p. 65, 67.

† Order of 6 January, 1653. " History of the Rise, Decline, and Fall of the Family of the Geraldines, Earls of Desmond ; to which is added the Persecution of the Irish by the English, by Friar Dominic de Rosario O'Daly, Head of the Dominicans in Portugal. Printed at Lisbon, 1655. Translated by Rev. C. P. Meehan, and republished at Dublin. James Duffy, Wellington-quay. 1847."

‡ $\frac{A}{5}$, p. 67.

sioners particularly desire they may be so employed as they may not return again where that sort of people are able to do much mischief, having so great an influence over the Popish Irish, and of alienating their affections from the present Government.* Yet these penalties did not daunt them, or prevent their recourse to Ireland. In consequence of the great increase of priests towards the close of the year 1655, a general arrest by the justices of peace was ordered, under which, in April, 1656, the prisons in every part of Ireland seem to have been filled to overflowing. On 3rd of May the governors of the respective precincts were ordered to send them with sufficient guards from garrison to garrison to Carrickfergus, to be there put on board such ship as should sail with the first opportunity for the Barbadoes.† One may imagine the pains of this toilsome journey by the petition of one of them. Paul Cashin, an aged priest, apprehended at Maryborough, and sent to Philipstown on the way to Carrickfergus, there fell desperately sick, and, being also extremely aged, was in danger of perishing in restraint for want of friends and means of relief. On 27th of August, 1656, the Commissioners having ascertained the truth of his petition, they ordered him sixpence a day during his sickness ; and (in answer probably to this poor prisoner's prayer to be spared from transportation,) their order directed that it should be continued to him in his travel thence (after his recovery) to Carrickfergus, in order to his transportation to the Barbadoes.‡

At Carrickfergus the horrors of approaching exile seem to have shaken the firmness of some of them; for on 23rd September, 1656, Colonel Cooper, who had the charge of the prison, reporting that several would under their hands renounce the Pope's supremacy, and frequent the Protestant meetings and no other, he was directed to dispense with the transporta-

---

* $\frac{A}{30}$, p. 115.   ‡ $\frac{A}{10}$, p. 102.   † $\frac{A}{12}$, p. 217.

M

tion of such of them as he could satisfy himself would do so without fraud or design, on their obtaining Protestant security for their future good conduct.*

But even in Barbadoes the Government did not seem to consider them secure, or perhaps the cost of transporting them may have been too heavy. For on 27th February, 1657, they referred it to His Excellency to consider where the priests then in prison in Dublin might be most safely disposed of; and thenceforth the Isles of Arran, lying out thirty miles in the Atlantic, opposite the entrance to the Bay of Galway, and the Isle of Innisboffin, off the coast of Connemara, became their prisons.† In these storm-beaten islands they dwelt in colonies during the three concluding years of the Commonwealth rule in Ireland, in cabins built for them by the Government, and maintained on an allowance of sixpence a day.‡ Yet still in all parts of the nation there was found a succession of these intrepid soldiers of religion to perform their sworn duties, meeting the relics of their flocks in old raths, under trees, and in ruined chapels,§ or secretly administering to individuals in the very houses of their oppressors, and in the ranks of their armies.

---

* $\frac{A}{10}$, p. 179.   † Ib., p. 277.

‡ "To Col. Thoˢ. Sadleir, Governor of Galway, the sum of £100 upon account, to be by him issued as he shall conceive meet for the maintenance of such Popish priests as are or shall be confined in the island of Buffin, after the allowance of sixpence *per diem* each. And for building of cabbins, and other necessary accommodation for them. *Dated 3rd July*, 1657." Treasury Warrants, p. 352.

§ In the bishops' returns appended to Primate Boulter's Report to the Lords' Committee on the present state of Popery in Ireland (A.D. 1732), it is common to find masses said in huts, in old forts, and at moveable altars in the fields. An English tourist writes in 1746 :—" The poorer sort of Irish natives are Roman Catholics, who make no scruple [toleration was advancing at this time] to assemble in the open fields. As we passed yesterday in a by-road, we saw a priest under a tree, with a

THIRD BURDENSOME BEAST, A TORY.

The great aim of the transplantation was to give security
to the English planters.* For this forty thousand of the most
active of the old English and Irish nobility and gentry and
commons, who had borne arms in the ten years' war, were
forced to abandon wife and children, home and country, and
embark for Spain ; for this their deserted wives and children, and all the remaining landed proprietors, their families
and next heirs,† their tenants, with their wives, sons, and
daughters, were forced into Connaught. With this view, the
country was laid waste, wherever the crops or cattle were
liable to afford support to the Irish who had not submitted to
be transplanted or transported ; and whole districts were put
out of protection, so that men or women found there were to

large assembly about him, celebrating mass in his proper habit ; and though
at a great distance from him, we heard him distinctly." Chetwood's "Tour
through Ireland," p. 163.   12mo.   London : 1746.

* " To the end, therefore, that the country of Ireland may be planted
and settled with security unto such as shall plant and inhabit the same."
Preamble to the Act for the Satisfaction of Adventurers and Souldiers,
passed 27th September, 1653.

† " And whereas the children, grandchildren, brothers, nephews, uncles,
and next pretended heirs of the persons attainted, do remain in the provinces of Leinster, Ulster, and Munster, having little or no visible estates
or subsistence, but living only and coshering upon the common sort of
people who were tenants to or followers of the respective ancestors of such
persons, waiting an opportunity, as may justly be supposed, to massacre
and destroy the English who as adventurers or souldiers, or their tenants,
are set down to plant upon the several lands and estates of the persons so
attainted," they are to transplant or be transported to the English plantations in America.   Act for Attainder of the Rebels in Ireland, passed
1656.   Scobell's " Acts and Ordinances."

be shot as spies and enemies, unless they had a pass or ticket of protection.*

But the kind of agrarian law under which the lands were distributed amongst the adventurers, and officers and soldiers of the Commonwealth army, took from property its sanctity, which depends much on antiquity of possession, and gave rise to agrarian crimes.†

The old English of Ireland, though themselves descended of an invading nation, whose title to their lands was anciently conquest, must have felt deeply their present wrongs, inflicted by men of their own blood and race. But deeper still must have been the sense of wrong amongst the native Irish. By them "property" (in the hands of the English in Ireland) must have been long looked upon as "plunder." Open force had been the means of extending the possessions of the English in early

* " Their custom was, by their proclamation to draw some imaginary line about a large tract of some depopulated country, inhibiting the natives to come within that circle ; and whensoever some ignorant or unwary person chanced (either for taking a short way to the place he intended to go to, or in pursuit of his cattle strayed or stolen) to pass those enchanted limits, he was knocked on the head by any officer or souldier that first met him, as Colonel Axtell did, having killed six women on the high road betwixt Athy and Kilkenny." "A Continuation of the Brief Narrative, and the Sufferings of the Irish under Cromwell." Small 4to. Printed in the year 1660. [By Father Peter Walsh, Author of the " Loyal Remonstrance."] Amongst the MSS. in the Library of Trinity College, Dublin, are notes taken on the trial of Colonel Axtell by court martial for this act. F. 3. 18.

† " The proclamation of Lord Canning for the confiscation of Oude was supposed to be a great stroke of policy. But no Mahometan conqueror, no British conqueror, had ever attempted to perform the dangerous operation which it projected. The design of confiscation was the most dangerous design which a conqueror could entertain ; and a shrewd observer had said, that it was never safe to confiscate a man's property unless you were prepared also to take his life." Sir James Graham, Bart., Parliamentary debate, May 21, 1858. He might have added, " Or to transplant him, or make him emigrate."

times,—force and fraud combined, in the century just elapsed. The English looked upon force and law (the will of the stranger) as the proper title to land and empire ; the Irish, to an enjoyment of it as the right of all the families of the country, as sons and descendants of the earliest occupants of the soil. The old English of Ireland had one reflection that moderated their bitter thoughts. Their turn was come. " What you do to another, another will do to you." And they still hated the Irish. The Irish, the most forgiving race under the sun, respected the old English, who had long suffered with them for their faith, but hated the English of the new plantations, who drove them from their lands, insulted their religion and country, and now tyrannized over the old English, whom the Irish had learned to respect and pity.

What, if Lord Roche of Fermoy had had a son, would have been his feelings at seeing his father and his sisters reduced to beggary, and forced to walk on foot to Connaught,* to end their days there in some cabin, while their ancient inheritance was divided between the cornet of some English regiment of horse and his troop ? What the feelings of John, the brother of Christian, Anstace, and Kate Roche, daughters of Jordan Roche of Limerick, to behold his sisters reduced from the affluence of a landed estate of £2000 a year to nothing to live on but what they could earn by their needles, and by washing and wringing—their father's lands in the Liberties of Limerick being divided amongst the gentlemen of Cromwell's Life Guard ?†

---

* See above, p. 74.

† " *To the Right Honourable yᵉ Commissioners of yᵉ Commonwealth of England for yᵉ Affairs of Ireland,*

" The humble peticōn of Christian Roche, Anstace Roche, Cate Roche, and John Roche, yᵉ children of Alderman Jordan Roche, deceased, sheweth yᵗ Alderman Jordan Roche decᵈ. dyed seized of a vast reall estate to yᵉ value of £2000 a year, and likewise of a considerable personal estate,

Or of John Luttrell, transplanted with his wife and children from the ancient family estate of Luttrellstown, near Dublin, worth £2500 a year in 1640,* where for four hundred years his ancestors had fixed their affections and their name, into the barony of Clare in Galway, and there to hear of his four sisters begging the Council Board for some relief, and given ten pounds a piece, and bidden for the future not to expect any further gratuity or allowance from that Board ?†

But how must the feelings of national hatred have been heightened, by seeing everywhere crowds of such unfortunates, their brothers, cousins, kinsmen, and by beholding the whole country given up a prey to hungry insolent soldiers and adventurers from England, mocking their wrongs, and triumphing in their own irresistible power !

Inspired by such sights, bands of desperate men formed themselves into bodies, under the leadership of some dispossessed gentleman, who had retired into the wilds when the rest of the army he belonged to laid down arms, or had "run out" again after submitting, and resumed them rather than transplant to Connaught.‡ He soon found associates, for the coun-

---

all which devolved and came to yᵉ publique : That your poore petitioners are in a sadd and deplorable condition for want of sustenance or mayntenance, and have nothing to live on but what they erne by their needles and by washing and wringinge."

They pray a competent provision out of their father's estate,—" an acte very charitable and suitable to yᵉ civility of yᵉ English government."

" Petition referred to the Commissioners of Limerick Precinct, to enquire and report in what qualification of the Act of Settlement this falls. *Dated April*, 1654." Records of the late Auditor-General's Office.

* $\frac{A}{12}$, p. 147.

† Treasury Warrants, p. 194; 6th April, 1657.

‡ "*27th August*, 1656. Notwithstanding the several orders wherein several days and times have been prefixed by which Papist proprietors of

try was full of swordmen, though 40,000 took conditions from the King of Spain. Others came back from Spain.* These were the Tories. The great regions left waste and desolate by the wars and transplantation gave them scopes for harbouring in ; and the inadequate numbers of the forces of the Commonwealth to fully control so extensive a country as Ireland left them at liberty to plan their surprises.

These outlaws were so daring and ¦desperate, that they attacked the new English tenants and purchasers within hail of the garrisons. In the month of March, 1655, a sad case occurred in the neighbourhood of the garrison of Timolin, in the county of Kildare : John Symonds and his family, who had lately come out of England with all their substance to plant in Ireland, by advice of friends settled at Kilnemarne, and had engaged twenty more families very suddenly to come and plant there, being encouraged by hopes of receiving protection from the garrison of Timolin, adjacent thereto ; soon after his arrival, he and his two sons, being about repairing of houses upon the premises, in the daytime (the deserted abodes, of course, of Irish gentlemen and their families, lately transplanted to Connaught), were waylaid and set upon by three Irishmen, being bloodthirsty and wicked persons, who fell upon him and his two sons, and cruelly murdered one of

---

lands were to remove themselves, as also their wives and children, to Connaught, whereto some have yielded obedience, and many others in several parts do refuse, and from thence have taken occasion to run out again into the boggs, woods, and other the fastnesses and desert places of the land, to commit murders and robberies upon the well affected." $\frac{A}{10}$, p. 171.

* " 24th January, 1656. That Irish Papists who had been licensed to depart this nation, and of late years have been transplanted into Spain, Flanders, and other foreign parts, have nevertheless secretly returned into Ireland, occasioning the increase of Tories and other lawless persons." $\frac{A}{5}$, p. 349.

them, and dangerously wounded the other. Both these sons had faithfully served the Commonwealth in England as soldiers since the beginning of the war, and the one murdered left behind him a poor distressed widow, an honest sober person, in an extraordinary poor condition, with very small children, for whom a charitable subscription was encouraged in the parish churches, by order of the Commissioners for the Affairs of Ireland.* Rigorous orders were immediately issued and enforced for transplanting all the Irish inhabitants of the town and neighbourhood of Timolin to Connaught, as a consequence of this murder.†

Six months afterwards, notwithstanding this signal chastisement, another murder took place, in the townland of Lackagh, in the same county. On 22nd October, 1655, Dennis Brennan, and Murtagh Turner, Protestants (persons lately in the service of the State and in the pay of the army), were barbarously murdered. All the Irish in the townland of Lackagh were seized ;‡ four of them by sentence of court martial were hanged for the murder, or for not preventing it ; and all the rest, thirty-seven in number, including two priests, were on the 27th November delivered to the captain of the "Wexford" frigate, to take to Waterford, there to be handed over to Mr. Norton, a Bristol merchant, to be sold as bond slaves to the sugar planters at the Barbadoes.§ Among these were Mrs. Margery Fitzgerald, of the age of fourscore years, and her husband, Mr. Henry Fitzgerald of Lackagh ; although (as it afterwards appeared) the Tories had by their frequent robberies much infested that gentleman and his tenants—a discovery that seems to have been made only after the King's restoration.‖

* $\frac{A}{6}$, p. 148.   † $\frac{A}{30}$, p. 42.   ‡ $\frac{A}{5}$, p. 260.   § Ib., p. 303.

‖ Pp. 7, 8, " Continuation of the Brief Narrative; and the Sufferings of Ireland under Cromwell." London : 1660.

But the main objects of the Tories were the cows and cattle of the Englishmen, to support them in their fastnesses. If a band of these outlaws came down from the hills, and drove off the horses, cows, and cattle of the stranger to their retreats where none dare follow them, satisfaction was to be made by the kindred of the Tories living under protection. These levies were called Kincogues,* or kindred moneys. But as it was often difficult to find out who the Tories were, and as it happened that when found out the kindred were too poor to make satisfaction, all the Irish of a barony where any murder, robbery, or other outrage was committed upon an Englishman, whether they were of kin or not of kin to the Tories, were to contribute equally with the kindred ; and not they only, but any Irish of any barony through which the Tories had passed or repassed on their way to or from the outrage, unless they had resisted them, or followed them with hue and cry, or given immediate notice to the nearest garrison.† These latter levies were called "prey moneys."

* "Kincogues," from "*cin*" (crime, debt, and liability), and "*comrogus*" (kindred, relations). By the Brehon law, unless the tribe outlawed an offender, one of their kindred, they were collectively liable for his crime. (The statement of the late John O'Donovan, LL. D.) Among the statutes objected to by Spenser was the 11th Edwd. 4, c. 4, whereby the custom of Kin-cogish (as he calls it) was made law. By that statute every head of every sept, and every head of every kindred, should be bound to bring forth every one of that sept or kindred charged with any crime. Spenser's "View of Ireland," p. 451.

† Proclamation of Colonel Jones, Governor of Dublin, for robberies committed by the Tories . . . within the English quarters, to be answered by the kindred of such as commit them. Dated 2nd November, 1647.

Proclamation of Colonel Hewson, Governor of Dublin, making the inhabitants, whether of kin or not of kin, and the inhabitants of the baronies through which the Tories passed, responsible. 25th February, 1650. MSS. Trin. Coll. Dub., F. 3, 18.

Instructions for putting the above in execution by the Commissioners for the Administration of Justice, and Commissioners of Revenue. $\frac{A}{82}$, p. 72.

But even in these measures of war which the newness of their conquest was their excuse for, the purpose was compensation, not vengeance, and they observed a kind of justice even in their injustice; for the inhabitants were allowed to appoint an advocate or agent, to appear and plead any just defence for them before the court martial. The whole system was the jurisprudence of conquerors. The conquerors, though possessed of all the power, and bound to provide for the security of the Irish no less than the English within their protection, laid the whole burden on the native race, and let all the English go free.

The effect of these laws was to increase the numbers of Tories. For though the Irish were bound to discover and resist the Tories under pain of death, they were not allowed arms to enable them to resist, nor could the English protect them, so that in either way they suffered death, either by the English or the Irish.[*]

The grinding taxation, the consequence of this law, upon the families under protection, together with the chance of being slain by the Tories if they resisted them, or by the English if they did not, drove numbers out of protection to take part with the Tories.[†]   At length it was found that the Irish inhabitants became so impoverished by paying for preys and losses done by their kindred in arms, that the contribution was in many places destroyed.   This, and not the injustice of this monstrous law, which punished the innocent and the guilty together, and oftenest none but the innocent, and that too for the crimes of the Government, which made men desperate by wrongs, caused it to be repealed or limited.[‡]   But it was re-enacted in penal laws after the Revolution, and was only abo-

---

[*] "The Great Case of Transplantation in Ireland Discussed," p. 28.

[†] Ibid.   [‡] $\frac{A}{84}$, p. 752.

lished about the time of the commencement of the American war, to be re-enacted in a new form in the Crime and Outrage Act of 1853.

The penalties against the Tories themselves were to allow them no quarter when caught, and to set a price upon their heads.* The ordinary price for the head of a Tory was 40s. ; but for leaders of Tories, or distinguished men, it varied from £5 to £30.

In a proclamation of 3rd October, 1655, there was offered to any that should bring in the persons hereafter named, or their heads, to the governors of any of the counties where the said Tories should be taken, the following sums, viz. :—for Donnogh O'Derrick, commonly called "Blind Donnogh," the sum of £30 ; for Dermot Ryan, the sum of £20 ; for James Leigh, the sum of £5 ; for Laughlin Kelly, the sum of £5 ; or for any other Tory, thief, or robber that should be hereafter taken by any countryman, and brought dead or alive to any of the chief governors of any county or precinct, 40s. ; and if taken and brought by any soldier, 20s.† Under a similar proclamation, there appears paid, by a Treasury Warrant, to Captain Adam Loftus, on the 12th May, 1657, the sum of £20, for taking Daniel Kennedy, an Irish Tory,—his head being sent to Catherlough, to set up on the castle walls, to the terror of other malefactors.‡ And in April of the same year, to Lieutenant Francis Rowlestone, the sum of £6 13s. 4d., the same being in consideration of the good services by him performed in December last, in killing two Tories, viz. : Henry Archer, formerly a lieutenant in the Irish army, then a chief leading Tory ; and William Shaffe, broguemaker, then under his command ; whose heads were brought to the town of Kilkenny, unto Major

* $\frac{A}{26}$, p. 27. † $\frac{A}{5}$, p. 241.

‡ Treasury Warrants, p. 240.

Redmond there, as appears by his certificate, dated 9th of April, inst.*

But there were other modes of dealing for the suppression of Tories. The English, whether as soldiers or planters, were inadequate to cope with these wild and lightfooted outlaws, who knew each togher (or footpath) through the quaking bogs, and every pass among the hills and woods. They were therefore under the necessity of calling in the aid of some of the countrymen of the Tories, who were equally skilled in the knowledge ef the country, and were familiar with the habits and secrets of these outlaws. They either dealt with some Irish gentleman for the guarding of some district, and pursuing of the Tories within it, on the terms of his being spared from transplantation for his services; or they found means to agree with any Tory not guilty of any actual murder, to kill by treachery any two of his comrades as the price of his own pardon.

Life at this time had become of little value; there was no public cause to maintain; the armies had surrendered. Men were like wolves lying out in the woods and bogs of this desolated island, their friends and families dead or banished. It is no wonder that, between threats and rewards, men should be tempted to betray and murder one another. Major Morgan's boast, however, that brothers and cousins cut one another's throats, is only one of those calumnies of which this ill-fated country has for ages been the victim. On the contrary, their inviolable fidelity throughout all ages to those that defend their cause has oftener afforded matter of reproach to their revilers.

Arms and ammunition were occasionally intrusted to Irish-

* Treasury Warrants, p. 224.

men to hunt and kill Tories,* just as they were employed occasionally to kill wolves. It is possible they may have sometimes killed others than Tories, but they could scarce go wrong in killing an Irishman.

As an instance of a gentleman obtaining his dispensation from transplantation to Connaught by engaging to keep a district against Tories, there is the case of Major Charles Kavanagh, one of the McMurrough family,—a family which long retained great possessions in the county of Carlow, in consideration of their being of those Irishmen that first brought Englishmen into Ireland,† but which they were now to forfeit. To reduce the Tories of the county of Carlow, the Government in the year 1656 came to an agreement with Major Charles Kavanagh to dispense with his transplantation to Connaught, and with that of thirteen Irishmen, of his own selection as his assistants, for the purpose of prosecuting and destroying Tories in that county, and in the adjoining counties of Wicklow, Wexford, and Kilkenny.‡ Major Kavanagh selected the stump of the old castle of Archagh (otherwise Agha), a waste place lying in the barony of Idrone, as the post for him and his band to inhabit, as being situate in the centre of the three counties of Wexford, Carlow, and Kilkenny ; and a lease was made of it by the State to Major Boulton (who seems to have been the medium of communication with Major Kavanagh), in order that he might assign it over to him for his residence

---

* " 14th October, 1659. Order empowering Colonel Henry Prettie to employ twenty Irish with guns and ammunition into the counties of Carlow and Kilkenny, for three months, to find and destroy the Tories in the said counties. $\frac{A}{17}$, p. 74.

Similar order for Lieutenant-Colonel Nelson in King's and Queen's Counties. Ib., ib.

† " State Papers of Henry VIII." (Ireland). Vol. ii., p. 571.

‡ $\frac{A}{12}$, p. 54.

and habitation.* This place lay four miles due east of Leigh-lin Bridge, and in some degree may have watched the approaches against the advance of any Tories from the Wicklow hills. Major Kavanagh was no Tory, but, having laid down arms, was quietly awaiting his transplantation.

But others, wilder and more desperate, "ran out :" amongst these was Gerald Kinsellagh, who appears in the survey of 1653 as forfeiting a large estate of 1420 acres, consisting of the lands of Kynogh, Kiledmond, Kilcoursey, and other lands in the county of Carlow. He became "a leading Tory," and with him the Government entered into terms for pursuing and destroying his fellow-Tories. The same Lieutenant Francis Rowlestone who was paid for the heads of two Tories killed by him, and who probably, in his frequent conflicts with them, had earned their respect and confidence (for the brave respect the brave), had a warrant from the State in 1659 to treat with this Gerald (or Garrett) Kinsellagh and two other Tories of the neighbourhood, "then abroad and on their keeping," and to promise them their security and liberty on condition of their hunting down other Tories who were abroad disturbing the public peace.†

But national hatred, as has been remarked, is the firmest bond of association and secrecy.‡ The Irish, who had seen their country desolated, and their ancient gentry driven off to Connaught to make way for strangers of a new creed and new manners, would give no assistance to the law. Those that would not themselves deal a blow against the new proprietors and their tenants, yet saw them with silent satisfaction terri-

---

* $\frac{A}{12}$, p. 55.   † $\frac{A}{17}$, p. 57.

‡ " The conspiracy [of the Greeks against the Latins, then in possession of Constantinople, A. D. 1205] was propagated by national hatred, the firmest bond of association and secrecy." Gibbon's " Decline and Fall of the Roman Empire," vol. x., ch. 61.

fied and bewildered at the sudden and secret attacks upon their neighbours. They gave private intelligence to the Tories to aid them to escape, or were simply passive ; and no penalties could force them to betray those whom they looked on as avengers of the wrongs of gentry and people alike. There remains a very graphic account of the constant danger in which the new settlers lived. So sudden and so frequent were the murders of the English planters, that it was stated that no person was able to assure himself of one night's safety, except such as lived in strong castles, and these well guarded, and they (adds the reporter) very liable to surprise too. And after referring to the instances of the several horrid murders lately committed in the counties of Wexford, Kildare, and Carlow, and elsewhere, he continues,—" Of which number one gentleman living in a strong castle, and sitting by the fire with his wife and family in the evening, heard some persons, whose voice he knew, call him by name to come to his gate to speak with him; the poor gentleman, supposing no danger in a country where no enemy was heard of, presently went to the door, and was there murthered, where he was taken up dead off the place. Another of them, walking in his grounds in the day time, about his business, was there found murthered, and to this day it could never be learned who committed either of them. And when these horrid murthers are done, the poor English that doe escape know not what means to use. As for his Irish neighbours, it's like he may not have one near him that can speak English ; and if he have an hue and cry (or hullaloo as they call it) to be set up, they will be sure to send it the wrong way, or at least deferr it until the offender be far enough out of reach ; and not unlike but the persons that seem busiest in the pursuit may be them that did the mischief."*

* " England's Great Interest in the Well Planting of Ireland with English People," p. 7. By Colonel Richard Lawrence. 4to. Dublin : 1656.

But a more effective way of suppressing Tories seems to have been to induce them, as already mentioned, to betray or murder one another,—a measure continued after the Restoration, during the absence of Parliaments, by Acts and Orders of State, and re-enacted by the first Parliament summoned after the Revolution, when in that and the following reigns almost every provision of the rule of the Parliament of England in Ireland was re-enacted by the Parliaments of Ireland, composed of the soldiers and adventurers of Cromwell's day, or new English and Scotch capitalists. In 1695 any Tory killing two other Tories proclaimed and on their keeping was entitled to pardon,*—a measure which put such distrust and alarm among their bands on finding one of their number so killed, that it became difficult to kill a second. Therefore, in 1718, it was declared sufficient qualification for pardon for a Tory to kill one of his fellow-Tories.† This law was continued in 1755 for twenty-one years, and only expired in 1776. Tory hunting and Tory murdering thus became common pursuits. No wonder, therefore, after so lengthened an existence, to find traces of the Tories in our household words. Few, however, are now aware that the well-known Irish nursery rhymes have so truly historical a foundation :—

" Ho! brother Teig, what is your story ?"
"I went to the wood and shot a Tory :"
" I went to the wood, and shot another;"
" Was it the same, or was it his brother?"

" I hunted him in, and I hunted him out,
    Three times through the bog, and about and about ;
    Till out of a bush I spied his head,
    So I levelled my gun, and shot him dead."‡

* 7 Will. 3 (Irish), c. 21.   † 9 Will. 3 (Irish), c. 9.
    ‡ Crofton Croker's " Sketches in the South of Ireland," p. 54. 4to. London : 1824.

At the Restoration, some of the gentry of old English descent, who had good interest at court, got back their estates. Others, of equal loyalty, obtained decrees of the Court of Claims to have back their ancient inheritances ; but as the adventurers and soldiers in possession were not to be removed without being first reprised, that is, provided with other lands of equal value, which the Commissioners were in no hurry to do, even if there had been lands enough to supply them, the dispossessed owners, especially the ancient Irish, were never restored, but wandered many of them about their ancient inheritances, living upon the bounty of their former tenants, or joined some band of Tories.* The poor Irish peasantry, with a generosity characteristic of their race and country, never refused them hospitality, but maintained them as gentlemen, allowing them to cosher upon them, as the Irish called the giving their lord a certain number of days' board and lodging. Archbishop King complains of the numbers thus supported, or by stealing and Torying. These pretended gentlemen, together with the numerous coshering Popish clergy that lived much after the same manner, were the two greatest grievances of the

---

* In a manuscript account of the state of the county of Kildare, A. D. 1684, is the following :—" In the open or plain countreys the peasants are content to live on their labour ; the woods, boggs, and fastnesses fostering and sheltering the robbers, Tories, and woodkernes, who are usually the offspring of gentlemen that have either misspent or forfeited their estates, who, though having no subsistence, yet contemn trade as being too mean and base for a gentleman reduced never so low, being *nusled* up by their priests and followers in an opinion that they may yet recover their lands to live on in their predecessors' splendour : yet the robberies, and burglaries, and other crimes usually committed in this kingdom, are not so numerous, but there are commonly sentenced to die in a monthly sessions att the Old Bailey more than in half a year's circuit in Ireland." Folio volume, endorsed " Detached Papers relating to the Natural History of Ireland." Press I., tab. i., vol. ii., p. 296, MSS. Trin. Coll. Dublin.

kingdom in this Archbishop's view, and more especially hindered its settlement and happiness.* The Archbishop and the possessors of the lands of these gentlemen complained much of their pride and idleness in not becoming their labourers. But the sense of injustice, and their use of arms, were against it. Their sons or nephews, brought up in poverty, and matched with peasant girls, will become the tenants of the English officers and soldiers; and, thence reduced to labourers, will be found the turf-cutters and potato-diggers of the next generation,—yet keeping, even in the low social rank they have fallen to, their ancient spirit and courage, and their intolerance of injury and insult. These dispossessed proprietors were the pretended Irish gentlemen that would not work, but wandered about demanding victuals, and coshering from house to house among their fosterers, followers, and others, described in the Act of 1707 " for the more effectual Suppressing of Tories," and who were (on presentment of any grand jury of the counties they frequented) to be seized and sent on board the Queen's fleet, or to some of the plantations in America.† The grandfathers of men now alive have seen the heir or representative of the old forfeiting proprietor of 1688 wandering about with his ancient title-deeds tied up in an old handkerchief,—these and the respect paid him by the peasantry being the only signs left to show the world he was a gentleman.

The Tories, however, notwithstanding all these provisions and precautions, continued to infest the new Scotch and English settlers during the whole of the Commonwealth period; they survived the Restoration; they received new accessions

---

* King's " State of the Protestants of Ireland under the Government of King James the Second," p. 87. 8vo. Dublin: 1730. See also " A Tour through Ireland." Dublin, 1748, p. 147.

† 6 Ann (Irish), c. 2.

by the war of the Revolution and the forfeitures of 1688 ; and they can be traced through the Statute Book to the reign of George III., during the whole of which period there were rewards set upon their heads ; and all their murders, maimings, and dismemberments, their robberies and spoils, were satisfied by levies on the ancient native inhabitants of the different districts.

After the Restoration, Colonel Poer in Munster, and Colonel Coughlan in Leinster, dispossessed of their hereditary properties, headed bands that gave infinite trouble. Redmond O'Hanlon, a dispossessed proprietor of Ulster, during the whole of the Duke of Ormond's and the Earl of Essex's Lord Lieutenancies, kept the counties of Tyrone and Armagh in terror, the farmers paying him regular contribution to be protected from pillage by other Tories. His history is characteristic of Ireland. The O'Hanlons and Magennises were the only friends of Queen Elizabeth in Ulster.* O'Hanlon was the chief of Orier in the county of Armagh, and claimed to be hereditary royal standard-bearer north of the Boyne. In 1595, in the war against Hugh O'Neil, in the march of the Deputy Sir W. Russel from Dundalk, the royal standard was borne the first day by O'Mulloy, and the next by O'Hanlon.† On the 17th November, 1600, he was slain at the pass of Carlingford, fighting on the English side, under the orders of Lord Mountjoy. For his loyalty and his services in this war against the Earl of Tyrone, King James I. bestowed upon his family seven townlands. These were, of course, taken from them by the orders of the English Parliament in 1653 ; and they were transplanted to Connaught, where the mother re-

* " Brief Declaration of the Government of Ireland, discovering the Discontents of the Irishry." By Captain Thomas Lee, A. D. 1594. " Desiderata Curiosa Hibernica," vol. i., p. 140.

† Sir Richard Cox's " Hibernia Anglicana," p. 407.

ceived some pittance of land for her support. At the Restoration Hugh O'Hanlon petitioned to have their lands restored,*
but in vain. Redmond O'Hanlon, who was probably a brother
of Hugh's, took to the hills. He principally haunted the Fews
Mountains, near Dundalk. He thought more than once of
withdrawing to France, where he was known to fame as Count
O'Hanlon, but was still kept back by rumours of a war, and
hopes of a French invasion.† Various attempts were made to
surprise him, and large bribes offered for his capture. But
all was of no avail. At last, the Duke of Ormond drawing secret instructions for two gentlemen with his own hand
(else this outlaw would be sure to get intelligence of the
plan formed against him), he was shot through the heart, while
he lay asleep, on the 25th of April, 1681; nor would the
Duke ever disclose by whose information he was enabled to
accomplish his destruction.‡   "Thus fell this Irish Scander-

---

* Petition of Hugh O'Hanlon, A. D. 1663, claiming as an "innocent
Papist," MS., folio (series of twelve volumes relating to Acts of Settlement
and Explanation,) vol. ii., B., p. 335.   Record Tower, Dublin Castle.

† " Present State of Ireland, but more particularly of Ulster," by Edmund Murphy, Secular Priest, and titular Chanter of Armagh, and one of
the first discoverers of the Irish Plot.   Folio.   London : 1681.

‡ Betrayed, perhaps, by his mistress, as Daniel O'Keeffe, a similar outlaw in the county of Cork, by Mary O'Kelly, whose treachery, however,
O'Keeffe avenged by plunging his dagger into her heart before taking to
flight, as in the following lines:—

> " No more shall mine ear drink
>   Thy melody swelling ;
>   or thy beaming eye brighten
>   The outlaw's dark dwelling ;
> Or thy soft heaving bosom
>   My destiny hallow,
> When thy arms twine around me,
>   Young Mauriade ny Kallagh.

beg," says Sir Francis Brewster, who had the relation of his death from the mouth of one of the gentlemen employed by the Duke, " who did things, considering his means, more to be admired than Scanderbeg himself."*

After the war of 1688, the Tories received fresh accessions, and, a great part of the kingdom being left waste and desolate, they betook themselves to these wilds, and greatly discouraged the replanting of the kingdom by their frequent murders of the new Scotch and English planters ; the Irish "choosing rather" (so runs the language of the Act) " to suffer strangers to be robbed and despoiled, than to apprehend or convict the offenders." In order, therefore, for the better encouragement of strangers to plant and inhabit the kingdom, any persons presented as Tories by the gentlemen of a county, and proclaimed as such by the Lord Lieutenant, might be shot as outlaws and traitors ; and any persons harbouring them were to be guilty of high treason.† Rewards were offered for the taking or killing of them ; and the inhabitants of the barony, of the ancient native race, were to make satisfaction for all

> " The moss couch I brought thee
> To-day from the mountain
> Has drunk the last drop
> Of thy young heart's red fountain
> For this good *skeane* beside me
> Struck deep, and rung hollow
> In thy bosom of treason,
> Young Mauriade ny Kallagh."

" Dublin Penny Journal," vol iv., No. 165 (August 29, 1835), p. 71.

Mauriade ny Kallagh is the Irish for Mary O'Kelly. " O" is " son of." Women used the prefix " ny," instead—as, " Honora ny Brien," " Katherine ny Donohue," "Sarah ny Donnel."

* Carte's " Life of James Duke of Ormond," vol. ii., p. 512.

† 9 Will. 3 (Irish), c. 9.

robberies and spoils.* If persons were maimed or dismembered by Tories, they were to be compensated by ten pounds ; and the families of persons murdered were to receive thirty pounds.†

As their leaders of gentle birth or blood died off, or were killed, they were not replaced ; but the ranks of these outlaws were still recruited from the lower and the poorer class.

In this state they presented, at the end of thirty years, to the historian of the war of the Revolution,‡ under the name of Rapparees, an aspect so fierce, so wan, and wild, that his commentator is appalled at the spectacle. He starts at the " hideous ferocity" of these Irish, " remaining untameable after so many ages, since British civilization was first planted in Ireland ; exhibiting man, like the solitary hyena that could neither be domesticated nor extirpated, prowling about the grave of society rather than its habitation§—Ireland thereby realizing the fate foretold for another nation—' I will bring your sanctuaries and your land into desolation . . . . and your enemies who dwell therein shall be astonished at it.' "‖

Like the same nation, too, the Irish of the seventeenth century were " scattered among all people, from one end of the earth unto the other," carrying with them into foreign lands their enduring hostility,—entering the armies of the enemies of their country, or (like the last of those accomplished gentlemen, the Moors of Spain, who, driven from their native An-

---

* 9 Will. 3 (Irish), c. 9.   † Ibid.

‡ "History of the late War" (1690-92), by Rev. W. Story.   4to. London.

§ " Res Gestæ Anglorum in Hibernia ab anno 1150 usque ad 1800 ; or, a Supplement to the History of England," prefixed to " the Liber Munerum Publicorum ; or, the Establishments of Ireland during 675 years ;" being the Report of Rowley Lascelles, of the Middle Temple.   Ordered by the House of Commons to be printed, 1814   Vol. i., p. 93.

‖ Leviticus, xxvi. 31, 32.

dalusia in 1610, became the first of those pirates called Sallee Rovers, in hatred of the injustice of the Christians),* manning French privateers, and robbing and insulting the coasts of the land of their birth, from which they had been cast out.†

* "Mahommedan Dynasties of Spain," by an African author of the year 1620, vol. ii., p. 392. 4to. Printed for the Oriental Society.

† 9 Will. 3 (Irish), c. 9, s. 5.

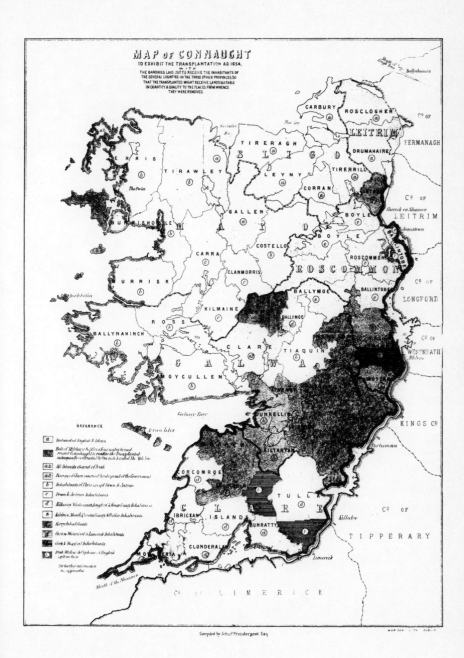

MAP OF CONNAUGHT
TO EXHIBIT THE TRANSPLANTATION A.D. 1654,
WITH
THE BARONIES LAID OUT TO RECEIVE THE INHABITANTS OF
THE SEVERAL COUNTIES IN THE THREE OTHER PROVINCES, SO
THAT THE TRANSPLANTED MIGHT RECEIVE LANDS SUITABLE
IN QUANTITY & QUALITY TO THE PLACES FROM WHENCE
THEY WERE REMOVED

APPENDIX.

No. I.

MAP OF CONNAUGHT.

THE first orders to the Irish nation, which were dated the 14th of October, 1653, directed the strongest and ablest of them to proceed immediately after Christmas, 1653, to Galway, and to present to the Commissioners of Revenue there inventories setting forth the names and number of persons in their families, the quantity of tillage on the lands they were leaving, and stating whether they were freeholders or leaseholders, in order that the Commissioners of Revenue might set them out lands competent to the stock that they had to bring into Connaught, and set them down on them as proprietors or tenants.*

Their families were to follow before the first of May; ·meantime they were to prepare housing for their reception. But before the time for moving arrived, Special Commissioners were appointed to perform this duty, as being too much for the Commissioners of Revenue. They were directed to sit at Loughrea instead of Galway, and thenceforth were known always as the Loughrea Commissioners.

On the 6th of January, 1654, they received their first instructions,† which seem to have been prepared by a standing Committee,

---

* Order of Commissioners for the Affairs of Ireland, 14th October, 1653, in Kilkenny Castle.

† " Instructions for Wm. Edwards, Edw. Doyly, Chs. Holcroft, and Hy. Greenoway, Esqrs., Commissioners appointed for the Setting out Lands in Connaught to the Transplanted Irish, who are to remove thither before the 1st of May next," $\frac{A}{85}$, p. 47.

consisting of Roger Lord Broghill, Colonel Hierome Sankey, Colonel Richard Lawrence, and ten others, who were appointed to sit in the long gallery at Cork House, which then adjoined the Castle of Dublin, every Monday, Wednesday, and Friday, to consider all matters referred to them, and amongst others, How the Great Worke of Transplantation might be managed and carried on with most advantage to the Commonwealth.*

These instructions directed that none of the inhabitants of Kerry, Cork, or Limerick were to be placed in Clare (as they might thence perhaps behold their native hills and plains, and be tempted to return, though the width of the Shannon would seem to have been enough to secure the Cork and Kerry inhabitants in their new abodes).

None of the inhabitants of Cavan, Fermanagh, Tyrone, or Donegal, were to be placed in Leitrim, as being too near Ulster, besides being a country full of fastnesses ; and, as a general rule, none of those inhabiting within ten miles of the Shannon on this side should be settled near, or have lands assigned to them within ten miles of the other side.

Care was also to be taken that the whole inhabitants of no one county, when transplanted, should have lands assigned to them in any one county in part of Connaught, but should be dispersed; and that the several septs, clans, or families of one name removing should be, as far as possible, dispersed into several places.

Some thoughtful persons, indeed, went so far as to propose to keep the transplanted Irish of English descent separate from the Irish. It was observed that the transplanted in Connaught were a disjointed people, both as to their principles and interest. " For though all of them," said Colonel Lawrence, " be equally Papist, they are not all equally Irish, but a considerable part of them (if not the most considerable) are of ancient English extract (alluding to the Butlers, Talbots, Barnewalls, Plunkets, &c.), who had been

* Order appointing the Committee, 1st Aug., 1653, $\frac{A}{84}$, p. 364.

of old, and until the late plantation of new English, determined enemies of the Irish."* And he proposed that the Irish should be kept still divided by being settled entirely, one of them at the one end, and the other at the other end of the province of Connaught. He proposed, also, that favours might be extended to the one, viz., the English-descended Irish (as by being planted near towns, &c.), that should not be to the other, by which means their joint agreement against the English interest would be much obstructed.† But plans of this nicety could scarce be carried out, considering the numbers passing into Connaught, and the constant taking away of lands by the Government for one cause or the other, so that in the end not a twentieth freeholder had any land assigned to him.‡

By the Act of Parliament which assigned Connaught for the habitation of the Irish nation, the only parts reserved from them were the towns, and a belt of ground four miles wide beginning at one statute mile round the town of Sligo, and so winging along the sea coast, to be planted with soldiers, in order to shut out relief by sea from abroad.§ This belt, however, was afterwards carried along the Shannon side, to prevent escape back to the other provinces.‖ Its breadth, as land became scarce, was reduced first to three miles, and finally contracted to one mile; and the circle of three miles drawn round Portumna, Athlone, Jamestown, Limerick, and the Pass of Killaloe, on the Connaught side, and of 100 acres round Shrule, Gort, and other garrisons given

---

* "Interest of England in the Well Planting of Ireland with English People Discussed," 4to, Dublin, 1656, p. 40.

† Ibid. p. 41.

‡ "A Continuation of the Brief Narrative and the Sufferings of the Irish under Cromwell," 4to, London, 1660, p. 9.

§ Act for Satisfaction of the Adventurers for Lands in Ireland, and of Arrears due to the Souldiery, 26th Sept., 1653. Scobell's "Acts and Ordinances," ch. xii.

‖ Additional Instructions to Commissioners at Loughrea, 16th June, 1655, $\frac{A}{26}$, p. 132. Colonel Ingoldsby and others to make the line, 8th April, 1656, $\frac{A}{10}$, p. 58.

up, the five miles round the town of Galway alone being still reserved.

The baronies of Tirrera, and Carbury in Sligo, then Tirrerril, Corran, and Leyney were first taken away, and set out to satisfy the disbanded.* And the transplanters who had received assignments there had to gather up their flocks and herds, and with their weary and heart-broken wives and children to begin their wanderings again.† The ancient proprietors, too, who had probably been comparing their happier lot with the poor transplanted, to lose only part of their lands to afford the exiles a maintenance, while they still kept their old mansions, had now to transplant to make way for the English soldiery.‡

It will be observed that the barony of Tirrera is bounded on the west by the fine estuary which leads up to Ballina, in Mayo. Opposite is the barony of Tyrawley, with a belt of fine, rich, feeding and grazing land along the estuary, commencing about Killala, near the mouth, and extending to Ballina. The rest, westwards to Erris, partakes of the nature of that barony, and is a waste of heath and bog. The officers now took a good part of Tyrawley, on the ground that by such an English plantation the sea coast would be greatly secured ; they left the bad half for the transplanters. The barony of Burren, and the district of Connemara, were for a time reserved from the Irish, as being near the sea‖ and great fastnesses, but were finally set out to the transplanted.

Leitrim, which had before been suspended from being set out on account of its being such a strong country, became filled in spite of the order with the Ulster Creaghts.¶ It was the first land they met with on entering Connaught, and they drove their herds of multitudinous small cows into its mountains and valleys

---

* $\frac{A}{90}$, p. 701.   † $\frac{A}{90}$, p. 704.   ‡ $\frac{A}{5}$, p. 60.   § $\frac{A}{90}$, p. 61.

‖ Propositions of Loughrea Commissioners Answered, $\frac{A}{85}$, p. 544.

¶ Id., ib.

and depastured them, suffering less, probably, from the transplantation than others, being accustomed to a wandering life, and to
pitch their frail booths, erected of boughs, covered with long strips
of green turf, where the pasture suited their herds. They received various summonses to retire. The county was at length
taken for the soldiery, to answer arrears before 5th June, 1649,
and the ancient proprietors were ordered to remove to the baronies
of Murrisk and Borrishool, in Mayo, most resembling Leitrim in
the opinion of the Loughrea Commissioners ;* but in the opinion of
the proprietors it probably only resembled it in its wildest and
worst parts.

These, however, were only the first rude essays in the great
work of transplantation during the first year. They were of less
consequence, as the assignments of land were *De Bene Esse*, or
conditional, and were only preliminary to the final settlements,
which were to be made by the court to sit at Athlone for discrimi-
nating the qualifications of the Irish.

These Commissioners, commonly called the Athlone Commissioners, or Court of Claims and Qualifications of the Irish, were appointed (as appears by their commission and instructions) on 28th
December, 1654.†

Their business was twofold; first, to discriminate the guilt of
every proprietor ; and, second, to ascertain the size and value of
the lands he lately held on the English side of the Shannon.

In the Act for Settling Ireland, passed 12th August, 1652,‡
there were eight different qualifications. By the first six, death or
banishment and forfeiture were declared against all the chief nobility (some of them Protestant Royalists, as the Earl of Ormond,
Primate Bramhall, and others), and all the gentlemen of Ireland
who had borne arms for the King. Swordmen under that rank
fell under the 7th qualification, and forfeited two-thirds. Gentlemen and others, who had borne no part in the war, but remained quiet, fell under the 8th qualification, as not having ma-

---

* $\frac{A}{30}$, p. 161.   † $\frac{A}{26}$, p. 53.   ‡ Scobell's " Acts and Ordinances."

nifested a constant good affection by some outward acts in favour of the Parliament and against the King. They forfeited one-third ; Protestants in like condition forfeited one-fifth. By the Act for Settling Ireland, all within these qualifications were to transplant, and receive their proportions of land in Connaught; but by an ordinance of the Protector and Council, Protestants were allowed to compound* for their one-fifth, and were dispensed with from transplantation. This was equal to two years' annual value, lands being then valued at ten years their annual profits.†

As the whole nation was declared guilty of rebellion, it lay on each claimant to prove both the quantity of his lands, and " the series of his carriages," or his course of conduct during the ten years' war. To check the claimants the Commissioners were furnished with the Civil Survey, which set forth the names and estates of all the proprietors in 1641,—with the Depositions, taken in 1642, of Protestants complaining of goods taken from them in the first year of the war, in which were entered every idle hearsay they chose to offer, the more monstrous the better. These were duly alphabeted and indexed, and were called the Crimination Books. They were also supplied with the books of the late Government of Confederate Catholics. According to the evidence thus afforded, and the testimony of witnesses, the Commissioners decreed that the claimant either had no claim, or fell under the 7th or 8th qualification, and so forfeited either two-thirds or one-third; or the claimant got a decree of Constant Good Affection, entitling him to be restored to his estate.

It now became the duty of the Loughrea Commissioners to set out lands to the transplanted in quantity according to the Athlone Decrees. The assignments thus made were called Final Settle-

---

* Dated 2nd September, 1654. Scobell's " Acts and Ordinances."

† Order of Council made on report of the Commissioners of Revenue on Lord Viscount Moore of Drogheda's Case, Records of late Auditor General, Custom House, vol. xviii., p. 9 ; on Teig O'Hara's case, ib., p. 19.

ments, to distinguish them from those which the transplanters first received for the support of their stock of cattle. The business having become more important, Sir Charles Coote, President of Connaught, and others, were joined to the other Commissioners at Loughrea.*

The Government early in this year directed the Loughrea Commissioners to give the first comers assignments, with houses and other accommodation, to encourage the nation to come on.† Instead of which (strange to say), they began with the baronies of Burren and Inchiquin, in the county of Clare, " generally known and reputed to be sterile," to the hindrance of the transplantation. Transplanters also were set down in counties totally different in character from those which they and their families had been accustomed to.‡

To remedy these inconveniences a committee was appointed on the 1st of February, 1656, in Dublin, consisting of Sir Hardress Waller, Sir Robert King, Major-General Jephson, and Colonel Hewson, and Colonel Sankey, to consider of the nature and quality of the soil of the respective baronies in the three provinces of Leinster, Munster, and Ulster, and what counties and baronies there were beyond the Shannon to which the transplanted Irish were to remove, that might bear a resemblance in proportion and quality of the lands they left in the other provinces, that they might be set down in lands of like quality and quantity in Connaught.§ And Sir Charles Coote, one of the Loughrea Commissioners, was joined to the committee on account of his experience acquired in Connaught in the business of setting down the transplanted.

On the 12th of February, 1656, this committee submitted their proposals in the form exhibited in the map. Besides resemblance, they took into consideration the distance from whence the proprietors were to remove, so that the inhabitants of one county

---

* 16th June, 1655, $\frac{A}{26}$, p. 99.   † $\frac{A}{30}$, p. 42.   ‡ Ib. p. 82.   § $\frac{A}{5}$, p. 351.

should not be removed to a greater distance from their former estates than others.*   These proposals follow :—

" Proposals in order to assigning certain Baronies in Connaught and Clare to certain Counties in the other Provinces.

" The inhabitants of the Province of Ulster (except the Counties of Down and Antrim) to be transplanted into the Baronies of Muckullen, Rosse, and Ballinihinsey, in the territory of Ere Connaught, and County of Galway (except what is reserved by the Lyne on the Sea), and into the Baronies of Moyrisk, Burryshoule, and the half Barony of Irish [Erris], parte of Tyrawley Barony (parte of it being given to the soldiers), and Costello Barony (except what is on the line aforesaid), and into Tyaquin Barony, in the Co. of Galway.

" The Inhabitants of the Counties of Corke and Wexford to be transplanted into the Baronies of Dunkellyn and Kiltartan, in the County of Galway (except what is on the lyne on the sea), and into Athlone Barony and the half Barony of Moycarnane (except what is on the lyne of the Shannon), in the County of Roscommon.

" The inhabitants of the County of Kerry to be transplanted into Inchiquin and Burren Baronies, in the County of Clare, and into the territories of Artagh, in the Barony of Boyle, in the County of Roscommon.

" The inhabitants of the Counties of Down and Antrim to be transplanted into the Baronies of Clanmorris, Carra, and Kilmaine, in the County of Mayo.

" The Inhabitants of the Counties of Kilkenny, Westmeath, Longford, King's County, and Tipperary, to be transplanted into the Baronies of Tullagh, Bunratty, Islands, Corcomroe, Clonderlau, Moyfartagh, and Ibrican, in the County of Clare, and into the half barony of Bellamo, in the County of Galway.

* $\frac{A}{26}$, p. 189.

" The inhabitants of the Counties of Catherlagh, Waterford, and Limerick, into the half Baronies of Loughrea and Leitrim, and the Baronies of Dunmore and Kilconnell, and the half Barony of Longford (except what is in the lyne), in the County of Galway.

" And the inhabitants of East Meath, Kildare, Queen's County, and Dublin, into the Baronies of Roscommon and Ballintobber, in the half Barony of Bellamo and the Barony of Boyle (except the territory of Artagh), in the County of Roscommon.

" Memorandum.—That Louth is reputed much better land than Wicklow, and to be accordingly estimated.

" *Dated at Dublin, 12th February, 1655–6.*

" HARDRESS WALLER.   CHARLES COOTE.   ROBERT KING.
JOHN HEWSON.   WM. JEPHSON.   HIEROME SANKEY."*

The plan of consigning to the four baronies of Ballintober in Rocommon, and Athlone in Galway, and Tulla and Bunratty in Clare, " Irish widows of English extraction" (by which are to be understood the widows of the nobility and ancient English gentry— ladies such as Viscountess Mayo, Lady Louth, Lady Grace Talbot, Lady Dunboyne, &c.), was the suggestion of the Committee of Transplantation, as early as 5th of May, 1654.† In the following year it was conceived that three would be enough, and Ballintober was cut off.‡

Notwithstanding the vast amount of Connaught already withdrawn from Transplanters, the Commissioners had orders to reserve one choice barony in Clare, and one in Galway, for the disposal of the Government.§

For the Lord Henry Cromwell, also, was reserved Portumna

* $\frac{A}{26}$, p. 189.

† Order Book of Council, Custom House Buildings, vol. vii.

‡ $\frac{A}{5}$, p. 111.   § $\frac{A}{10}$, p. 55.

Castle, park, and gardens, the ancient seat of the Earls of Clan-
rickard, with 6000 acres next adjoining.*

Sir Charles Coote, Colonel Sadleir, Major Ormsby, and others
did not think it beneath them to still further diminish the fund
of land† for the support of the exiled Irish nation, and got grants
in Connaught. Two-thirds of Mayo was taken to answer soldiers'
arrears of Cromwell's army of Ireland, incurred in England before
the 5th of June, 1649 ; and as the remaining third was moun-
tainous and maritime, the Commissioners of Parliament thought
they might as well make a clean sweep of Mayo ; the Loughrea
Commissioners were therefore ordered to take care that no Irish
should set down within that county either as proprietors or tenants, to the end it should be planted with English,—that import-
ing most of public safety and advantage.‡ This, however, would
seem to have been given back when they found that all disposable
lands had been set out, except the two reserved baronies, and
except what was waste and remote;§ and that many Irish proprietors and their families, who had left fine estates, were still
unaccommodated, and reduced to little better than a starving condition.

The rule of Settlement now became impracticable. Mr. Thomas
Shortal‖ and Mr. Richard Nugent,¶ and others, complained that
their Athlone decrees were not satisfied in the baronies appointed
for those in their capacity. Maurice Lord Viscount Roche, of
Fermoy, was sent off on his wearisome and fruitless journey on
foot to the Owles, in the wildest and remotest part of Connaught**
(and had nothing but his labour for his pains), instead of being set
down with the inhabitants of the county of Cork, in the baronies
of Kiltartan and Dunkellin in the county of Galway, or of Athlone
or Moycarnon, in Roscommon.

It remains to observe that the present baronies of Frenchpark
and Castlerea were not then known. They formed part of the ba-

---

* $\frac{A}{10}$, p. 277 ; and see Letter of Henry Cromwell, *supra*, p. 56, n. *ib.*

† $\frac{A}{10}$, p. 266.   ‡ Ib., p. 123.   § $\frac{A}{26}$, p. 233.   ‖ $\frac{A}{12}$, p. 230.

¶ Ib. ib.   ** *Supra*, p. 75.

rony of Boyle, in the county of Roscommon. The territory of Artagh was part of the same barony.

The barony of Galway was not then known. It has been formed out of parts of Moycullen and Dunkellin. The baronies of Clare, Athenry, Kilconnel, and Clonmacnowen, in the county of Galway, are not mentioned in the scheme of 12th February, 1656. Clare was excepted by an almost contemporaneous order,* and was perhaps one of the two choice baronies reserved for Government disposal.

"THE OWLES."

This territory is thus marked on the present map in the baronies of Borrishool and Erris, after an ancient map among the MSS. of Trinity College Library, Dublin, of the time probably of Queen Elizabeth or James I., showing the division made of Connaught into baronies by Sir Henry Sydney.

The Irish name of this territory was Umhall, and it was divided into two—Umhall ioghtragh, i. e. Lower Umhall, the ancient name of the barony of Borrishool ; and Umhall uaghtragh, i. e. Upper Umhall, the ancient name of the barony of Murrisk.

These latter divisions are marked on an ancient map, from the Book of Lecan, prefixed to the "Tribes and Customs of Hy Fiachrach."† This was the country of the O'Mailleys. Grace O'Mailley, that famous Amazonian sea rover of Queen Elizabeth's day, is commonly known as Granuaille, or Grace of Umhall. The English called the territory " The Owles," another name for the " The Umhalls."

---

* $\frac{A}{10}$, p. 55.

† Translated and annotated by John O'Donovan, Irish Archæological Society's Publications, 4to, Dublin, 1844.

II.

MAP OF THE COUNTY OF TIPPERARY, AS DIVIDED BETWEEN THE ADVENTURERS AND SOLDIERS.

(See pp. 24 and 25, and 113.)

An account having been taken of the lands forfeited in the several baronies of the ten counties, and the counties divided by baronies into two equal parts,* a lot was drawn for the Adventurers by Alderman Avery, and for the Soldiers by Colonel Hewson (appointed to that office by the Lord General Crowwell); and the several baronies in the county of Tipperary forming the two parts of the county fell to the Adventurers and Soldiers, respectively, as exhibited in the map.†

The Adventurers' baronies in the county of Tipperary were to be charged with not more than £60,000. Bodies of Adventurers who might wish to plant together might join in a lot, no one lot to exceed £5000.‡

The Committee were then directed to subdivide the several baronies appropriated to the Adventurers equally by lot, according to the proportions due to each of them ; and if any barony should prove deficient to answer the sum which was apportioned to it, a supply was to be made out of some redundant barony in the same county.§ In consequence of disputes, the Lord Protector and his Council of State, on the 6th of August, 1654, appointed the com-

-----

  * P. 25, *supra*.

  † Analysis of the Act for Satisfaction of Adventurers and Soldiers of 26th April, 1653, MSS. in Library of Trinity College, Dublin, F. 3. 16.

  ‡ Act of Parliament of 26th Sept. 1653.   § Ib.

mittee mentioned in the Adventurers' certificate (at p. 113), empowered, when many lots were upon one barony, to settle a way by lot who should remain, and who should remove ; and to settle a way by lot for ascertaining the subdivision of Adventurers' proportions that should continue in the several baronies.

The committee arranged a settled method, and made a declaration for their explanation of it,* which unfortunately has not yet been found. Enough, however, remains in Dr. Petty's account of the Down Survey, and the certificates of the Committee, to show that they quartered the baronies in the manner exhibited on the Map of Tipperary.†

The following list of Adventurers in that county is evidently compiled from the certificates furnished to each Adventurer by the Committee at Grocers' Hall, pursuant to the Act of 26th of September, 1653.

It will be observed that in many instances the same amount of money gives a different amount of land. The conditions varied. Adventurers under the first of the Acts of Subscription, passed in 1642, commonly called the Adventurers Act, were to be satisfied in lands by English measure. By the doubling ordinance, as it was called, made on the 14th of July, 1643,‡ sums advanced were to be satisfied in double the quantity in the first Act, that is to say, the lands were to be rated at four shillings the acre instead of eight in Munster, and at two shillings instead of four in Ulster, and the measure was enlarged to Irish measure. And any original Adventurer who should within three months pay in a further sum, equal to a fourth part of the sum he had first subscribed, was to have the old and new adventures counted together at one sum, to be repaid at the new rates.

The entire sums charged on the county, according to the accompanying list, amount to £68,858 6s. 0d., thus exceeding (it

* Analysis of Act of 26th Sept., 1653, MSS. T. C. D., F. 3. 16.
† And see *supra*, p. 112.
‡ Scobell's " Acts and Ordinances."

would seem) the amount permitted by the Act by £8858. However unsatisfactory it be not to have the means of explaining this
difficulty, it yet leads to the conclusion that the list is a complete
one, and contains the names of all the Adventurers for the county
of Tipperary.

It does not appear how the Adventurers equalized or rated the
different counties and baronies between one another. The rates
set by the officers upon those which they subdivided are already
given at page 87, and the following pages.

The Quarterings and Subquarterings of the Adventurers' Baronies, as expressed upon the Map, have been made according to
the description given by Dr. Petty of their proceedings,* and will
serve to explain the references to the Divisions and Subdivisions
into which each Adventurer's lot is described to fall in the following Table. The authentic Maps have been, it is feared, lost ; for
all the documents relative to the Adventurers preserved in Gold-
smiths' Hall, London, were, on the 23d of September, 1671, ordered
to be delivered by Sir Joseph Williamson to Sir James Shaen,† who
was Keeper of the Papers connected with the execution of the Acts of
Settlement,‡ and they were probably burnt among so many others
in the fire that destroyed the Council Office in Dublin in 1711.

* *Supra,* p. 112.

† Letter of Mr. Kingston, of the Record Office, London, July, 1862.

‡ Patent of 13 Charles II., 30th March, 1661–2. Lib. D. p. 63, Record Tower,
Dublin Castle.

"ACCOUNT OF THE ADVENTURERS IN THE COUNTY OF TIPPERARY."*

BARONY OF MIDDLETHIRD.

Divisions.	Subdivisions.	Adventurers.	Sums of Money.			Irish Measure.			English Measure.		
			£	s.	d.	A.	R.	P.	A.	R.	P.
North-East Quarter, No. 1.	1	William Watts; Rowland Hill, assignee to William Watts,	300	0	0	666	2	6	1079	3	21
	2	Francis Allen,	100	0	0	222	0	34	359	3	31
	3	Robert Eldred,	400	0	0	888	3	22	1439	3	16
	4	Henry Elinston,	100	0	0	222	0	34	359	3	31
	5	Corporation of Exeter,	25	6	8	55	2	8	89	6	37
			1883	6	8	2583	2	32	4185	0	29
South-East Quarter, No. 2.	North-East, No. 1. 1	Thomas Eyres,	200	0	0	444	1	30	719	3	26
	2	Colonel John Owen, assignee to William Watts,	500	0	0	1111	0	17	1799	3	9
	South-East, No. 2.	William Webster,	300	0	0	666	2	26	1079	3	21
		James Yeates,	400	0	0	718	3	6	1164	1	10
		John Hall,	600	0	0	1333	1	13	2159	3	4
	South-West, No. 3.	Thomas Moore,	150	0	0	333	1	13	539	3	30
		Mary or Robert Garland,	750	0	0	1666	2	26	2692	2	34
South-East Quarter, No. 3.	No. 1.	Richard Clutterbuck,	900	0	0	2000	0	0	3239	2	27
		George Snell,	350	0	0	777	3	3	1259	1	22
		Abigail Lloyd, assignee to Alderman Ridges,	100	0	0	222	0	34	359	3	31
	No. 2.	Nicholas Bond,	100	0	0	222	0	34	359	3	31
		Charles Roberts,	1400	0	0	3111	0	17	5039	1	36

* From the Books of Dudley Loftus in the Library of St. Patrick's Cathedral, Dublin, commonly called Archbishop Marsh's Library, V. 3. 1. 35.

BARONY OF MIDDLETHIRD—*continued.*

Divisions	Subdivisions	Adventurers.	Sums of Money.			Irish Measure.			English Measure.		
			£	s.	d.	A.	R.	P.	A.	R.	P.
	1	Samuel Northcott,	50	0	0	68	2	14	111	0	17
	2	Thomas Dennis,	50	0	0	68	2	14	111	0	17
	3	Mary Page and Anne Shepcott,	100	0	0	222	0	35	359	3	31
	4	Thomas Wallis,	50	0	0	111	0	17	179	3	35
	5	Sarah Shortt,	150	0	0	333	1	13	539	3	30
		John Shortt,	225	0	0	500	0	0	809	3	26
	6	Richard Hayden,	750	0	0	1666	2	26	2699	2	34
	7	Thomas Moore,	300	0	0	411	2	11	666	2	26
North-West Quarter, No. 4.	8	Christopher Towse and Nathaniel Witham,	200	0	0	444	1	30	719	3	26
	9	Rowland Hill,	250	0	0	555	2	8	899	3	23
	10	William Squire,	100	0	0	222	0	35	359	3	33
	11	Matthew Rutton,	200	0	0	444	1	30	719	3	26
	12	Joshua and Caleb Pearce,	30	0	0	41	0	24	66	2	26
	13	Ahasuerus Regiment,	100	0	0	222	0	35	359	3	33
		William Ridges,	120	0	0	266	2	25	431	3	29
		Mary Daire,	600	0	0	1333	1	13	2159	3	4
		Cor⁵. Burgess,	700	0	0	1555	2	8	2519	2	35
		Richard Scott,	520	0	0	1155	2	8	1871	3	8
		George Clarke,	1000	0	0	2222	0	34	3599	2	18
						28,090	2	29			

BARONY OF IFFA AND OFFA.

Divisions.	Subdivisions.	Adventurers.	Sums of Money. £ s. d.	Irish Measure. A. R. P.	English Measure. A. R. P.
East, No. 1.	North, No. 1, and North, No. 2. {	William Bereton,	100 0 0	222 0 35	359 3 33
		Colonel William Bosville,	400 0 0	888 3 21	1439 3 14
	1	Thomas Combe,	20 0 0	27 1 29	44 1 34
	2	John Clay,	60 0 0	133 1 13	215 3 34
	3	Abraham Barnabye,	25 0 0	55 2 8	89 3 37
	South Middle, No. 3. { 4 {	Simon Lumnery,	95 0 0 }	225 2 8	413 3 24
		Joseph Clifton,	20 0 0 }		
	5	William Musgrave,	20 0 0	27 1 29	44 1 31
	6	Ion Fisher,	25 0 0	55 2 8	89 3 37
	South, No. 4. 4	Bartholomew White,	300 0 0	666 2 26	1079 3 19
East Middle, No. 2.	1	Yarmouth Corporation,	600 0 0	1333 1 13	2159 3 4
	2	Humphrey Towne,	600 0 3	1333 1 13	2159 3 4
	3	Giles Moore,	25 0 0	34 1 6	55 2 8
West Middle, No. 3.	1	Peter Chaveney,	100 0 0	137 0 30	222 0 35
	2	John Seager,	200 0 0	444 1 30	719 3 26
	3 {	Charles Crooke,	225 0 0	500 0 0	809 3 31
		Roger Whitehall,	100 0 0	222 0 34	359 3 26
	4	Francis Finch,	200 0 0	444 1 30	719 3 26
	5	Humphrey Bedingfield,	200 0 0	444 1 30	719 3 26
	6	Philip Musgrave,	20 0 0	44 1 31	71 2 12

BARONY OF IFFA AND OFFA—continued.

Divisions.	Subdivisions.		Adventurers.	Sums of Money.			Irish Measure.			English Measure.		
				£	s.	d.	A.	R.	P.	A.	R.	P.
East, No. 1.	West, No. 4.	1	John Dawson,	300	0	0	496	2	13	804	1	21
		2	Anthony Bosfield,	180	0	0	400	0	0	647	3	29
		3	Samuel Clarke,	300	0	0	666	2	26	1079	3	21
		4	Peter Radcliffe,	25	0	0	55	2	8	89	3	37
		5	Joshua Sturny,	40	0	0	88	3	22	143	3	36
		6	Robert Price,	100	0	0	222	0	34	359	3	34
		7	John Pitts,*	100	0	0	222	0	34	359	3	34
	East No. 1.	1	John Wheatley,	125	0	0	277	3	2	449	3	30
			Henry Langham,	340	0	0	755	3	8	1223	3	18
		2	Ephraim Bishop,	20	0	0	27	1	29	44	1	31
		3	Roger Sear,	100	0	0	222	1	34	359	3	33
		4	John Amyos,	66	13	4	91	1	32	148	0	23
		5	Richard Haddilove,	50	0	0	111	0	17	179	3	35
		6	James Blatt,	133	6	8	182	3	1	296	0	7
		7	William Almond,	100	0	0	222	0	34	359	3	31
		8	Thomas Valentine,	100	0	0	222	0	34	359	3	31
East Middle, No. 2.	No. 1.	1	John Boyse,	100	0	0	222	0	34	359	3	31
	East Middle, No. 2.	2	Elizabeth Cooke,	100	0	0	222	0	34	359	3	31
	No. 2.	3	Richard Newtowne,	300	0	0	666	2	26	1079	3	21
			Charles Alcock,	500	0	0	1111	0	17	1799	3	9
West Middle, No. 3.	No. 1.	1	Hugh Radcliffe,	650	0	0	1444	1	30	2339	2	37
		2	Thomas Chewning,	245	0	0	544	1	27	881	3	18
	No. 2.		Thomas Jackson,	100	0	0	222	0	35	359	3	23
	No. 3.		Jerome Sankey,	50	0	0	111	0	17	180	0	35

* For an incident in this Devonshire Adventurer's experience of the county of Tipperary, in 1656, see p. 126, *supra*.

BARONY OF IFFA AND OFFA—*continued.*

Divisions.	Subdivisions.	Adventurers.	Sums of Money. £ s. d.	Irish Measure. A. R. P.	English Measure. A. R. P.
East Middle, No. 2.	1	Laurence Peacock,	50 0 0	111 0 17	179 8 35
	2	Thomas Woodley,	166 13 4	370 1 14	599 3 21
		William Richardson,	50 0 0	111 0 17	180 0 35
	3	Simon Ashe,	100 0 0	222 0 34	359 3 31
		George Clarke,	350 0 0	777 3 33	1259 3 17
	4	Jerome Sankey,	200 0 0	444 1 28	719 3 22
	5	William Rogers,	50 0 0	111 0 17	179 3 35
West Middle, No. 3.	1	Abraham Alexander Benco,	1250 0 0	2777 3 4	4499 2 5
	2	Alderman George Withern,	750 0 0	1666 2 26	2699 2 34
	3	Richard Hutchinson,	760 0 0	1466 2 25	2375 3 2
	4	Thomas Barnardiston,	625 0 0	1388 3 21	2249 3 1
	5	Alderman John Kendricke,	700 0 0	1555 2 8	2519 2 57
West Quarter, No. 4.		Thomas Addys,	361 5 0	802 3 4	1300 1 18
		Robert Hamon,	143 15 0	319 1 31	517 1 31
		Sir William Brereton,	1200 0 0	1646 2 37	2666 2 22
		Gilbert Lambelle,	625 0 0	1388 3 21	2249 3 1
		The Lady Ingram,	1000 0 0	1371 3 20	2222 0 35
		Humphrey Towne,	1200 0 0	2666 2 27	4819 2 19
		The said Sir William Brereton,	500 0 0	1111 0 17	1799 3 9
		John Seed,	200 0 0	444 1 30	719 3 26
		Thomas Bigg,	100 0 0	222 0 35	359 3 33
		William Tibbs,	1102 0 0	2418 0 18	3916 3 30
		Richard Kitlebutler,	25 0 0	34 1 6	55 2 8
				39,507 2 12	

THE BARONY OF CLANWILLIAM.

Divisions	Subdivisions	Adventurers	Sums of Money £ s. d.			Irish Measure. A. R. P.			English Measure. A. R. P.		
North-East Quarter, No. 1.	North-East, No. 1.	Richard Thrale,									
		Christ' Foster,									
		Samuel and Daniel Brewster,	600	0	0	1333	1	13	2159	3	3
		John Hart,									
		Abraham Miller,									
		Ann and Elizabeth Ffrancis,	50	0	0	68	2	14	111	0	17
		John Curtise,	40	0	0	44	3	19	88	3	25
		Richard Allen,	200	0	0	444	1	28	719	3	22
		Thomas Gower,	62	10	0	138	3	21	224	3	35
	South-East, No. 2.	Thomas Gower,	600	0	0	1333	1	13	2159	3	30
		Theophilus Biddolph,	100	0	0	222	0	34	359	3	30
		Theophilus Birkenhead,	100	0	0	222	0	34	359	3	30
	South-West, No. 3.	Thomas Stock,	600	0	0	1333	1	13	2159	3	30
		Richard Hill,	250	0	0	555	2	8	899	3	23
	North-West, No. 4.	Alexander Popaham,	1000	0	0	1371	3	20	2222	0	35
South-East Quarter, No. 2.	North-East, No. 1.	Henry Box,	400	0	0	888	3	21	1439	3	14
		John Offeild,	500	0	0	1111	0	17	1799	3	9
		Thomas Briscoe,	100	0	0	222	0	34	539	3	31
		Joseph Ruthorne,	250	0	0	555	2	8	899	3	23
	South-East, No. 2.	John Player,	25	0	0	55	2	8	89	3	37
		Peregrine Prettie,	200	0	0	444	1	28	719	3	22
		Zachariah Worth,	100	0	0	222	0	34	359	3	22
		Joseph Ling,	100	0	0	222	0	34	359	3	31
		William Almond,	25	0	0	55	2	8	89	3	37

THE BARONY OF CLANWILLIAM—*continued.*

Divisions	Subdivisions		Adventurers	Sums of Money. £ s. d.	Irish Measure. A. R. P.	English Measure. A. R. P.
South-East Quarter, No. 2.	South-West, No. 3.		Daniel Waldoe,	600 0 0	1333 1 13	2159 3 4
			John Raymoun,	300 0 0	666 2 26	1079 3 21
	North-East, No. 4.		Joseph Jaques,	750 0 0	750 0 0	1666 2 26
			Richard Symons,	100 0 0	222 0 34	359 3 31
	North-East, No. 1.	East, No. 1. 1	Hezekiah Woodward,	100 0 0	137 0 29	222 0 35
		2	Samuel Blackwell,	38 0 0	84 1 30	136 3 3
			Samuel Blackwell,	200 0 0	274 1 18	444 1 30
		3	Rawleigh Clapham,	30 0 0	41 0 24	66 2 26
		4	John Man,	250 0 0	555 0 8	899 3 23
South-West Quarter, No. 3.	South-East, No. 2.	East, No. 1. 1	James Webster,	50 0 0	68 2 14	111 0 17
		2	Roger Lazingbye,	100 0 0	222 0 34	359 3 31
		West, No. 2. 3	George Clarke,	200 0 0	448 1 30	719 3 26
			Erasmus Smith,	300 0 0	666 2 26	1079 3 18
	South-West, No. 3.	West, No. 2.	John Ash,	800 0 0	1777 3 2	2879 2 29
		1	Jane Blande,	200 0 0	444 1 30	719 3 26
		2	John Dawson,	600 0 0	1333 1 13	2159 3 4
	South-West, No. 4.		Edward Ash,	400 0 0	888 3 21	1439 3 14
			Sir Richard Onslowe,	400 0 0	548 3 0	888 3 22
North-West Quarter, No. 4.	East, No. 1.		Erasmus Smith,	1345 0 0	2988 3 22	4841 2 1
	West, No. 2.		George Clarke,	2000 0 0	4444 1 31	7199 1 2
						29659 3 0

BARONY OF ELIOGARTIE.

Divisions.	Subdivisions.		Adventurers.	Sums of Money.			Irish Measure.			English Measure.		
				£	s.	d.	A.	R.	P.	A.	R.	P.
North-East Quarter, No. 1.	No. 1.	1	John Temple,	200	0	0	274	1	20	444	1	30
		2	William Sheares,	300	0	0	411	2	9	666	2	26
	2	1	Thomas Mathew,	150	0	0	333	1	13	539	3	30
		2	Andrew Broughton,	100	0	0	222	0	35	359	3	33
		3	James Mathew,	100	0	0	222	0	34	359	3	31
		4	John Lake,	200	0	0	444	1	30	719	3	26
		1	Thomas Kinnaye,	400	0	0	888	3	21	1439	3	14
		2	Grace Heathcott,	25	0	0	34	1	6	55	2	8
		3	Edward Barker,	600	0	0	1333	1	13	2159	3	4
South-East Quarter, No. 2.	No. 1.	1	John Trelawney,	150	0	0	333	1	13	539	3	30
		2	Nicholas Herring,	900	0	0	2000	0	0	3239	2	27
	No. 1.	1	Robert Trelawney,	450	0	0	1000	0	0	1619	3	13
		2	John Winspeare,	75	0	0	166	2	26	269	3	30
	No. 2.	1	John Soame,	300	0	0	666	2	26	1079	3	21
		2	Benjamin Atkins,	50	0	0	111	0	17	179	3	35
		3	Margaret Shakspeare,	100	0	0	222	0	35	359	3	33
			Peter Atkins,	25	0	0	34	1	6	55	2	8

BARONY OF ELIOGARTIE—*continued.*

Divisions.	Subdivisions.	Adventurers.	Sums of Money. £ s. d.	Irish Measure. A. R. P.	English Measure. A. R. P.
South-West Quarter, No. 3.	No. 1.	William Lambert,	100 0 0	222 0 34	359 3 31
		Roger Lambert,	300 0 0	581 2 20	942 0 21
		Robert Kircombe,	50 0 0	111 0 17	179 3 35
	No. 2.	John Turbington,	120 0 0	266 2 25	431 3 29
		Samuel Ball,	125 0 0	277 3 2	449 3 30
	East, No. 1.	James Phillips,	200 0 0	444 1 28	719 3 22
	No. 3.	Joshua Northcott,	100 0 0	137 0 30	222 0 34
		William Tillaslye,	100 0 0	222 0 34	359 3 31
	West, No. 2.	Edward Austin,	100 0 0	222 0 34	359 3 34
North-West Part, No. 4.	North-East, No. 1.	Nicholas Howard,	100 0 0	222 0 34	359 3 31
		William Allen,	550 0 0	1222 0 35	1979 3 6
	South-East, No. 2.	Richard Rogers,	650 0 0	1444 1 30	2339 3 39
		George Underwood's Children,	100 0 0	222 0 34	359 3 31
		Thomas Barker,	50 0 0	68 2 14	111 0 17
		Benjamin Underwood,	50 0 0	11 0 17	179 3 35
	South-West, No. 3.	John Hunter,	100 0 0	222 0 35	359 3 31
		James Hayes,	100 0 0	222 0 35	359 3 31
		William Skrimshawe,	50 0 0	111 0 17	179 3 35
		Alderman William Underwood,	350 0 0	777 3 33	1259 3 17
		Martin North,	1040 0 0	2311 0 17	3743 2 17
		John Hawes,	400 0 0	888 3 21	1439 3 14

BARONY OF ILEAGH.

Divisions.	Subdivisions.	Adventurers.	Sums of Money. £ s. d.			Irish Measure. A. R. P.			English Measure. A. E. P.		
North-East Quarter, No. 1.		Richard Boughton, Thomas White, and John Dowleing,	345	16	8	1213	3	2	1964	3	26
South-East Quarter, No. 2.		Robert Crawley, Richard Tyler,	250 0 0 } 250 0 1 }			1111	0	17	1799	3	9
South-West Quarter, No.3.		Richard Boughton, Thomas White, and John Dowleing,	272	13	4	606	0	0	982	3	11
		Joseph Blackwell,	337	1	0	750	0	0	1214	3	20
North-West Quarter, No. 4	1	George Starrshiers,	200	0	0	444	1	30	719	3	26
	2	Susan and Thomas Daniel,	100	0	0	222	0	35	359	3	23
	3	Elizabeth and Sarah Swinnock,	250	0	0	555	2	8	899	3	23
	4	John Mosyer, fformerly claymed by John and Ann Lound,	100	0	0	137	0	28	222	0	34
	5	James Fletcher,	200	0	0	444	1	30	719	3	26
		Thomas Guy,	200	0	0	444	1	30	719	3	26
						5929	0	4			

BARONY OF IKERRIN.

Divisions.	Subdivisions.	Adventurers.	Sums of Money. £ s. d.	Irish Measure. A. R. P.	English Measure. A. R. P.
North-East Quarter, No. 1.		John Blackwell, Senior,	300 0 0	666 2 26	1079 3 21
		John Blackwell, Junior,	1350 0 0	2914 3 33	4721 2 39
South-East Quarter, No. 2.	1	Alderman John Ffoulkes,	600 0 0	1333 1 13	2159 3 4
	2	Doctor Roger Drake,	500 0 0	1111 0 17	1799 3 8
	3	William Thornburie,	200 0 0	444 1 30	719 3 26
	1	Mary Hubbert,	100 0 0	222 0 35	359 3 33
	4 { 2	William Heather,	50 0 0 }		
		The said William Heather,	75 0 0 }	277 3 2	449 3 30
South-West Quarter, No. 3.		Anthony Radcliff,	300 0 0	666 0 34	1079 3 21
		Simon Middleton,	1200 0 0	2666 2 26	4319 2 8
	North-East, No. 1. { 1, 2, 3	Thomas Bayley,	150 0 0	333 1 13	539 3 30
		Thomas Woodcock,	100 0 0	222 0 34	359 3 31
		Alderman William Ridges,	150 0 0	205 3 4	333 1 12
	South-East, No. 2. {	Gerrard Boate,	468 15 0	847 3 20	1372 0 37
	1	Symon Cressy,	10 0 0	22 0 30	35 3 6
	2	Robert Wallis,	125 0 0	277 3 2	449 3 30
	South-West, No. 3. { 3	William Heather,	100 0 0	222 0 34	359 3 31
		Oliver Brunskell,	20 0 0	44 1 31	71 3 38
	4	Henry Goddesden,	100 0 0	222 0 34	359 3 31
South-West Quarter, No. 4.	South-West, No. 4. {	Katherine Boate,	156 5 0	282 1 20	437 1 14
		Robert Malthies,	150 0 0	333 1 13	539 3 30
		Henry Day,	350 0 0	777 3 3	1259 1 22
				13,984 3 14	

Signed by order of the Committee of Adventurers for Lands in Ireland, sitting at Grocers' Hall, London,

Per RICHARD DEACON, Clerk to yᵉ said Committee.

	Sums paid. £ s. d.	Value upon Doubling. £ s. d.	Letters differencing yᵉ Measure.	Irish Measure. A. R. P.	English Measure. A. R. P.
In yᵉ Barony of Middlethird, &c. Robert Hamon, of London, merchant, assignee of Cornelius Burgess, Doctor in Divinity, and late Vicar of Waterford, in yᵉ county of Hartford.	700 0 0	. . . . . .	I	1555 2 8	2519 2 35
George Clarke, of London, merchant, assignee of Richard Sallway, Esq.	1000 0 0	. . . . . .	I	2222 0 34	3599 2 18
In yᵉ Barony of Iffa and Offa. Richard Kittlebutler, of St. Peter's Vincles, within yᵉ liberties of the Tower of London, cittizen, cutler,	25 0 0	. . . . . .	E	34 1 6	55 2 6
In yᵉ Barony of Clanwilliam. Nathaniel Lacey, eldest sonne of Nathaniel Lacey, and nephew and next heir of Richard Lacey, late of London, haberdasher, deceased.	200 0 0	. . . . . .	I	444 1 30	719 3 26
In yᵉ Barony of Ikerrin. Henry Day, of London, mercer.	225 - 0 0	530 0 0	I	777 3 3	1259 1 22

26th *October,* 1658.

This page above written conteyneth all yᵉ Claymes of and for such Adventurers as have been by us allowed, and not incerted in either of yᵉ two former Books by us certified under our hands, and sent into Ireland.

NATHANIEL MANTON, JOHN FFENTON, ROBERT HANON, ELIAS ROBERTS.

COUNTY of TIPPERARY
AS DIVIDED BY LOT BY BARONIES
Between
THE ADVENTURERS & SOLDIERS
Pursuant to Act of 23rd September 1653

The Adventurers Baronies are colored Blue
The Soldiers   "   "   Red

LOWER ORMOND

IKERRIN

OWNEY & ARRA

UPPER ORMOND

ILEAGH

ELIOGARTY

KILNAMANAGH

SLIEVE ARDAGH

MIDDLETHIRD

CLANWILLIAM

IFFA & OFFA

III.

SALE OF DEBENTURES BY THE COMMON SOLDIERS TO THEIR OFFICERS.

(See p. 95.)

By the Act for the Settlement of Ireland, passed at the King's Restoration, innocent Papists were to be restored forthwith, and the soldier who was dispossessed to be reprised. But the soldiers looked upon reprisals as mere notional or moonshine, and to retain their possession was what they looked to. Innocency or nocency was not their concern, but "shall I lose my lands?"*

This produced a conspiracy, commonly called the "Phanatic Plot of 1663," to seize the Castle and overturn the Government. The temper of the times appears by such instances as the following, which are taken from depositions sworn after the plot had been defeated, and the Duke of Ormond was seeking for evidence :—

One swore that upon St. Luke's Day, in the year 1662, he did come into a house in Kilbeggan, where one Sergeant Beverly and some others were in company, and one of them did say unto the said sergeant, that he was called "One of Cromwell's doggs;" whereupon Beverly answered, "they should let Cromwell alone, for he was the best man that ever reigned in the three nations, or that ever would, either of King, Prince, or any other; and if the King thinks to take away our lands that we gained by Cromwell and our swords, and to give it to those that are now come into the land, he shall be deceived; for we will join our heads together again, and have one knock for it first, my life for it."†

---

* Michael, Bishop of Cork, to the Duke of Ormond, 29th of May, and 5th of June, 1663. Carte MSS., G. G., pp. 296, 322, Bodleian Library, Oxford.

† Examination of John Flinn, of Rahan, taken by John Hallam, Esq., J. P. for King's County, 3rd Nov. 1663. Ib., B. 4to "Letters," p. 261.

Of the same mind were the officers. Major Alexander Jephson, and Colonel Edward Warren, died in defence of the same cause. Major Jephson, in his dying speech upon the gibbet, declared that they rose because of the corrupt acting (as he called it) of the Court of Claims, "turning poor Englishmen unjustly out of their lands ;— *out of that which they have been a-getting and keeping by Englishmen's blood and purses this five hundred years.*"*

The officers now began to regret that they had not kept their former comrades in the war as fellow-planters and neighbours, instead of purchasing up debentures to make themselves large proprietors. One was heard to say, he had rather than his estate that the soldiers that served Oliver Cromwell in Ireland had not sold their lands to the officers; and that, if they had kept them, neither the King nor the Duke of Ormond durst try their qualifications.†

By the Act of Settlement every one who had received lands under the Usurper's rule was obliged to send in his claim. The following is one out of many hundreds that escaped the great fire of 1711.

It shows how largely the officers bought up the soldiers' debentures. Conveyances from the soldiers, similar to the one given above, page 96, n., were, of course, produced to the court. It is the report of the officer to whom the claim was referred, probably John Petty, Surveyor-General, on the claim of Captain Tandy.

" *To the Honble. His Majesty's Commissioners appointed for putting in Execution the Act of Settlement and the Act of Explanation of ye same.*

" May it please Yr. Honnours,

" Pursuant to your Honnours' instructions we have compared and examined the Peticon and Schedule of Captain Thomas Tandy,

---

* Major Alexander Jephson's last speech upon the gibbet, July 15, 1663. Carte MSS., Ireland, vii., p. 258.

† " Edmond Morres, of Kerryhill, in the county of Kilkenny, being in company with Charles Minchin, of Knockagh, in the county of Tipperary, on the 18th of August, 1662, he said, Charles Minchin did say," &c. Carte MSS., F. F., p. 281, Bodleian Library.

who claymes in right of a Souldier, and doe report thereupon as
followeth :—

" Vizt.

Souldiers' Names in Collonell Clarke's Regt.	£	s.	d.	Souldiers' Names in Collonell Clarke's Regt.	£	s.	d.
Capt. Thomas Tandy . .	29	9	1	Wm. Golde	5	7	9
Id.	8	5	8	Hugh Griffith	6	7	1
Capt. Ed. Allen	193	3	8	Wm. Grantham.	6	7	1
Ensign Js. Ashley. . . .	65	7	11	Wm. Gardiner	5	7	9
Sergt. Wm. Stephens . .	15	13	4	John Gillmer	6	9	7
Sergt. Symon Peckham .	15	13	4	Thos. Grey	4	16	5
Captn. Edwd. Peratt . .	23	9	7	Danl. Hull.	5	7	9
Captn. W. Robinson . .	7	13	7	John Hutchins	5	7	9
Corporal Thos. Smyth . .	7	13	7	Arthur Mannyfold . . .	15	5	1
Wm. Reveson, Drummer .	7	13	7	Robt. Maurice	7	5	6
Robert Dawson, Drummer	7	13	7	Griffin Morgan	5	7	9
John Armstronge	5	7	9	Thos. Mason	5	7	9
Rd. Bradshawe	5	14	10	Wm. Moncke	5	7	9
Thos. Margott	7	13	7	John Mosse	5	7	9
Thomas Browne	5	7	9	George Howell	4	16	5
Francis Bradley	5	7	9	John Newmans	5	7	9
Thos. Ball, alias Bull . .	5	7	9	Jas. Oakford	5	7	9
Stephen Bastard	5	7	9	Chr. Palmer	5	7	9
Jas. Hayward	5	7	9	Robt. Pidle	4	16	5
Anthony Downton . . .	5	2	6	John Rogers	10	13	0
Philip Doyle	3	17	11	Thos. Shinkins	5	7	9
John Davis	6	7	1	John Summers	5	7	9
Js. Dermond	9	14	7	Thos. Skelton	5	7	9
Chas. Caprett	5	7	9	Henry Toler	5	7	9
Wm. Evans	5	7	9	Philip Thomas	5	7	9
Thos. Evans	13	11	3	John Turner	5	7	9
Hugh Edwards	7	18	9	Peter Thornton	11	11	5
David Edwards.	7	15	9	Ethelbert Unite	5	7	9
John Freese	5	7	9	George Woodburnes . . .	5	7	9
John Ffenne	5	7	9	Anthony Whalley. . . .	15	5	7
Rd. Ffarmerly	5	7	9	Robert Whyte	6	7	1
John Gilbert	4	16	5				

Souldiers' Names in Captn. Sandy's Company.	£	s.	d.	Souldiers' Names in Captn. Sandy's Company.	£	s.	d.
John Browne	5	7	9	Edwd Hackyn	6	7	1
John Browne	5	7	9	Rd. Hewson	6	7	1
John Benson	6	7	1	Wm. Hewson	6	7	1
Wm. Pettily	6	7	1	John Hill	6	7	1
Thos. Bate	6	7	1	Wm. Hill	6	7	1
Edw. Bryan	6	7	1	Mereda Jones	6	7	1
Symon Beslin	5	7	9	John Kelly	6	7	1
Thos. Crofts	5	8	6	Robt. Longe	4	16	1
Richd. Croutche	5	7	9	Walter Halley	8	10	1
John Coll	5	7	9	J. Lenningstown	5	7	9
John Cleane	5	7	9	Thos. Lowe	6	7	7
Henry Cooke	5	7	9	Roger Large	5	7	9
Thos. Claydon	5	7	9	Ralph Lee	6	7	1
Ralph Capper	5	14	10	John Lickgoe	5	2	6
John Cooke	4	4	1	Js. Lownd	6	7	1
Thoms. Clement	6	7	1	Rd. Leadbeater	6	7	1
Rd. Cooke	6	7	1	Ricd. Mollineux	6	7	1
Hersy Druitt	5	7	9	John Wardle	6	7	1
Robert Haywood	5	7	9	J. Hutchinson	15	5	1
Anthony Huddlestone	5	14	10	Patk. Wingfield	9	14	7
Rich. Hill	5	7	9	Patk. Smyth	15	17	4
Edwd. Kearne	5	7	9				

MEATH COUNTY.—KELLS BARRONY.

	£	s.	d.
Thos. Day	16	12	8
Robt. Cooper	9	2	4
Patk. Helton	16	12	8
Hugh Gill	9	14	7
Wm. Avery	5	7	10
Total of the said Company's debt	1059	19	2

The 12s. 3d. whereof are £649 4s.

		A.	R.	P.	
Plunket of Tat'rath.	Great Drewstowne	185	1	2	Claimant in possession.
	Little Drewstowne	189	0	0	
	Part of Gorly, the whole being	100	0	0	

ROBT. BLAKE, Esq.,
a Nominee.*

* Elect 18A. per estimation.

		A.	R.	P.		A.	R.	P.
Moore of Grenans-town,	Gilbertstown ..	70	6	6		70	0	10
		152	0	0				
	Total .	623	1	0	which, at 11*s.* per acre, pays £342 15*s.* 9*d.*			

A re-survey of this town by order of the Commissioners to the Surveyor-General, and upon the return found to be but 70A. 0R. 6P., and so allowed.

WESTMEATH COUNTY.—DELVIN BARONY.

George Nugent.—The town and lands of Ballinlough-bevil, *alias* Ballinlogh bemoyle.

	A.	R.	P.
	197	1	0
	194	1	20
	2	3	20

John Nugent, 8th May, 35th yeare of His Majesties reign, was left to law for recovery of this parcell. Entered.

J[OHN] P[ETTY].

Confirmed: placed to account by order of the 6th July, 1666.
Deficiency since placed to account by Paul Brazier, Esq., and in his certificate.

	A.	R.	P.
Earl of Westmeath.—Part of Martenstown, the whole 205 ..	181	0	0
Total ...	487	3	0

Which, at 12*s.* per acre, pays £306 5*s.* 9*d.*

Souldiers' Names in Collonell Clarke's Regt.	£	s.	d.	Souldiers' Names in Collonell Clarke's Regt.	£	s.	d.
Stephen Combes	37	14	10	Jas. Cooke	5	7	10
Hy. Roberts	5	7	10	Henry Morgan	5	7	10
Thos. Miller	14	18	11	Rich. Collington	16	12	8
Robt. Massey	16	6	5	Anth. Tongue	7	11	8
Thos. Evans	5	7	10	Dan. Suillevane	2	7	4
Thos. Baker	5	7	10	Benjn. Harvey	5	7	10
Roger Baker	1	2	9	John Pally	5	7	10
Symon Northcot	6	18	4	Henry Martin	5	7	10
Paule Reynolds	13	0	6	Jno. Bastone	5	7	10
Philip Grinster	5	7	10				

Souldiers' Names in Capt. Hardiar's Company.	Sums of Money.			Souldiers' Names in Capt. Hardiar's Company.	Sums of Money.		
	£	s.	d.		£	s.	d.
Thos. Rendall	5	7	10	Wm. Stephens	5	7	10
Martin Keffard	4	15	5	Sam. Seward	5	7	10
John Scott	12	9	10	Rd. Hicke	5	7	10
Rd. Singley	15	13	3	Thos. Selby	5	7	10

WESTMEATH COUNTY.—FFARBILL BARRONY.

	£	s.	d.
T. Wilkes	16	12	8
J. Pierce	14	12	9
T. Duke	5	7	10
Edward Hayden	16	12	9
J. Patterson	5	14	10
T. Merritt	5	7	4
Totall	£292	9	3
The 12s. 3d.	£185	5	4

To George Fitzgerald, 22nd June.

Sir Luke Fitzgerald, of Ticroghan—Part of Joristown, 240A. 3R. 0P., at 16s. per acre, requires [£192 0s. 0d.]

In possession '59. Died January, 166[ ]. Sells to yᵉ Claimant.*

As illustrative of the dealings of the army with the lands, there is appended a statement of the arrears due to Colonel Phaer's Regiment. It was found among the papers of the Phaer family by William J. O'Donnavan, Esq., of The Cloisters, Temple, a descendant of Colonel Phaer's, who has furnished it as explanatory of the subject.

The amount of forfeited land not extending, according to computation made in 1655, to satisfy the whole, the officers agreed to take lands for 12s. 3d. in the pound, on the 22nd May, 1654, and to have them admeasured and set out to them by Dr. Petty to that

---

* Endorsed, " Report of Captain Tandy, Westmeath."

From the volumes entitled " Claims in the Office of the late Surveyor-General," Custom House Buildings, Dublin.

extent, hoping still, as further lands might be discovered to be applicable to their debt, to obtain two-thirds, or 13*s.* 4*d.*, in the pound.*

Collonel Phaer's Regiment. The whole Debt of each Company.† The Money satisfied. The Acres satisfying.

	Total of the Debt.			The 12*s.* 3*d.* satisfied.			Acres satisfying.		
	£	*s.*	*d.*	£	*s.*	*d.*	A.	R.	P.
His owne Company . .	6643	19	8¼	4069	8	9¾	6782	1	24
Captain Radford . . .	1879	14	9¼	1151	6	9¾	1918	3	24
Colonel Robert Saunders .	2935	12	11¾	1798	1	8¾	2996	3	10
Lt.-Col. Wheeler . . .	2755	5	9	1687	12	3	2832	12	30
Major Dennison . . .	3016	11	6¾	1847	13	0¾	3079	1	20
Capt. Coakley	2492	7	11	1526	11	9¼	2544	1	10
Capt. Alex. Barrington .	2434	6	6	1491	0	5½	2485	0	7
Capt. Jervoise	2455	0	10¾	1503	14	3	2506	0	20
Capt. Gale	2489	11	2¾	1524	17	1¼	2541	1	28
Capt. Wakeham . . .	2109	12	7¼	1292	2	10½	2153	2	11
Added Debentors . . .	249	3	2½	152	12	2½	254	1	16
Totall. . .	£29,461	6	11¼	£18,045	1	4	30,075	0	0

* Petty's "Down Survey, by Larcom," ch. ix., p. 63.

† Captain Cartrett's company of Colonel Phaer's Regiment was satisfied in the barony of Bantry, county of Wexford. *Supra*, p. 99.

IV.

PETITIONS FOR DISPENSATION FROM TRANSPLANTATION INTO CONNAUGHT.

As the documents in full often convey a better notion than any abstract, a few orders made on the petitions for Dispensation from
Transplantation are here given. It would require to inspect the
many volumes full of them to realize the amount and variety of
misery suffered by the inhabitants of Ireland during the government
of the people of England.

The Lord Baron Brittas.

" Upon reading the petition of Theobald Lord Baron of Brittas,
touching his transplantation into Connaught, and the report of the
Commissioners of Revenue of Dublin thereupon, whereby it appears
that the petitioner hath in the year 1645 taken the oath of association with the Confederate Rebells (*alias* Catholics) : It is therefore ordered that the Governor and Commissioners of Revenue of
Limerick do proceed in the Petitioner's case according to the printed
instructions and declarations given for direction in this and
cases of like nature.

" *Dublin*, 29*th May*, 1654.

" THOMAS HERBERT, Clerk of the Council."*

Idem.

" Upon consideration had of the further petition of the
Baron of Brittas, it is ordered that the petitioner be allowed what
sheafe is due unto him according to the rule, and as by the Commissioners of Revenue upon the place is given to others in like
cases. And the Commissioners at Loughrea are to take care that

* $\frac{A}{85}$, p. 410.

the petitioner be provided for in Connaught answerable to his age and other qualifications.

"*Dublin, October* 13*th,* 1654.

"THOS. HERBERT, Clerk of the Council."*

Piers Creagh, of Limerick.

"Upon consideration had of the petition of Piers Creagh, of Limerick, desiring a dispensation from being transplanted into Connaught, and a liberty to enjoy his estate where it lies, and of the report of the Committee of Officers thereupon, whereby it appears' that upon serious reflection they have had of the petitioner's harmless carriages, and of his manifold affection to the present Government, which was heretofore more fully certified to the Commissioners of the Commonwealth from the officers of the army: They offer it as their opinion that the petitioner be allowed to remain in any part of the county of Limerick (except the city) till the 1st of May next. And for those lands the petitioner desired a fourth sheafe, if the said lands be in the Commonwealth's possession he be allowed the said fourth sheafe. And it was further certified by the said officers, that in regard they were persuaded that for his former known inclination to the English Government the petitioner, is hated by his countrymen, and that therefore he might be permitted to reside in such secure place in the county of Clare (not being within a garrison), neare the English quarters as the petitioner should make choice of in the disposal of the State; unto which said report the Lord Deputy and Council do agree, and therefore do hereby order, that the petitioner be dispensed with from transplantation till the 1st of May next, and that he do receive the fourth sheafe of and from those lands claymed by him in his petition, if in the possession of the State; and that he likewise be permitted to make choice of a convenient place to reside in from the 1st of May forward, neare the English quarters, in the county of Clare, provided it be not in any garrison. And hereof the Commander in Chief of Limerick and

* $\frac{A}{4}$, p. 51.

the county of Clare, and Commissioners of Assessments, and all others concerned are to take notice.

"*Dated at Dublin, the* 28*th of October*, 1654.

"THOS. HERBERT, Clerk of the Council."*

Lady Dowager of Louth.

"Upon considering the petition of the Lady Dowager of Louth, and consideration had thereof, and of the petitioner's great age and impotency; It is ordered, that it be referred to the Officer Commanding in Chief and Commissioners of Assessments for the precinct of Tredagh, to consider of the allegations thereof, and to dispense with the petitioner's transplantation into Connaught till the 1st of May, next. And that towards her present maintenance they do allow her two-third parts of the profits that arise to her out of the thirds of her estate till the 1st of May aforesaid. And that in case the said estate be already disposed of, they are to certify the same, to the end she may be otherwise provided for during the time the petitioner is dispensed with from transplantation; and then further care shall be taken of her with others of her condition, according to such rules as shall be held forth for that purpose.

"*Dublin,* 25*th October,* 1654.

"THOMAS HERBERT, Clerk of the Council."†

Elinor Butler.

"Upon consideration had of the petition of Elinor Butler, widow, and the order of the Commissioners of Revenue at Waterford touching her and the report of Colonel Lawrence thereupon (unto whom it was referred), it being thereby set forth that the petitioner's allegations are confirmed by a certificate of a person of good credit; and it being the said Colonel Lawrence's opinion upon the whole that the petitioner's own person and her helpless children should be dispensed with as to their present transplantation, and that she be permitted to bring back her cattle from Connaught towards the maintenance of herself and children; we, the said

---

* $\frac{A}{4}$, p. 122.   † Ib., p. 96.

Deputy and Council, do therefore agree and consent unto the said report, and do hereby order that the petitioner be accordingly permitted to bring back her said cattle without molestation. Whereof the said Commissioners of Revenue at Waterford, the Commissioners sitting at Loughrea, and all others concerned, are to take notice.

"*Dated at Dublin, the* 16*th of October,* 1654.

"THOMAS HERBERT, Clerk of the Council."*

Mary Thorpe, otherwise Dillon.

"Upon consideration had of the within petition of Mary Thorpe, otherwise Dillon, a Protestant ; and forasmuch as by her husband's recusancy comprising him within the order made that proprietors, &c., do transplant themselves into Connaught, he is to remove accordingly, to have lands set out to him there by the Commissioners sitting at Loughrea, according to his qualification. Further considering the merit of the petitioner, and that she is reputed to be a person fearing God and affecting His worship and ordinances, It is therefore ordered, that the Commissioners at Loughrea do forthwith sett out to the petitioner's husband lands as near Athlone or other place in Connaught, where she shall desire (not repugnant to former general orders), to the end that it may afford the petitioner the better conveniency of repairing neare to such places where the Gospel is preached.

"*Dublin,* 6*th October,* 1654.

"THOMAS HERBERT, Clerk of the Council."†

The Lady Trimleston.‡

"Ordered, that it be referred to the Commissioners at Loughreagh to consider of the within petition, and upon examination of the allegations, and finding them to be true as therein is set forth, they are to permit the petitioner's husband, the Lord Trimleston, to return into some place in the province of Leinster, for such time as shall be thought necessary for the recovery of his health, and so continue at the said place without removal above a mile from

* $\frac{A}{4}$, p. 62.　　　　　　　† Ib., p. 29.

‡ See pages 41 and 77, *supra.*

the same, without license from the Commander in Chief of the said precinct where he shall reside as aforesaid ; provided he return into Connaught within three months.

" *Dublin*, 8*th of August*, 1654.

" Signed in the name of the Lord Deputy and Council,

" MILES CORBETT."*

Mary Archer.

" Upon consideration had of a petition presented unto this Board by Mary Archer, in behalf of her aged father, Thomas Archer, and of the certificate thereunto annexed, deposed upon oath before Dudley Loftus, Esq., one of His Highness's Justices of the Peace for this county, that the said Thomas Archer is above 60 years of age, and that his transplantation into Connaught will infallibly endanger his life, if not suddenly bring him to his grave, wanting his former accustomed accommodations; It is therefore ordered, that he, the said Thomas Archer, be, and he is hereby dispensed with from transplantation into Connaught for the space of two months from the date hereof, to the end that at present he may not want the accommodations aforesaid, and thereby enable himself to travel into the transplantation quarter, according to rule.

" *Dublin Castle*, 19*th of May*, 1654.

" THOMAS HERBERT, Clerk of the Council."†

" *The Lord of Ikerrin.*‡

" Upon reading the petition of the Lord of Ikerrin, and consideration had thereof, and the report of the Standing Committee of Officers thereupon ; It is thought fit and ordered, that the petitioner (in regard of his weakness and infirmity of body) be permitted to repair to the Bath in England (according to his physician's advice), in order to the recovery of his health, for the space of six weeks. And it is further ordered, that the said Lord of Ikerrin's lady be dispensed with from her transplantation into

---

* $\frac{A}{85}$, p. 522.　　　† $\frac{A}{12}$, p. 71.　　　‡ See p. 71, *supra*.

Connaught for the space of two months from the 1st day of May next ; and that her servants be also dispensed with from their transplantation until they have gathered in their next harvest.

" *Dublin, the 24th of April*, 1654.

" CHARLES FLEETWOOD, MILES CORBETT, JOHN JONES."*

Edmund Magrath.†

" Upon consideration had of the within petition of Edmund Magrath, complaining that the woods upon the lands set out unto him in the county of Clare (pursuant to his qualification), are daily cut and destroyed by the Irish there, who bear him malice for his good services to the English, and by others, to his great damage and discouragement, and therefore praying relief in the premises ; It is ordered that it be referred to the next Justices of the Peace in that county, or any two of them, who are to consider of the allegations, and to examine the matter of fact, and to take such care for the petitioner's relief in the premises as shall be agreeable to law.

" *Dublin Castle, 20th May*, 1656.

" THOMAS HERBERT, Clerk of the Council."‡

" *Old Native Inhabitants of Limerick.*

" Upon reading the petition and papers of the old native inhabitants of Limerick, it being alledged by the petitioners that they have laboured as much as in them lay to preserve the English interests in that city, and to surrender to the English, whereby they became odious to the Irish, and therefore desired some place upon the River Shannon to be assigned unto them for their residence.

---

* $\frac{A}{85}$, p. 304.

† This Edmund Magrath, of Ballymore, Barony of Kilnemanagh, county of Tipperary, acted as a spy from the beginning of the Rebellion, and for his good service obtained Cromwell's special Letter of Dispensation from Transplantation, and had order to have his estate, not exceeding 800 acres, plantation measure, restored to him. Letter dated Whitehall, March 11th, 1657-8. " Letters of the Lord Protector," p. 121, Record Tower, Dublin Castle.

‡ $\frac{A}{12}$, p. 64.

And upon consideration had thereof, and of the report of the Committee of Transplantation, It is ordered that the petitioners as to their merits and qualifications be referred unto the officers commanding in chief and the Commissioners of Revenue within the precinct of Limerick, who are to proceed therein, according to the tenor of the late printed declaration of 27th of March last; and as to their place of residence, it is further referred to the Commissioners sitting at Loughreagh, who are to consider thereof, and to do therein as shall be agreeable to the rules and instructions given them in that behalf.

"*Dublin, 4th of April*, 1654.

"CHARLES FLEETWOOD, MILES CORBETT, JOHN JONES."*

Richard Christmas, of Bristol, Merchant.

"Upon consideration had of the petition of Richard Christmas, of Bristol, merchant, desiring that one Edward Browne, an Irish Papist, who hath been hitherto entrusted with the management of all his affairs in and about Waterford, hath been faithful unto him, and best understands and is acquainted with the petitioner's debts and credits, may be permitted to continue in Waterford, and follow his occupations as formerly; It is hereby ordered, that the said Edward Browne be permitted to reside in Waterford for and during the space of six months from the date hereof, and no longer, he giving good security to the Governor of Waterford that he will not act anything to the prejudice of His Highness and the State: And hereof all whom it may concern are to take notice.

"*Dublin, 18th August*, 1656.

"THOMAS HERBERT, Clerk of the Council."†

Dame Mary Culme.

"Upon reading the within petition of Dame Mary Culme, setting forth that her servant, Cornelius Brady, is upon some information transplanted into Connaught, being not liable thereunto,

---

* $\frac{A}{83}$, p. 244.   † $\frac{A}{12}$, p. 184.

and that the said Cornelius is her agent to sell and let her lands, and manage her necessary suits at law, &c., and thereupon praying that his transplantation might be dispensed with. And forasmuch as the respective Governors of Limerick, Galway, and Athlone, have power to give licences in the case, the Council think not fitt to do anything thereon, but leave the petitioner to make her application to the said Governors, who are to proceed in the case as shall be thought fitt.

“ *Dated at the Council Chamber, Dublin, 29th of August,* 1656.

“ THOMAS HERBERT, Clerk of the Council.”*

Lady Grace Talbot.

“ Upon reading the petition of Lady Grace Talbot, wife of Sir Robert Talbot, of Malahide, desiring a subsistence for her and her five children out of her estate in the county of Wicklow (alledged to be 1700 acres), or otherwise out of her husband's estate in Meath, and consideration had thereof, and of the report of Sir Hardress Waller, Sir Charles Coote, Commissary-General Reynolds, and Colonel Lawrence, whereby it appears that they humbly offer it as their opinion that, in regard of the petitioner's husband Sir Robert Talbot's civil carriage during the late rebellion, and his great charge, with the considerableness of his estate in the Province of Leinster, from whence he is to be transplanted ; and likewise the petitioner's incapability of receiving lands in Connaught, according to the rule of stock given out, that there be settled 500 acres of land in some convenient place in Connaught upon the said Lady Talbot and her children. And in case that her said husband's claim be allowed, and of right ascertained to a greater proportion, that then the said 500 acres be part thereof. And they further offer, that in regard the petitioner is an Englishwoman, and reduced to a poor condition, being without relief, and likely so to continue until the lands in Connaught shall yield her subsistence, that for six months yet to come the petitioner may receive the contribution

* $\frac{A}{12}$, p. 214.

Q

falling due thereon. It is further thought fitt and ordered, that the said Lady Grace Talbot do receive the quantity of 500 acres of land in Connaught; and that the petitioner do enjoy one moiety of the present profits arising out of her said husband's estate in Leinster (paying contribution) for the space of six months from the date hereof.

" *Dublin, 17th November,* 1654.

" Thomas Herbert, Clerk of the Council."*

* $\frac{A}{4}$, p. 438.

V.

THE MALLOW COMMISSION.—A. D. 1656.

IT was before a court at Athlone that the Irish nation had to appear to receive each man his doom. An exception, however, was made in favour of "the Ancient inhabitants of Cork, Kinsale, and Youghal,"* for whose trial a court was held at Mallow by the same judges as sat at Athlone, and these Ancient inhabitants were granted the peculiar privilege, that they were not in the mean time forced to transplant like the rest of the nation, but were permitted to reside in the county of Cork until the sitting of the court.

The conduct which entitled them to this signal distinction was their loyalty to the English interest, as it was called ; for though they were all Roman Catholics, they united themselves to the English and Protestant forces, shut the gates, manned the walls, and kept watch and ward with them against their own countrymen and religionists.

One would expect that the judgment of the Commissioners, if it did not mark them out for further favour, would at least have declared that they were not to be included in the dreadful doom pronounced on the rest of the nation.

But by the proceedings of the Court, of which there remains a full account under the hands of the Commissioners themselves, it will be seen that it was easier for a camel to go through the eye of a needle than for an Irish adversary of the English rebels, dwelling in Ireland, to escape transplantation to Connaught.

When the rebels of England, at the end of the year 1643, in-

---

* The case of the ancient natives of Youghal is not given in the Mallow Commissioners' Report ; but it would seem that they were turned out of that town at the same time as the natives of Cork—p. 143, *supra.*

duced the rebels of Scotland by a gift of £100,000 to invade England a second time to help them against the King, the King turned to Ireland to obtain forces, and Lord Ormond, at his command, sent him over considerable bodies of troops.

But the King placed his chief hopes in the aid he expected to derive from the Confederate Catholics upon the conclusion of a treaty for a peace; preliminary to which he directed Lord Ormond to enter into a cessation of arms with them. The new English of Ireland, composed chiefly of planters since Queen Elizabeth's time, whose hatred and fear of the Irish, on account of the injuries they had inflicted on them, far exceeded their loyalty to the King, could not endure the idea of the King's vanquishing the rebels of England by such aid. " Where would the Protestant religion be," they asked, " if the King conquered by the aid of the Irish?"* Or, rather (for this was the religion they thirsted after), where would the lands of the ancient nobility, gentry, and people of Ireland be in that case, which, to the extent of 2,500,000 acres, the Parliament had already confiscated by anticipation, while the Puritan rebels and their followers had still in view the swallowing up of the rest ? The Earl of Inchiquin, who commanded large forces in Munster for the King, and had his head-quarters at Cork, now turned over for this cause to the Parliament side. He wrote to his brother Henry, who held Wareham with his (Inchiquin's) regiment, for the King, to deliver that town to the Parliament, and bring the regiment to Ireland; and wrote letters to Colonel Mynn, Colonel Poulet, and Colonel St. Leger, urging them also to bring their forces over to Munster.† He impressed upon them his conviction that "deserving men would have the estates of their enemies conferred upon them by the Parliament at the end of this war, as it was at the end of the last war, i. e.

---

* " A Letter from the Right Hon. the Lord Inchiquin and the other Commanders in Munster to His Majestie, expressing the Reasons for not holding the Cessation any longer with the Rebells, &c. ; with several other Letters to Friends here in England advising them to return to their former Charges in Ireland, &c. Published by authority." 4to. London : 1644.

† Ib.

Tyrone's wars."* This could not be expected if the King were to put down the rebellion of England by the aid of the Irish. Meantime he drove out all the Old English inhabitants of Irish birth, pretending he could not be safe with them because they were "Irish" and Catholic, though they had shut the gates against the Irish in 1641, and had ever since joined with the King's forces, defending the town against them. At the same time he wrote over to England, suggesting that the Parliament should give the houses and lands of the expulsed inhabitants to the English remaining in the city of Cork.†

As Irish evidence is not to be believed unless it be to the prejudice of the nation (according to the maxim that an Irishman's oath is of no value except to hang another), the loyalty of the Ancient natives of Cork would probably not be credited unless upon English testimony. Against the calumnious and interested charges of Lord Inchiquin, therefore, there is to be set the solemn report of the Duke of Ormond, the Earl of Anglesey, and Sir George Hamilton (no friends of the Irish), made at the order of the King, on the petition of these expelled inhabitants, who prayed at the Restoration to be restored to their lands and former habitations.

By this report it was certified that the ancient natives of Cork had at all times from the breaking out of the troubles and disturbances acted with and for the English interest equally with the English Protestants; that when they were put out of their houses and from their habitations, they, to hold still firm to their loyalty, had immediate recourse, and only refuge, by their mayor, Robert Coppinger, to the Lord Marquis of Ormond, as the proper centre, in whose hands they deposited the badges of their privileges, namely, the sword, mace, and cap of maintenance; and his Lordship, in acknowledgment of such faithful and loyal deportment, knighted the said Robert Coppinger; and then promised, in the behalf of his late Majesty, to render unto them in seasonable time the said sword, and mace, and cap of maintenance, and to testify to

* "A Letter," &c., as before, p. 228, *supra*   † Ib.

their advantage how properly they had deposited the same in due time.*

They further reported that it appeared by two several letters from his late Majesty of ever-blessed memory, in the years 1643 and 1644, directed to the mayor, aldermen, and commons of that city, that they had, towards the maintenance of His Majesty's army, issued in loans and otherwise the sum of £30,000, besides their other sufferings mentioned in their former petition, amounting to £60,000; and when their stock in corn was totally exhausted, they willingly gave up their plate, household stuff, and moveables, to advance his late Majesty's service, which the said late King declared himself so sensible of, that he said the same should be in due time remembered to their great advantage, and returned to their loyal bosoms.†

The case of the ancient inhabitants of Kinsale is to be found in the report of Cromwell's Commissioners. The Court was opened on the 22nd of July, 1656. On the 29th, the case of Thomas Toomey (otherwise Thomas) was heard. Most of the claims depended upon it. The judges heard it at great length. They adjourned to the following morning, to allow the counsel at the bar to speak to it. The claimant owned a house in Kinsale, under a lease made in 1635. He was a shipwright, and worked in the King's dockyard there. It was proved that he shut the gates against the Irish in 1641; that he served as a corporal under Captain John Farlo; that he kept watch and ward when the rebels besieged the town. It came out, however, that after Inchiquin revolted from the Parliament, in 1649, and returned to the King's side, contribution was collected by the magistrates, and paid by Toomey‡ (as by all the other inhabitants) to his receivers; that distresses were taken on everybody; none durst refuse payment of contribution to Inchiquin. This, however, was the claimant's ruin. It deprived him of the plea of Con-

* Report, dated 13th February, 1661, Liber D., of a series of twelve volumes, folio, relating to the Act of Settlement, in the Record Tower, Dublin Castle.

† Ib.

‡ It would seem from this that the ancient inhabitants of Kinsale continued to dwell there during the whole war.

stant good affection, which but for this he might have maintained. He had resided in the enemies' quarters, and this brought him within the Eighth qualification. The consequences appear from the following special report of these proceedings made by the Commissioners to the Government:—

" COURT AT MALLOW FOR THE QUALIFICATIONS OF THE IRISH THAT FORMERLY INHABITED THE TOWNS OF CORKE, YOUGHAL. AND KINSALE.

" *29th of August*, 1656.

" This day the claimants' counsel demanded the judgment of the Court upon the point of Constant good affection; and first in the case of Thomas Toomey of Kinsale, whether upon proof he hath manifested Constant good affection.

" MR. JUSTICE COOKE.—Negative.

" MR. JUSTICE HALSEY.—Negative.

" It is adjudged that Thomas Toomey hath not manifested Constant good affection; but falls within the eighth qualification, to have two parts of his estate in Connaught.

" COURT.—The counsel for Thomas Toomey is to proceed upon his title.*

" MR. SILVER.—He is resolved not to go into Connaught.

" MR. HOARE.—And so they are all.

" MR. SILVER.—My clients do further demand the judgment of the Court, whether they, and how many of them, have proved their Constant good affections?

" COURT.—We have seriously considered of the several cases and several claimants named, as George Gold Fitz-William, Dominick Sarsfield, David Terry, Patrick Galway, James Gough, Patrick Meagh, Stephen Coppinger, Patrick Roth, John Coppinger, James Murro, John Levallyn, James Levallyn [and so all the claymants were named particularly].

---

* That is, to prove what lands he was formerly possessed of, in order to regulate the quantity to be now set out to him in Connaught.

"JUSTICE HALSEY.—If you demand of us any further judgment in any particular client's case, you shall have it; though you see we have run over them all.

"CLAIMANTS' COUNSEL.—We humbly demand the judgment of the Court upon the whole, whether any claimant hath proved Constant good affection ?

"JUSTICE COOKE.—Negative.

"JUSTICE HALSEY.—Negative.

"Resolved by the Court, that not any one of a Popish claimant hath proved Constant good affection.

"JUSTICE COOKE.—Now proceed upon the title distinctly.

"CLAIMANTS' COUNSEL.—Not one of our clients will proceed.

"COURT.—You had best to advise your clients what to do. We shall stay your leisure. Therefore adjourn till the afternoon.

"Saturday Afternoon.

"JUSTICE COOKE, present; JUSTICE HALSEY, present.

"COURT.—Will the counsel, or any of the attorneys for any of the claimants, proceed to their titles?

"MR. SILVER.—James Gough, Patrick Meagh, Stephen Coppinger, Patrick Roth, John Coppinger, James Murro, John Levallyn [and so all the claimants were named particularly].

"COURT.—We have considered of the several causes of every claimant in Court, and have singled out about thirty which may come nearest to Constant good affection. And we cannot find that any of them hath manifested Constant good affection according to the strict rule of law, but all fall short in some point or other.

"CLAIMANTS' COUNSEL.—We hope in equity our clients shall not be sent into Connaught among their enemies.

"COURT.—We must proceed, as our Commission requires, according to law; and we cannot find how the Irish can be in a better condition than the English, who are to forfeit a fifth for their delinquency had it not been for His Highness' Ordinance of Indemnity.*

* Protestants who had not shown a Constant good affection to the cause of the rebels of England were liable to forfeit one-fifth. But by an ordinance of 2nd Sep-

" CLAIMANTS' COUNSEL.—Our clients would willingly lose a great deal more.

" COURT.—We cannot alter the law, but must judge according to law.

" MR. SILVER.—Our clients will not take any lands in Connaught. We have demanded the judgment of the Court concerning the several estates of our clients that are Protestants, as, namely, Mr Robert Southwell, William Chidley, William Howell, Christopher Sugar, and others, who were Protestants and proprietors at the time of the Act of Settlement.

" COURT.—We shall consider of the several cases of the Protestant claimants who had *bonâ fide* purchased from Papists before the Act of Settlement, as to that point only, whether they can be in a better position than those from whom they claim.

" JUSTICE COOKE.—Proceed, therefore, to the titles of your Irish clients.

" CLAIMANTS' COUNSEL.—We have advised with our clients, and they are resolved not to take any lands in Connaught.

" The first proclamation was made.

" COURT.—Crier, make proclamation again that all persons who have any business here to do may come in and be heard.

" Second proclamation was made.

" COURT.—Will you proceed before the last proclamation be made, or else it will be too late?

" CLAIMANTS' COUNSEL.—We humbly pray the Court to adjourn till Munday, that we may better advise with our clients.

" COURT.—Adjourn till Munday, at 8 of the clock.

" *Munday, Sept.* 1, 1656.

" COOKE, present; HALSEY, present.

" COURT.—Will any of the claimants proceed upon their titles, that they may have their proportions in Connaught?

tember, 1654, they were allowed to compound for two years' annual value of their real and personal estates, which was equal to one-fifth as lands were then rated, viz., at ten years' purchase.

" CLAIMANTS' COUNSEL. There being only present Mr. Hoare and Mr. Silver, Attorneys (Mr. Fisher, Mr. Jones, Mr. Barber, and all the other Protestant practizers having left the Court),

" MR. SILVER.—The claimants will not a man of them proceed unless they may enjoy their own estates; they will not go into Connaught.

" COURT.—They must transplant according to law.

" The Court urged them several times to proceed, but they would not.

" COURT.—Make proclamation, requiring all that have any business at this Court to come in and proceed.

" Third proclamation made.

" Nothing moved.

" The claimants made a noise, some of them saying they had rather go to the Barbadoes than into Connaught amongst the rebels.

" COURT.—We shall consider of the claims of the Protestants, and they shall know our judgment thereon.

" The Court arose, and day to* ——

" MAY IT PLEASE YOUR LORDSHIPS,

" Upon mature and deliberate consideration (so far as the Lord hath enabled us) we have proceeded to judgment in the causes depending before us, and have not adjudged Constant good affection to any one of the claimants; but the law will be clear for most of them to have two parts in Connaught. There remains only one question concerning the interests of Protestants, which they purchased from Papists since 1641, and before the Act of Settlement [of 12th August, 1652], wherein we humbly crave the opinions of the Lords the Judges as to the matter of law before we give judgments.

" The matter of fact being as followeth :—

" A., a Papist, upon the trial of his Qualifications is found to be neither aider, abettor, countenancer, nor promotor of the rebellion

---

* Blank in the Report.

within the Act of September;* but fails to make out Constant good
affection, by reason of the general defection of Inchiquin, &c.; so for-
feits a third part, as a Papist within the Eighth qualification, having
conveyed the land to a Protestant.

" The question is, whether B. is to lose a third part of the estate,
and take the other two parts in Connaught?"

On the part of the Commonwealth it was contended, that the
purchasers must lose one-third, and take two-thirds in value in Connaught, because they could be in no better condition than him from
whom they purchased. The Protestant purchasers insisted that, as
the persons whose lands they purchased had never aided nor coun-
tenanced the rebellion, and had constantly dwelt amongst the English, they must be deemed to have shown a Constant good affection,
and therefore should suffer no forfeiture. But the Mallow Commissioners submitted that the proof that was offered "was only in the
negative, doing nothing, neither good nor bad, and was not sufficient to prove Constant good affection, which must appear by outward signal demonstration of the affection of the heart, and not in
sitting still," and accordingly referred it to the judgments of their
Lordships.

The Report concludes thus:—
" If we could have foreseen the tenth part of the difficulties
which we have met with in this business, we should have been ear-
nest and humble suitors to your Lordships for more assistance, our
brother Santhy being gone into Kerry, Limerick, and Clare, that
the counties might not be disappointed; wee have endeavoured to
the utmost of our apprehensions to convince and satisfy the claimants
and standers by of the legality and justice of our proceedings; and
because in so great an expectation we feared that, if all should be
transplanted it might seem to carry some face of rigour, we spared
no pains to distinguish the merits of each case; and as we were selecting ten or twenty that might best pretend to be legally restored

* Properly of August 12th, 1652.

to their own estates, the next claimants had instantly as much to say for themselves; and when we had named and weighed about eighty-six cases, which possibly might come nearest to the mark of Constant good affection, presently the claimants' counsel named others to us, which we in our reason could not deny but that they did equally merit with the rest; so as we found an absolute necessity to deny Constant good affection to all or none (some very few exceptions that will fall within 1st or 7th qualification); and that which turned the scale was their residence with Inchiquin after his revolt.

" We have called upon them to proceed to their titles, and adjudged the 8th qualification to many of them, which for the present they decline and refuse, and will not proceed upon their titles, so as we can proceed no further therein.

" They make great asseverations that they dare not go into Connaught for fear of their lives, and that they had rather be sent to the Barbadoes, which we tell them are vain and frivolous allegations, and that by law they are transplantable. So most of them have left us. We have caused several proclamations to be made that if any person have anything to do he may come in and be heard; and shall stay so long as any of them will proceed. Having done according to our Commission, to the best of our skill and knowledge, and so we humbly remain,

" Your Lordships' most humble
" And faithful Servants,
" JOHN COOKE, WM. HALSEY.

" P. S.—If your Lordships shall be pleased to enlarge our Commission until the 29th inst., my brother Santhy and myself will have ended the circuit (God willing), by the 16th inst., and be at Moyallo by the 18th inst., where we have ordered the clerk to stay for us.

" J. COOKE.

" To the Honourable the Lord Deputy and Council
    for the Affairs of Ireland."*

---

* From a quarto volume in limp sheepskin cover, in the Record Tower, Dublin Castle, endorsed, " Mallow Proceedings."

VI.

OF THE SEIZING OF WIDOWS AND ORPHANS, AND THE DESTI-
TUTE, AND TRANSPORTING THEM TO BARBADOES, AND THE
ENGLISH PLANTATIONS.

WHILE the Government were employed in clearing the ground
for the Adventurers and Soldiers (the English capitalists of that
day), by making the nobility and gentry yield up their ancient
inheritances, and withdraw to Connaught, " where they could wish
the whole nation,"* they had agents actively employed through Ireland, seizing women, orphans, and the destitute, to be transported
to Barbadoes and the English Plantations in America. It was a
measure beneficial to Ireland, which was thus relieved of a population that might trouble the planters; it was a benefit to the
people removed, who might thus be made English and Christians;†
and a great benefit to the West India sugar planters, who desired
the men and boys for their bondmen, and the women and Irish
girls in a country where they had only Maroon women and Negresses to solace them. The thirteen years' war, from 1641 to 1654,
followed by the departure of 40,000 Irish soldiers, with the chief
nobility and gentry, to Spain, had left behind a vast mass of widows
and deserted wives with destitute families. There were plenty of
other persons, too, who, as their ancient properties had been confiscated, " had no visible means of livelihood." Just as the King of
Spain sent over his agents to treat with the Government for the Irish
swordmen, the merchants of Bristol had agents treating with it for

---

* " The garrison of Roscommon Castle yielded upon that which we adjudged moderate terms amongst us, which is, for the Government to transport a regiment for
Spain, *where we could wish the whole nation.*" Letter from Athlone, 12th April,
1652. " Severall Proceedings in Parliament," &c., p. 2146.

† Letter of Henry Cromwell, 4th Thurloe's " State Papers."

men, women, and girls, to be sent to the sugar plantations in the West Indies. The Commissioners for Ireland gave them orders upon the governors of garrisons, to deliver to them prisoners of war; upon the keepers of goals, for offenders in custody; upon masters of workhouses, for the destitute in their care, "who were of an age to labour, or if women were marriageable and not past breeding;" and gave directions to all in authority to seize those who had no visible means of livelihood, and deliver them to these agents of the Bristol sugar merchants, in execution of which latter direction Ireland must have exhibited scenes in every part like the slave hunts in Africa. How many girls of gentle birth must have been caught and hurried to the private prisons of these men-catchers none can tell.* But at last the evil became too shocking and notorious, particularly when these dealers in Irish flesh began to seize the daughters and children of the English themselves, and to force them on board their slave ships; then, indeed, the orders, at the end of four years, were revoked.

Messrs. Sellick and Leader, Mr. Robert Yeomans, Mr. Joseph Lawrence, and others, all of Bristol, were active agents. As one instance out of many:—Captain John Vernon was employed by the Commissioners for Ireland into England, and contracted in their behalf with Mr. David Sellick and Mr. Leader, under his hand, bearing date the 14th September, 1653, to supply them with two hundred and fifty women of the Irish nation above twelve years, and under the age of forty-five, also three hundred men above twelve years of age and under fifty, to be found in the country within twenty miles of Cork, Youghal, and Kinsale, Waterford, and Wexford, to transport them into New England.† Messrs. Sellick and Leader appointed their

---

* Daniel Connery, a gentleman of Clare, was sentenced, in Morison's presence, to banishment, in 1657, by Colonel Henry Ingoldsby, for harbouring a priest. " This gentleman had a wife and twelve children. His wife fell sick, and died in poverty. Three of his daughters, most beautiful girls, were transported to the West Indies, to an island called the Barbadoes ; and there, if they are alive, they are in miserable slavery." P. 287. Morison's " Threnodia Hiberno-Catholica," Innsbruck : 1659.

† $\frac{A}{84}$, p. 663.

shipping to repair to Kinsale; but Roger Boyle, Lord Broghill (afterwards Earl of Orrery), whose name, like that of Sir C. Coote, seems ever the prelude of woe to the Irish, suggested that the required number of men and women might be had from among the wanderers and persons who had no means to get their livelihood in the county of Cork alone. Accordingly, on the 23rd of October, 1653, he was empowered to search for them and arrest them, and to deliver them to Messrs. Sellick and Leader, who were to be at all the charge of conducting them to the water side, and maintaining them from the time they received them; and no person, being once apprehended, was to be released but by special order in writing under the hand of Lord Broghill.*

Again, in January, 1654, the Governors of Carlow, Kilkenny, Clonmel, Wexford, Ross, and Waterford, had orders to arrest and deliver to Captain Thomas Morgan, Dudley North, and John Johnson, English merchants, all wanderers, men and women, and such other Irish within their precincts as should not prove they had such a settled course of industry as yielded them a means of their own to maintain them, all such children as were in hospitals or workhouses, all prisoners, men and women, to be transported to the West Indies. The governors were to guard the prisoners to the ports of shipping; but the prisoners were to be provided for and maintained by the said contractors, and none to be discharged except by order under the hand and seal of the governor ordering the arrest.† It is easy to imagine the deeds done under such a power! On the 22nd December, of the same year, orders were issued prohibiting all the shipping in any harbour in Ireland bound for Barbadoes, and other English plantations, from weighing anchor until searched, in order that any persons found to have been seized without warrant should be delivered.

All measures, however, were vain to prevent the most cruel captures as long as these English slave dealers had recourse to Ireland. In the course of four years they had seized and shipped about 6400

* $\frac{A}{84}$, p. 663.   † $\frac{A}{85}$, p. 66.

Irish, men and women, boys and maidens, when on the 4th of March, 1655, all orders were revoked. These men-catchers employed persons (so runs the order) "to delude poor people by false pretences into by-places, and thence they forced them on board their ships. The persons employed had so much a piece for all they so deluded, and for the money sake they were found to have enticed and forced women from their children and husbands, — children from their parents, who maintained them at school; and they had not only dealt so with the Irish, but also with the English,"—which last was the true cause, probably, of the Commissioners for Ireland putting an end to these proceedings.*

Yet not quite an end.

In 1655 Admiral Penn added Jamaica to the empire of England; and, colonists being wanted, the Lord Protector applied to the Lord Henry Cromwell, then Major-General of the forces in Ireland, to engage 1500 of the soldiers of the army in Ireland to go thither as planters, and to secure a thousand young Irish girls ("Irish wenches" is Secretary Thurloe's term), to be sent there also.† Henry Cromwell answered that there would be no difficulty, only that force must be used in taking them;‡ and he suggested the addition of from 1500 to 2000 boys of from twelve to fourteen years of age. "We could well spare them," he adds, "and they might be of use to you; and who knows but it might be a means to make them Englishmen—I mean, Christians?"§ The numbers finally fixed were 1000 boys, and 1000 girls, to sail from Galway in October, 1655,‖—the boys as bondmen, probably, and the girls to be bound by other ties to these English soldiers in Jamaica.¶

* $\frac{A}{10}$, p. 283.   † 4th vol. Thurloe's "State Papers," p. 75.
‡ Ib., p. 23.   § Ib., p. 40.   ‖ Ib., p. 100.
¶ Müller, the painter at Berlin, was stated to be engaged in 1859 on a picture representing the seizing and transporting of these Irish girls to the West Indies. See the Newspapers of the 21st Feb., 1859.

VII.

PETITIONS OF MAURICE VISCOUNT ROCHE, OF FERMOY, AND OF JORDAN ROCHE'S CHILDREN.

(Page 74, *supra*.)

*To the Right Hon. the Lords Justices of Ireland, the humble Petition of Maurice Lord Viscount Roche, of Fermoy,**

MOST HUMBLY SHEWETH,—That your Petitioner hath been seaven yeares agoe dispossessed of his wholl estate, havinge the chardge of Foure young daughters, unpreferred, to whose misery was added the losse of their mother, your Petitioner's wife, by an unjust illegal proceeding, as is knowne and may be attested by the best Protestant Nobility and Gentry of the Countie of Corke, who have heard and seen it, and whose charitable compassion it moved ; That your said Petitioner and his said children ever since have lived in a most disconsolate condition, destituted of all kind of subsistence (except what Almes some good Christians did in charity afford them), by occasion whereof one of your Petitioner's daughters, falling sick about three years ago, died, for want of requisite accommodacon, either for her cure or diett ; That your Petitioner hath often supplicated those in authority in the late Government for releefe, who after ten months attendance in Dublin gave him no other succor but an order to the Commissioners in Connaught to set outt some lands for him, *De bene esse,* there or in the county of Clare ; That your Petitioner being necessitated to goe from Dublin afoote to attende on them in Athlone and Loughreagh for six moneths more (in which prosecution and attendance he ran himself £100 in debt), yet at last had but 2500 acres, part in the Owles, in Connaught, and part in the

---

* Order Book of the Commissioners for Executing the King's Declaration, late Auditor-General's Office, Custom House Buildings, vol. xvii., p. 112.

remotest parts of Thomond, all wast and unprofitable, at that time assigned him, both which, before and after, were by the sayd Commissioners disposed of by Finall settlements to others, who evicted your Petitioner thereout before he could receive any maner of profitt, soe as that colour of succor and reliefe proved rather an increase and addition of misery to your said Petitioner, who is now in that very low condition that he cannot in person attend on your Lordships, much less make a jorney to his sacred Majesty to sett forth his sufferings and to implore releefe :

The premises tenderly considered, and for that it hath beene unheard of in all former ages that a Peere of the Realm of English extraction, though never so criminous, should be reduced to such extremitie of misery, his cause not heard, and without conviction or attainder by his Peeres or otherwise, contrary to the known lawes of the land, and the rights and privileges of the Nobilitie and Peerage; and for that your Petitioner is in that forlorne condition that he cannot any longer hould out unless speedily releaved, your Lordships may be pleased to afford your said Petitioner some present succour and releife, and to enable him to discharge the said £100 debt.

And hee will pray, &c.

TO THE RIGHT HONOURABLE THE COMMISSIONERS OF THE COMMON-
WEALTH OF ENGLAND FOR THE AFFAIRS OF IRELAND.

The humble Petition of Christian Roche, Anstace Roche, Cate Roche, and John Roche, the Children of Alderman Jordan Roche, deceased,

SHEWETH—That Alderman Jordan Roche, deceased, dyed seized of a reall estate to the value of £2000 a year, and likewise of a considerable personal estate, all which devolved and came to the publique; That your poore Petitioners are in a sadd and deplorable condition for want of sustenance or mayntenance, and have nothing to live upon but what they erne by their needles, and by washing and wringing. The humble request of your petitioners is that your Honnours

may be pleased to cast a favourable eye of compassion on the starve-
ing condition of your poore Petitioners; and accordingly to be
pleased to graunte unto them such a competent alimony out of
their father's estate, or otherwise, as to your Honnours in your approved judgments shall be thought most fitt, being an act very
charitable, and suitable to the civilitie of the English Government.

And your poore Petitioners, as in duty bound, shall pray.*

The Commissioners for Ireland referred it to the Commissioners for
Setting out Lands to the Transplanted sitting at Loughreagh, to in-
quire in what Qualification of the Act of Settlement they fell, and to
grant them such relief as should be agreeable to the said Act and to
their instructions : in other words, they refused them relief, and
"left them to the rules."   Order dated April, 1654.

---

* Council Book, in the Records of the late Auditor-General's Office, Custom
House Buildings, vol. vii.

VIII.

TRANSPLANTERS' CERTIFICATES.
(See page 23, *supra*.)

By the Commissioners within the Precincts of Clonmell.

No. of Certificate, and Tyme of Presenting.

No. 1, folio 1.

WEE, the said Commissioners, do hereby certifye that John Hore, of Ballymacmaag, and Mathew Hore, of Shandon, in the county of Waterford, hath, upon the 23rd day of January, 1653, in pursuance of a Declaration of the Commissioners of the Parliament of England for the Affairs of Ireland, bearing date the 14th day of October, 1653, delivered unto us in writing a particular, containing therein the names of himself and such other persons as are to remove with him, with the quantities and qualities of their respective stocks and tillage, the contents whereof are as followeth :— viz.—1. John Hore, of Ballymacmaag, adged seventy ; gray haired, tall stature; freeholder ; ten cows, five garrans. 2. Edmund Hore, son to the said John, adged ten years, brown haire. 3. Owen Crumpon, of the same, adged thirty; black; middle stature; servant. 4. James Daton, of the same, adged sixteen; flaxen haire; servant. 5. Morish Caffon, of Ballidonnack, adged thirty-foure; brown; low, servant. 6. Mathew Hore, of Shandon, adged thirty-one ; browne; middle; freeholder ; eight cows, two hundred sheepe, seventy-nine garrans, five cows; forty-two acres of wheate and beare, seven of pease. 7. Mary Hore, wife of the said Mathew, aged twenty-five ; white, tall. 8. Mary Hore, daughter of the said Mathew, adged nine ; flaxen ; three cows, two heifers. 9. Margaret Hore, daughter to the said Mathew, foure ; flaxen ; low; three cows, two bullocks. 10. Bridget Hore, daughter to the said Mathew, adged two ; white;

two cóws, and two bullocks. 11. John Hore, son to the said Mathew, adged seaven; white; lowe; three cows, and two yearlings. 12. Patrick Hore, son to the said Mathew, adged five; white; lowe; five cows, and one yearling. 13. Martin Hore, adged three; flaxen; ten cows, and one yearling, and thirty-six sheepe. 14. Murtagh Morrochoe, of Grage, aged thirty-seaven; browne; middle; tenant; two cows, and one yearling, fifteene sheepe, one garran. 15. Nicholas Power, of Shandon, sixtie; graye; middle; servant. 16. Edmund Kelly, of the same, thirty; black; middle; servant. 18. Thomas Kelly, of the same, thirty-nine; black; lowe; servant. 19. Thomas Fitzgerald, of the same, nineteen: white; tall; servant. 20. William Roch, of the same, servant. 21. Henry Tobin, of the same, thirtie; browne; low; servant. 22. Thomas Donnell, of the same, fortie-foure; browne; low; servant. 23. Morris Offelahan, of the same, fiftie; graye; middle; servant. 25. John O'Morrissee, of the same, seventeen; brown; low; servant. 26. Morish O'Morrissee, of the same, fifteen; dark; low; servant. 27. William O'Tuscan, of Ikart, thirtie; dark; middle; servant; two cows, ten sheepe, one garran; five acres of wheate, [   ] beare. 28. Nicholas White, of the same, sixteene; white; low; servant. 29. James Murphy, of the same; thirtie-four; brown; low; tenant; seaven sheepe, one garran. 30. Michael Conry, of Ballinacourty, thirtie-seaven; middle; tenant; three cows, sixteen sheepe, nine garrans; six acres of wheate, and two of pease and beans. 31. John O'Kelly, of the same, twentie; white; low; servant. 32. Richard [   ], of Ballyduff, thirtie-nine; black; middle; tenant; one cow, seven sheepe, three garrans; two acres of wheate and beare, and two of pease and beans. 33. Morish Ffallon, of Killdagan, fortie; graye; low; tenant; four cows, fifteene sheepe, eleven garrans, seaven acres of wheate and beare. 34. Patrick Ffallon, of the same, twentie; brown; middle; tenant. 35. Walter Power, of Ballinrode, twentie-five; brown; tall; tenant; five cows, fortie-three sheepe, eight garrans; ten acres of wheate and beare. 36. Darby Ffollowe, of Ballyhannick, fortie-four; black; tall; tenant; two cows, four sheepe, six garrans; five acres of wheate and beare. 37. Darby Powsye, of the same, thirtie-two; brown; tall; tenant; one cow, eleven sheepe, ten garrans; two acres of wheate and beare. 38. Mary Russell, the relict of Patrick Russell, of Dungarvan, burgess. fiftie-three; yellow; middle; three cows, fiftie sheepe, one garran, 39. John Fitzgerald, of the same, fortie; black; low; tenant; three cows, ten sheepe, one garran; one acre of wheate and beare. 40. Morish Roch, of the same, twenty-five; brown; middle; tenant; two cows, ten sheepe, two garrans; two acres of wheate, beare, and beans. 41. Morish Fitzgerald, of Grenane, twenty-five ; white; middle; servant. 42. Patrick Ffollowe, of Ballyhormock, thirteen; brown; servant. 43. William Wray, of the same, fourteen; brown; servant. 44. Morish Cowden, of Inchindrislye, thirtie-six; black; middle; tenant; one cow, ten sheepe, two garrans; one acre of wheate and beare. 45. Robert Pirquett, of the same, fiftie ; brown ; low; tenant; one cow, one garran, one acre of wheate and beare. 46. John Pirquett, of the same, twentie; browne; low; servant. 48. John Nagle, of Donnemainstragh, thirty-two ; brown ; tall; freeholder; two cows, ten sheepe, three garrans; three acres of wheat and beare, and one of pease. 49. James How fitz Thomas of Dungarvan, ten; blacke; low; burgess. 50. John Lea, of Dungarvan, sixteen; tall; white; freeholder. 51. John Coppinger the elder, of the same, fiftie-five; graye; tall; freeholder. 52. Philip Power, of Ballinrode, thirtie-five; brown; low; tenant; one cow, ten sheepe, two garrans; two acres of wheate and beare. 53. John O'Morrissee, of Ballinkelly, twenty-six; brown; middle; tenant; eight cows, twentie sheepe, ten garrans; five acres of wheat, two of pease. 54. Margaret, his wife, twenty-four; white; middle. 55. Philip Flyn, of the same, fifteen; brown; servant. 56. Donagh Corbane of the same, thirtie; blacke; low; servant. 57. Thomas Power, of Kildagan, adged twenty-seven; blacke; low; three cows, twelve sheepe, three garrans; two acres of wheate and beare. 58. Connor Gambon, of Inchindrisley, thirtie-two; brown; middle; tenant; three cows, twelve sheepe, three garrans; ten acres of wheate and beare. 59. John McPhilip, of Kildagan, thirtie; browne; middle; tenant. 60. William Morrissee, of Inchindrisly, eighteen; white; middle; servant. 61. David McDonagh, of Knock-an-power, sixtie-three ; graye ; middle ; freeholder ; ten cows, twenty-seaven sheepe, fifteen garrans; thirteen acres of wheate and beare. 62. Giles Mulcahy, fifty-three ; brown; low. 63. Margaret Mulcahy, his daughter, eighteen ; brown; middle ; spinster. 64. Ellen Mulcahy, his daughter, seventeen; brown; middle; spinster. 65. Ellinor Mulcahy, his daughter, ten; brown; spinster. 66. Thomas Shane, of the same, eighteen; brown; middle; servant. 67. John Offernan, of the same, sixteen; brown; servant. 68. Daniell Henery, of the same, thirtie; browne; middle; servant. 69. Richard Breenagh, of the same, twelve ; brown ; servant. 70. Thomas fitz John, of Ballinlea, forty-three; brown; tall; tenant; three cows, twenty sheepe, eight garrans; eight acres of wheate and beare. 71. James Forde, of Ballyduffmore, fifty-three; brown; low; mortgagee ; two cows, two garrans; two acres of wheate and beare. 72. John O'Kelly, of Knock-an-power, thirty; black; middle; tenant; two cows; two acres of wheate and beare. 73. James Ronayne, of the same, sixty ; graye, middle; tenant ; one cow. 74. Morish Ronayne, of the same, twenty; brown; middle. 75. John O'Glassine, of the same, twenty; black; middle; tenant; two cows, one garran. 76. Donagh Mulcahy, of the same, twenty-foure ; black; servant. 77. Connor O'Keirnane, of the same, thirty-five ; black ; middle ; servant. 78. Dermod O'Keirnane, of the same, twenty ; black; middle ; servant. 79. Ellen Prendergast, of the same, thirty-five ; brown; tall; widdowe; two cows, two garrans. 80. Onora Flanagan, of the same ; forty; black; middle; widdowe; three cows, twelve sheepe, three garrans; two acres of wheate and beare. 81. Thomas Kernane, of the same, twenty ; black; servant. 82. Thomas Prendergast, of the same; twelve; white; servant. 83. Donagh O'Hutterie, of Ballymartie, thirtie; black; middle; tenant; four cows, ten sheepe, three garrans; four acres of wheate and beare. 84. Morish Mulrery, of the same, twenty; dark ; middle; servant. 85. Derby O'Brien, of Inchindrisly, thirty ; brown ; low; four cows, thirty sheepe, seaven garrans; seaven acres of wheat and beare. 86. William Brennagh, of the same, twenty; white; low; servant. 87. John Kennedy, twenty; brown; servant. 88. William Kenny, of Kilknockane, fifty-four, graye; low; burgess; six cows, twenty

sheepe, nine garrans; fifteen acres of wheate, beare, and pease. 89.
Anne Kenny, wife of the said William, sixtie; brown; low. 91. James
Meregagh, of the same, thirtie; black; middle; servant. 92. Donagh O'Brien, of the same, thirty; dark; low; tenant; three cows,
five garrans; twelve acres of wheate and beare. 94. Richard Butler,
of Garrinlowe, thirty; flaxen; tall; tenant; six cows, twenty sheepe;
twelve garrans; three acres of wheate and beare. 95. Giles Butler,
his wife, twenty-four; brown; low. 96. Meaghlin Hogan, of the
same, twenty; dark; middle; servant. 97. Morish Dower, of the
same, twenty; yellow; middle; servant. 98. Daniel O'Phelane, of
the same, eighteen; black; low; servant. 99. Donogh O'Kerwick, of
the same, sixteene; dark; low; servant. 100. Ellen Magner, of
Donnemainstragh, fifty-seaven; black; middle; three cows, twenty-
six sheepe, two garrans; four acres of wheate, beare, and pease.
101. Thomas Butler, of Knockneagcarah, twenty-eight; yellow;
middle; tenant; thirty-one cows, one hundred sheepe, twenty-four
garrans, six oxen; twenty-eight acres of wheate and beare, and four
of pease. 102. Katherine, his wife, twenty-five; black; tall. 103.
Piers Butler, of the same, fiftie; graye; middle; servant. 104.
Edmund Butler, of the same, eighteen; black; low; servant. 105.
Walter Fanning, of the same, twenty-three; black; low; servant.
106. Daniel Mourye, of the same, fifteen; yellow; low; servant.
107. William Hodnett, of Grange, thirty-two; black; middle; tenant; three cows, five sheepe, three garrans; seventeene acres of
wheate and beare. 108. James Power, of Inchindrisly, twenty-
three; dark; middle; tenant; three cows, five sheepe, three garrans; seventeene acres of wheate and beare. 109. Thomas Gough,
of Dungarvan, forty; black; tall; burgess; one cow, ten sheepe,
two garrans. 110. James Fitzmorresh-Gerald, of Crushea, forty;
flaxen brown; middle; tenant; five cows, twenty-five sheepe, eight
garrans; ten acres of wheate and beare. 111. John Coppinger, of
Dungarvan, the younger, thirty-seaven; brown; middle; burgess.
112. Michael Hore, of the same, thirty; black; low; burgess. 113.
John McCreagh, of Inchindrisly, twenty; brown; middle; servant.
114. John Butler, son to Thomas Butler, of Knockneagcarah, above-

mentioned; flaxen. 115. Margaret Hodnett, wife to William Hodnett, abovementioned, thirty; flaxen; tall. 116. Garrett Hodnett, his son, four ; flaxen. 117. Teige O'Moane, thirty-six ; black ; middle; servant. 117. Bryan Moane, his son, four; browne. 117. Murtagh O'Boghan, forty-three; black; tall; servant. 118. John O'Boghan, fourteen; flaxen; servant. 118. Connor Carty, twenty; black; low; servant. 119. Morish [   ]; black ; low; servant. 120. Walter Grange, twenty ; black ; tall. 121. William Brennagh, thirty-five ; red; servant; middle. 122. Connor O'Farrelly, forty; brown; middle; servant. 123. Morish fitz John, twenty-five; brown; servant. 124. John Power, fifteen; brown; servant. 125. Murtagh Kenagh, forty ; brown ; middle ; servant. 129. Thomas Gorman, thirtie; black ; middle ; servant. 130. David Roch, of Dungarvan, twenty-two ; brown ; low ; servant. 131. Thomas Wyse, of Ballinavarie, forty; brown; middle; freeholder.

The substance whereof we believe to be true. In witness whereof, we have hereunto sett our hands and seals, the 26th day of January, 1653–4.

CHARLES BLOUNT, SOLOMON RICHARDS, HENRY PARIS.*

Ireland.—By the Commissioners of the Revenue within the Precinct of Limerick.

We, the said Commissioners, do hereby certify that James Bonfield, of the city of Limerick, burgess, hath upon the 20th day of December, 1653, in pursuance of a Declaration of the Commissioners of the Parliament of the Commonwealth of England for the Affairs of Ireland, bearing date the 14th day of October, 1653, delivered unto us in writing the names of himself and of such other persons as are to remove with him, with the quantities and qualities of their stocks and tillage, the contents whereof are as followeth : viz.—The said James Bonfield, of the city aforesaid, aged thirty-eight years; tall stature; browne flaxen hair. Catherine Bonfield,

* Book of Transplanters' Certificates, Records of the late Auditor-General, Custom House Buildings.

his wife, aged thirty-eight years; red haire.   John Hynane, aged twenty years; middle stature; black haire.   Gabriel Creagh, Gennett Creagh, Anthony Creagh, and James Creagh, small children, under the age of eight years.   Bridget Bonfield, daughter to the said James, aged eight years; brown haired.   Ellen ny Cahill, maid servant, aged forty years; middle stature; brown haire.   Mary ny Liddy, aged forty years; black haire; middle stature.   His substance— foure cows, foure garrans; and desires the benefit of his claim.   The substance whereof we believe to be true.   In witness whereof we have hereunto set our hands and seals the 20th day of December, 1653.*

Connollagh Barony.

We, the said Commissioners, do hereby certify, that John Fitzgerald of Finntanstown, in the county and barony aforesaid, hath upon the 10th day of January, 1653, in pursuance of a Declaration of the Commissioners of the Parliament of the Commonwealth of England for the Affairs of Ireland, bearing date the 14th day of October, 1653, delivered unto us in writing the names of himself, and of such other persons as are to remove with him, with the quantities and qualities of their stocks and tillage, the contents whereof are as followeth : viz.—The said John Fitzgerald, aged thirtie-five years; middle stature; black hair.   Sarah, his wife, aged twenty-six years; brown hair; tall stature.   David Fitzgeraid, aged four years; black hair.   His two daughters, called Joan and Mary, under the age of of two years, flaxen hair.   Edmund Fitzgerald, tenant, aged thirty years; tall stature; flaxen hair.   Ellen, his wife, aged forty years; tall stature ; brown hair.   Elleanor, Margaret, and Eliza, three daughters of the said Edmund, all under the age of four years.   David Wolfe, gentleman, aged twenty-four years ; black hair; middle stature.   Mauria Manning, aged twenty-six years; middle stature ; black hair.   Dermod Halpin, aged twenty-four years; tall stature; flaxen hair.   Donough McCarty, aged thirty-six years; middle stature; black hair.   Ann ny McNamara, servant, aged

---

* Book of Transplanters' Certificates in the Record Tower, Dublin Castle.

forty years; black hair; tall stature. His substance—twenty-four garrans, three cows, two sows; four acres of winter corn. The substance whereof we believe to be true. In witness whereof we have hereunto set our hands and seals, the 10th day of January, 1653.*

Citty of Limerick.

We, the said Commissioners, doe hereby certify that Margaret Heally, *alias* Creagh, the relict of John Heally, Esq., dead, of the county of Limerick, hath upon the 19th day of December, 1653, in pursuance of a Declaration of the Commissioners of the Parliament of the Commonwealth of England for the Affairs of Ireland, bearing date the 14th day of October, 1653, delivered unto us in writing the names of herself and of such other persons as are to remove with her, with the quantities and qualities of their stocks and tillage, the contents whereof are as followeth : viz.—The said Margaret, adged thirty years; flaxen hair; full face; middle size. In substance, two cows, three ploughs of garrans, and two acres of barley and wheate sowen. John Neal, her servant, adged twenty-eight years; red haire; middle stature; full face. Gennet Comyn, one of her servants, adged twenty-four years; brown haire; slender face; of middle stature. Joan Keane, servant, adged thirtie-six years; brown haire; middle seize; full face; and her little daughter, adged six yeares. Out of the above substance she payeth contribution. In witness whereof we have hereunto set our hands and seals, the 19th day of December, 1653.

* Book of Transplanters' Certificates, Record Tower, Dublin Castle, p. 8.

INDEX OF SUBJECTS.

———◆———

ARMY—*continued.*

and the regiments of each province for counties and baronies, 83.

Commission to Lord Broghill and others for setting out lands in the county of Cork, for arrears, 86.

list of officers set down in Munster, Leinster, and Ulster, 90–94.

ASSESSMENT,

in 1653, double the amount of rent in time of peace, 17.

soldiers throw up their farms, unable to bear the weight of it, ib.

ASSIGNMENT OF DEBENTURES BY COMMON SOLDIERS TO THEIR OFFICERS,

See DEBENTURES, 95.

ASSIGNMENTS OF LANDS TO TRANSPLANTERS *De bene esse,* 33.

ATHLONE COMMISSIONERS,

appointed on 28th December, 1654, 189.

their court called " The Court of Claims and Qualifications of the Irish," ib.

the Eight Qualifications, ib.

their " Crimination Books," 190.

the Athlone Decrees called Final Settlements, as compared with the Assignments of Lands *De bene esse* of the Loughrea Commissioners, 190.

the Loughrea Commissioners commissioned to set out lands acccording to the Athlone Decrees, 190.

ATKINSON, LADY MARGARET,

prays to be dispensed with from transplantation, 39.

"of great age, and no one to support her but her son, Sir G. A., a Protestant," 39.

AXTELL, COLONEL RICHARD,

shoots six women on the high road betwixt Athy and Kilkenny, 164, n.

BARBADOES,

gentlemen transported to, in numbers, for not transplanting, 142.

BARNEWALL, NICHOLAS, OF TURVEY, COUNTY OF DUBLIN,

and Bridget, Countess of Tyrconnell, his wife, plead (against being transplanted) their great age and infirmities, 41.

BARNEWALL, MARGARET,

applies to be dispensed with from transportation, as "long troubled with a shaking palsy," 38.

BENTHAM, JEREMY,

defines Law as the will of the Strongest, 7, n.

CARTHAGINIANS,
> the desolation of Ireland by the English in 1652 likened to the state of Sicily under the Carthaginians, 144.

CASHEL,
> to be cleared of Irish, 137.

> citizens of, dispensed from Transplantation; but God, better knowing their wickedness, burnt down the town, 23rd May, 1654, sparing only the English, 49.

CHEEVERS, WALTER,
> of Monkstown Castle, near Dublin, is transplanted, and Ludlow is given his castle, 68.

> his transplanter's certificate, 69.

> the Council order him in vain a good house in Connaught, 70.

CHURCH OF CHRIST,
> " sitting, at Chichester House, in College-green, Dublin," in 1659, 24.

CLONMEL,
> ordered to be cleared of Irish by 25th March, 1655, 137.

COMYN, SIR NICHOLAS,
> of Limerick, his certificate on transplanting, 32.

> " numb at one side of his body of a dead palsy," ib.

CONNAUGHT,
> Strafford confiscates it, in order to found a noble English Plantation, lxxiii.

> intends to take half of each man's estate, ib.

> the Parliament of England angry with Charles I. for not carrying out the plan, lxxii.

> by Act of 26th Sept., 1653, reserved "for the habitation of the Irish nation," 25.

> selected because it is an island all but ten miles, 29.

> a four-mile belt of English military planters round Connaught, 29, 187.

> transplanters have to bribe the officers and the Commissioners at Loughrea if they would get a good allotment, or speedy despatch, 67.

> in 1654 a waste, 47.

> the first transplanters scared at the sight, 48, 191.

> Sligo county taken from the transplanted, and given to the soldiers, 188.

> the best part of the barony of Tyrawley, in the county of Mayo, given to the soldiery, ib.

> Leitrim taken for arrears before 5th June, 1649, 189.

> certain baronies in, appointed to receive the inhabitants from the different counties in the other three provinces, 65, 192.

"CROMWELL'S DOGGS,"
    answer of Serjeant Beverley when so called in 1663, 211.

CULME, LADY,
    prays that her Irish servant may be dispensed with from transplantation, 39.

CUSACK, MARGARET,
    pleads (against being transplanted) that she is seventy-eight, and dropsical, 40.

DEBENTURES,
    given up on lands being assigned, and certificates given in their stead, 85.
    sale of, by the common soldiers to their officers, frequent, through distress, consequent upon delay in assigning lands, 95.
    though forbidden by Act of Parliament, ib.
    sale of, by common soldiers to their officers ; deed of assignment by thirty-four soldiers to their ensign, 96, n.
    advances made by Government on, to starving widows of soldiers, 97.
    various instances, 98, n.
    sold for the greater part by the common soldiers to their officers before the assignment of lands to the army, 99, 213, 214.

DEBENTURE BROKERS, 99.

DESOLATION,
    such, that (in 1652) wolves were hunted in the suburbs of Dublin, 144.
    Ireland in ruins, like Sicily from the tyranny of the Carthaginians, ib.
    wandering orphans (1653) preyed upon by wolves, 149.
    twenty and thirty miles (1652-53) without a living thing—man, beast, and bird, all dead or fled, ib.
    such was the depopulation that great part of it, it was believed, must lie waste many years—much of it for many ages, 150.
    whole districts laid waste, and put out of protection (1650-59), so that any found within the limits were liable to be shot on the spot, 164, n.

DISPENSATIONS FROM TRANSPLANTATION,
    various applications for, 38.
    orders of Council on petitions for, 218-226.
    on the petition of Lord Brittas, 218.
        of Piers Creagh, 219.
        of Dowager Lady Louth, 220.
        of Mary Thorpe, 221.
        of Lady Trimleston, 221.

FEUDAL SYSTEM,

FEUDAL LAW,

FEUDAL SLAVERY,

FIVE COUNTIES, THE,

FLEETWOOD,

FLOGGING OF WOMEN,

GAULS—*continued.*

Antiochus called Soteer, or Saviour, for rescuing Asia Minor from them, 30.

song of three Ionian young ladies, who quit life for fear of them, xxix, n.

the chosen soldiers of Pyrrhus, ib.

Gauls of France, weighed down with Roman taxes and ruined by large landed estates, welcome the barbarian invaders, xxxi.

GIRALDUS CAMBRENSIS,

on the liveliness and freedom of the Irish, 56.

on the coldness of men of Saxon and German stock, ib.

how strangers are immediately enchanted by the country, ib.

calls the English the most degraded of all races under heaven, xxxiv, n.

the most treacherous and murderous, ib.

doubts whether their servile habits arise from long slavery, or the natural dulness of the Saxon race, xxxix.

GOOKIN, SIR VINCENT,

in 1634 publishes an invective against all the inhabitants of Ireland, who would have hanged him if they could, 56.

GOOKIN, VINCENT,

son of Sir Vincent, returned as representative of Kinsale and the adjoining towns to the Little Parliament in 1653, 55.

his national land hunger satisfied, he learns to love the Irish, ib.

opposes Transplantation by his book, " The Great Case of Transplantation Discussed," 54–60.

fury of the officers of the army at his book, 60.

GRAHAM, SIR JAMES, BART.,

declares confiscation to be the most dangerous design a conqueror can undertake, he had better take their lives if he would take their lands, 164, n.

HANGING, DEATH BY, FOR NOT TRANSPLANTING,

the officers tender of, but had no scruple of sending the offending Irish proprietors to West Indies, 52.

Daniel Fitzpatrick and another condemned to death at Kilkenny, 53.

Mr. Edward Hetherington hanged at Dublin with placards on back and breast, ib.

Irish gentry choose to be hanged rather than remove from their wonted habitations, 54.

HARP,

the old English families of the Pale had each their Irish harp in 1688, lxi, n.

LEITRIM—*continued.*

> taken for the soldiery, though assigned by the Act to the Irish, as being too fast a country, 189.

LOUGHREA COMMISSIONERS,

> directed to set out lands to the transplanted according to the Athlone Decrees, 191.

> they dishearten the transplanters by setting them down in places totally unlike the places they came from, 48, 191.

LOUTH, DOWAGER LADY OF,

> prays to be dispensed with from transplantation, for her "great age and impotency," 39, 220.

LOUTH, THE COUNTY OF,

> laid aside for a supply for the Adventurers in case of a deficiency in the ten half counties, 115.

> the officers claim it, insisting that the Adventurers are overpaid by the ten half counties, ib.

> Dr. Petty appointed to examine the Adventurers' proceedings, ib.

LUTTREL, THOMAS, OF LUTTRELSTOWN, NEAR DUBLIN,

> his wife dispensed for six weeks, for her great charge of children, and stock not in a condition to drive, 36.

> proves much good, but not "Constant good affection," 35.

> turned out in 1649 for Lord Broghill, 36.

> is transplanted, ib.

LUTTRELL, JOHN,

> being transplanted from Luttrellstown, near Dublin, worth £2500 a year, his four sisters are given ten pounds a piece, and bidden like common Irishwomen no further to trouble the Council, 166.

LYNCH, JOHN,

> his "Alithinologia cited," 22, n. ; 30, n.

MAD,

> driven mad at the order to transplant, 76.

MALLOW COMMISSION,

> to try the claims and qualifications of the Ancient native inhabitants of Cork, Kinsale, and Youghal, 227.

> notwithstanding their loyalty to the English interest, they are turned out by orders of the Earl of Inchiquin, in 1644, 228.

MALLOW COMMISSION—*continued.*

the Commissioners report to the Council that they had granted to none of the Ancient inhabitants of Cork, Kinsale, or Youghal a decree of Constant good affection, 234.

their graphic account of the scene, 231.

the claimants declare they had rather go to Barbadoes than amongst the Irish, their enemies, in Connaught, 234.

MAP,

one such as Dr. Petty was bound to furnish every officer with, is now in possession of Major Waring, of Waringstown, Co. Down, 108, n.

MARCH LAW,

the mixture of English law and the Irish law of Kincogish, administered by the barons of English descent dwelling beyond the Pale, lix.

MARRIAGE,

every feudal landlord claimed the right of marrying to whom he would his tenant's orphan heir, or heiress, xlv.

an heiress once a king's ward was always a ward, and must marry again, or remain a widow, at his orders, xlvi.

people become burghers to have freedom of marriage, ib.

MARRIAGES,

any Englishman of the birth of Ireland taking an Irish girl for wife or mistress to be (by Statute 40th Ed. III.), half strangled, disembowelled while yet alive, and to undergo other horrors unmentionable, 105, n.

MARRIAGES BETWEEN ENGLISH AND IRISH,

caused the English planters of Queen Elizabeth's day to have become Irish in 1641, 61.

"the land is an unclean land,"—"ye shall not therefore give your sons to their daughters, nor take their daughters to your sons" (Officers' petition), 61.

the officers and soldiers of Ireton's army take Irish wives even before peace proclaimed, 128.

Major-General Ireton's Proclamation of 1st May, 1651, against intermarriages of English officers and soldiers with Irishwomen, 106, n.

the soldiers always pretend that the girls are converts to English religion, 105.

Ireton orders that the girls pass an examination into the true state of their hearts before a board of military saints, 106.

the board to ascertain whether the change be a real work of God upon the heart, or (as is to be feared), for some carnal ends, 106, n.

MARRIAGES BETWEEN ENGLISH AND IRISH—*continued.*

> Commissioners of Revenue of the Precinct of Galway to inquire after intermarriages, 129, n.
>
> W. Moreton, Clerk of Revenue Commissioners, dismissed his office by order of Council of 14th July, 1654, for marrying an Irishwoman, ib.
>
> " the children of Oliver's soldiers in Ireland, many of them (in 1697), their fathers having married Irishwomen, cannot speak a word of English," 130, n.
>
> the children of King William's soldiers in the same case, ib., ib.
>
> Sir Jerome Alexander's care by his will that his daughter should not marry any Irish Lord, Archbishop, or Bishop, &c., nor any Knight, Squire, or Gentleman born and bred in Ireland, or having his relations and means of subsistence there, 130, n.

MASSACRE OF 1641,

> an historical falsehood, 4.
>
> the guilty conscience of the English made them expect one, ib.
>
> the Irish have ever lacked gall to supply a wholesome animosity against the eternal enemies and revilers of their name and nation, ib.
>
> proved false by contemporaneous English accounts, 5.
>
> by the proclamation of the Lords Justices, 8th February, 1642.
>
> of some English in 1642, by Sir Phelim O'Neil's followers in a few towns in Ulster, in revenge for arson and massacre by English, 7, and n., ib.
>
> English propose to massacre the Irish, and not to spare infants, 8.
>
> how and why invented, and why kept up, 7.

MIDWIVES, IRISH,

> malicious calumnies of the English (1651) against the poor Irish midwives, 139.
>
> an English one imported, and all officers, civil and military, ordered to be aiding her in the performance of her duty, ib.

" MILE LINE, THE,"

> a belt of land four miles wide, (afterwards reduced to one), winging along the sea coast of Connaught and Shannon, 29, 187.
>
> reserved for English military planters, to shut out foreign relief or escape, ib.

MURDER,

> killing by law (which is the will of the strongest) no murder, 7, and n., ib.
>
> English, being the strongest, make killing the Irish no murder, ib. and xlix.

MURDERS,

> by the English of their French landlords, xxxiii.
>
> fines imposed on district for, ib.

MURDERS—*continued.*

of Cromwellian settlers frequent (A. D. 1654), even though dwelling in strong castles, 175.

the Lackagh murder, Co. Kildare, 22nd October, 1655, 168.

all the inhabitants transported for it, to the Barbadoes, ib.

including H. Fitzgerald, Esq., and his wife, near eighty years of age, ib.

the consequence of the kind of agrarian laws by which the lands of Ireland have been dealt with by the English, 164, n.

NAPOLEON CODE,

the blessings of it, with its abolition of primogeniture and entail, and equal partibility of landed inheritances, xxxii.

O'CONNOR FAILEY'S COUNTRY,

called by the Irish "the Door of the Pale," and O'Connor "their key," 117.

OFFICERS OF CROMWELL'S ARMY,

suggest that arrears be paid in land, 100.

some dissatisfied, 104.

Lieut.-Col. Scott arrested for agitating the disbanded companies sitting down in the county of Wexford, by treasonable words against His Highness, 104.

in January, 1652, propose that they be set down together with the Adventurers, and have lands for their arrears, 21.

and at "the Act," or Adventurers' rates, because of the difficulty and cost of surveying, ib.

the lands being waste, the inhabitants destroyed, and none to give evidence of value, ib.

their attempts to take advantage of one another in the setting out of the lots, 109.

Colonel Warden seeks to leave out all the coarse land in his lot, and encroach on the good land in Quartermaster Farr's lot, ib.

Colonel Le Hunte seeks to appropriate 1500 acres in Liberties of Wexford, applicable to Major Sam. Shepherd's company, 110.

list of those set down in different baronies in Leinster, Ulster, and Munster, 90–94.

kinder masters than the Adventurers, 127.

were six years settled in Ireland before the Adventurers came over, 128.

captivated by Irishwomen, they take them to wife, even before peace proclaimed, ib.

Ireton's order in 1651 against intermarriages, ib.

PETTY, DR. WILLIAM,

employed by the Army and State to survey the lands, 81.

joins Colonel Thomlinson in a solemn seeking of God for a blessing on the Down Survey, 81.

"individually" is a freethinker, 82.

considers sects to be maggots in the guts of a Commonwealth, ib.

considers the gathering of churches to be the listing of soldiers, ib.

appointed to examine into Adventurers' proceedings in setting out their lands, 115.

his mode of compensating deficient Adventurers, ib.

forms two parallel lists of deficient and redundant baronies, the first deficient to be repaired out of the first redundant, ib.

PHYSICIANS, IRISH,

the English, according to their national custom of reviling other nations (*i. e.* weak ones), vent their calumnies (A. D. 1650) against the Irish physicians, 138.

yet obliged to testify to their great skill and fidelity, 138.

Dr. Richard Madden, of Waterford, and Dr. Anthony Mulshinogue, of Cork, ib.

the latter to remain near, not in, the city of Cork, for his ability, ib.

PLANTATION, THE NEW, OF IRELAND,

proposal that Ireland be formed into three separate Plantations or Pales,—an Irish, an English, and a Mixed, 116.

a pure Irish Plantation or Pale in Connaught, a pure English within the line of the Boyne and the Barrow, and a Mixed in the intermediate and central parts of Ireland, suggested, 116.

Connaught selected for a pure Irish Plantation or Pale as being an island all but ten miles, 117.

a pure English Plantation or Pale proposed within the line of the Rivers Barrow and Boyne, 117.

whose head waters rise within five miles of each other, and the whole easily made into one line, ib.

similar project in Richard II.'s day, 118.

in Henry VIII.'s time, ib.

in the mixed Plantation, lying between the pure Irish and English Plantations or Pales, the Irish to give up their names of Teig or Dermot, to speak no Irish, to send their children to learn English religion, to build chimneys, 119.

PLOT, "THE PHANATICK,"

in 1663 the Cromwellian officers conspire to overthrow the Government, because of the proceedings of the Court of Claims, 211.

RATES OF LAND,

by the Acts of Subscription, called the Act Rates, 1000 acres plantation measure (equal to 1600 English measure), in Leinster for £600, adventure or arrears; in Munster, for £450, ditto; in Ulster for £300, ditto, 78.

set upon the several counties in Leinster, Munster, and Ulster, by the army, 88.

of certain baronies in Leinster and Munster, 89.

set by the officers of a troop or company, on the several seats, estates, and holdings within the lot of the troop or company, 94.

REAPE-HOOKS AND RUBSTONES,

implements of war (with the Bible) amongst the English forces in Ireland, 14.

REBELLION OF 23RD OCTOBER, 1641,

breaks out under Sir Phelim O'Neil in Ulster, 3.

terror of the planters, ib.

no cock heard to crow, nor dog to bark for the first three nights, ib.

RECUSANTS,

fined in January, 1616, for "refusing" to attend the Protestant service, 3.

fines in county of Cavan alone amounted to £8000 in 1616, ib., n.

penalties on obstinate juries for refusing to "present" their coreligionists for fines in one term in 1616, amounted to £16,000, ib.

RELIGION,

provincials always more stupidly religious than people at head quarters, 61.

RELIGION OF THE PURITANS,

hatred of bodies and principles of Papists, *passim.*

but love to their souls, 106, n.

and to their lands, 228.

RICHARDS, COLONEL SOLOMON,

prosecutes Captain Williamson for suspicion of fornication committed with a woman of the county of Tipperary during his time of service there, 105, n.

ROCHE, JORDAN,

his three daughters reduced from a landed estate of £2000 a year to nothing to live on but what they could earn by their needles and washing and wringing, 165.

SOLDIERS OF THE BIRTH OF IRELAND —*continued.*

Sir John Norris, a General of Queen Elizabeth's, and who had served in many armies and countries, was wont to say, *that there were fewer fools and cowards there than in any other kingdom*, 22.

SOLDIERS OF CROMWELL'S ARMY,

not so anxious to be paid their arrears in land as the officers, 100.

it was with the officers that the scheme originated, ib., and 104.

cheated by their officers, 107.

a whole troop sell their lots to Capt. Bassett for a barrel of beer, 108.

in 1649 fourteen regiments, after a solemn seeking of God by prayer, try which should go to Ireland by lots drawn from a hat by a child, 100.

found in Ireland no beer, no cheese; had no ploughs, nor horses, nor money to buy them, which renders them loth to become planters, 104.

for any amours with Irish girls, they are severely flogged, 104.

sentences of courts martial on different soldiers for fornication, ib., n.

if, after being disbanded, they married any of these attractive but " idolatrous" daughters of Erin, they must march after them to Connaught, 107.

are forbidden to take Irish girls to wife, even though they be " converts," unless the girls pass an examination before a board of military saints into the state of their hearts, to try if their conversion be a real work of God upon their hearts, or that they only so pretend (as is to be feared) for carnal ends, 106, n.

taking Irish girls to wife are to be reduced,—if dragoons, to foot soldiers; if foot soldiers, to pioneers, without hope in either case of promotion, 106.

whole troops and companies assign their debentures to their officers, 95.

deed of assignment of their debentures by 36 soldiers of Colonel Daniel Axtell's regiment to Arnold Thomas, their ensign, 96, n.

the many traditionary stories in Ireland, like that of " The white horse of the Peppers," that such and such an estate was given for a white horse, are founded on fact, and are sometimes probably true, 108.

the design of forming a yeomanry of them in Ireland suggested to Cromwell by Major Wildman's " Letter from an Officer of the Army in Ireland," 109, n

the idea stolen from Harington, author of " Oceana," ib.

Serjeant Beverley, on being called, in 1663, " One of Cromwell's doggs," says " Cromwell was the best man that ever reigned in the three nations," 211; adding, " If the King intends to take away our lands, gained by our swords, we will have one knock for it first," ib.

in 1663, Charles Minchin, of Knockagh, in Co. Tipperary, says, " He had rather than his estate that the soldiers of Cromwell had not sold their lands to their officers: if they had kept them, neither king nor duke durst try their qualifications," 212.

WAR, ENGLISH METHOD OF,

in Ireland, 12.

Spenser's description of, in Munster, in 1580, ib.

country wasted till man and beast died, ib.

children killed for food, 13.

Archbishop Ussher knew women to drag a rider from his horse to devour it, ib.

difficulties of, in Ireland ; islands in bogs, secure fortresses to Irish, nearly inaccessible, and whence they could escape at pleasure, 15.

WARING, MAJOR W., OF WARINGSTOWN, CO. DOWN,

possessed of one of the estate maps which Dr. Petty was bound to furnish to every officer, 108, n.

WATERFORD,

(among other seaports), with 1500 acres contiguous, offered for sale by Parliament in July, 1643, to English and foreign merchants, for £30,000 fine and £625 rent payable to the State, 136.

WEXFORD,

debt of £3697 satisfied by houses in, the English State creditor taking them orderly up one side of the street, and down the other, without picking and choosing, till satisfied, 145.

(among other seaports) with 6000 acres contiguous, offered for sale by Parliament to English and foreign merchants for £5000 fine and £156 4s. 4d., rent payable to the State, 136.

WHITE, ANNE,

of the town of Wexford, pleads (against being transplanted), her charity and good affection to English officers quartered in her house, 40.

WIDOWS AND ORPHANS, AND THE DESTITUTE,

seized and sent to the Barbadoes, 237.

the men and boys for bondmen, ib.

the girls for companions for the planters, instead of Maroon women and Negresses, ib.

Bristol merchants deal with the Government for supplies of them, 238.

names of some of the contractors, ib.

Broghill, afterwards Earl of Orrery, undertakes to find crowds in the county of Cork alone, 239.

1000 boys and 1000 girls, " Irish wenches" (the latter seized by force by order of H. Cromway), sent from Galway for the use of 1500 soldier planters, 240.

WIDOWS, IRISH,

whether men marrying transplantable widows become themselves transplantable ? 46.

WIDOWS, IRISH, OF ENGLISH EXTRACT,

Commissioners are asked to define what they mean by ? 46.

are to be set down in the four baronies of Ballintobber, Athlone, Tulla, and Bunratty, 193.

Ballintobber afterwards withdrawn from them, ib.

WILLIAMSON, CAPTAIN WILLIAM,

tried for fornication with a woman in the county of Tipperary during his service there, 105, n.

WIVES AND YOUNG CHILDREN OF TRANSPLANTERS,

in the absence of their protectors away in Connaught building huts for them, spared by the tenderness of those in authority (27th February, 1655), from transplanting till 1st May, on account of the immoderate rains, order for, 50, n.

WOLVES, PRIESTS, AND TORIES,

" the three burdensome beasts on whose heads were laid rewards," 150.

WOLF DOGS,

and hawks of Ireland, of old, fit presents for kings, 151.

taken from the officers departing (1654), for Spain, on account of the plague of wolves, ib.

WOLVES,

public hunt for, ordered in the suburbs of Dublin, 1652, 144.

increase upon the English, from exterminating the Irish too rapidly, contrary to the wise injunction of Jehovah in the case of the killing of all the Canaanites by the Jews, 151.

public hunts organized, and deer toil brought from England, ib.

increase of, charged by Cromwell (conqueror's logic), on the priests, 152.

rewards for head of a bitch wolf, £6; of a dog wolf, £5; of every cub that preyeth by himself, 40 shillings; of every sucking cub, 10 shillings, 153.

lands near Dublin (1653), leased by the State on condition of lessee's keeping two packs of wolf hounds—one at Dublin, the other at Dunboyne, and yielding a certain number of wolf heads, ib.

INDEX OF NAMES.

—◆—

Explanation of Conventional Marks.

A name in Italics signifies that the person is an author whose work is cited from. But where the man is both actor and author, as in the case of Colonel Richard Lawrence, Doctor William Petty, and other such, who were as much (or indeed considerably more) actors than writers, the former character is preferred, and the name is not distinguished.

A. signifies English, Scotch, and Foreign "Adventurer for Lands in Ireland," confined only, however, to the class encouraged by the "Acts of Subscription," between 1642 and 1646.

O. means "Officer of Cromwell's Army" entitled to be satisfied in Irish land according to the amount of his Arrears stated in his Debenture, and in those of his men, which he had bought up "by what aweings we leave to consideration." It might perhaps appear needless to put "O." after Colonel Prettie or Colonel Lehunte; but as there are cases where Officers were Royalists (of English and Irish birth and religion, respectively), it is not altogether superfluous.

S. means Common Soldier of Cromwell's Army, in which it is not necessary to look for ancestors, because they are mostly those that assigned their Debentures, and took themselves back to the place from whence they came, and this without impeachment of any : for Bastards and Common Soldiers have been the Progenitors of some of the best and oldest lines of Kings in Europe, the first of whom was but a fortunate soldier, or Soldier of Fortune.

P. means Irish Proprietor. Almost every Irish Proprietor (as the term "Irish" was then understood in England) had to transplant with his sons and his daughters, his men servants and his maid servants, his cattle, and his little flaxen-haired children, into Connaught; and this class might therefore, without any logical impropriety, have been included in the next, of "Transplanters." It has been thought more convenient, however, to separate the gentry from the lower orders, in order to enable the reader consulting the Index to pass the latter by. Under the term "Proprietors" he will find the Lord Trimleston, the Lord Fingall, the Lord and Lady Dunsany, the Marquis of Westmeath,—people that one is ˌnaturally interested about.

Tr. means "Transplanter ;" but transplanter of the lower class, such as Farmers, Burgesses, Peasants, &c. ; in fact they were common Irish, that one can take no more interest about than about the thousands of the same kind of people that are transplanting under "the Law of Level" every day before our eyes, without inspiring us with any other care than a wish that they should take themselves off as quickly as possible, and leave the country to persons of skill, and capital, and true religion.

Pr. means Priest (not Protestant), but of the Irish Roman Catholic Religion.

To. means Tory, with whom the Priests in those days kept company (necessarily), and without betraying them.

THE END.